2005

P9-AOA-041

OXFORD TELEVISION STUDIES
General Editors **Charlotte Brunsdon**
John Caughie

New Media and Popular Imagination

New Media and Popular Imagination: Launching Radio, Television, and Digital Media in the United States

William Boddy

OXFORD
UNIVERSITY PRESS

Great Clarendon Street, Oxford OX2 6DP

Oxford University Press is a department of the University of Oxford.
It furthers the University's objective of excellence in research, scholarship,
and education by publishing worldwide in

Oxford New York

Auckland Bangkok Buenos Aires Cape Town Chennai
Dar es Salaam Delhi Hong Kong Istanbul Karachi Kolkata
Kuala Lumpur Madrid Melbourne Mexico City Mumbai Nairobi
São Paulo Shanghai Taipei Tokyo Toronto

Oxford is a registered trade mark of Oxford University Press
in the UK and in certain other countries

Published in the United States
by Oxford University Press Inc., New York

British Library Cataloguing in Publication Data

Data available

Library of Congress Cataloging in Publication Data

Data available

ISBN 0–19–871146–8
ISBN 0–19–871145–x (pbk.)

1 3 5 7 9 10 8 6 4 2

Typeset by Graphicraft Limited, Hong Kong
Printed in Great Britain
on acid-free paper by
Biddles Ltd,
King's Lynn, Norfolk

Oxford Television Studies

General Editors
Charlotte Brunsdon and **John Caughie**

OXFORD TELEVISION STUDIES offers international authors—both established and emerging—an opportunity to reflect on particular problems of history, theory, and criticism which are specific to television and which are central to its critical understanding. The perspective of the series will be international, while respecting the peculiarities of the national; it will be historical, without proposing simple histories; and it will be grounded in the analysis of programmes and genres. The series is intended to be foundational without being introductory or routine, facilitating clearly focused critical reflection and engaging a range of debates, topics, and approaches which will offer a basis for the development of television studies.

For Alison

Acknowledgements

RESEARCH FOR THIS book stretched across many sites over a long period of time; in New York, I owe debts to the staffs of the Newman Library at Baruch College (especially Louisa Moy of the interlibrary loan office), the CBS Reference Library, and the New York Public Library's Research Library and its Science, Industry and Business Library. In Washington, DC, I received help from the Library of Congress and the Archives Center of the Smithsonian National Museum of American History, and in London, the staffs at the British Library and the British Film Institute Library were invaluable. My research assistants at Baruch College, Nilimesh Baruah and Vikram Kamath, worked untiringly to track down material, and I am also grateful to a number of media executives, especially Ken Ripley, formerly of TiVo, and Noah Meiri of Orad Hi-Tech Systems Ltd., for generously sharing their time and experience with me in personal interviews.

Institutional support from the City University of New York facilitated the research and writing of this book, and I would like to thank Robert Myers, Chair of the Department of Communication Studies, Dean Myrna Chase, and former Deans Lexa Logue and Dennis Slavin of the Weissman School of Arts and Sciences of Baruch College. Stella Varveris at Baruch College's Media Services and Kristin McDonough of the New York Public Library's Science, Industry and Business Library were indispensable in making possible the book's illustrations. Grant support from the PSC-CUNY research awards programme and the Skirball Foundation through the Wiessman Center for International Business at Baruch College aided research travel.

Many friends and family members also supported this project in diverse venues and ways, including Ruth Baumgarten, Sarah Berry, Evelyne Boddy, Jonathan Buchsbaum, Scott Bukatman, Thomas Elsaesser, Anne Friedberg, Nicholas Friendly, Sara Friendly, Eric Gander, Val Griffiths, Tom Gunning, John Hanhardt, John Hartley, Henry Jenkins, Paul Kerr, Brian Larkin, Jon Lewis, Annette Michelson, Toby Miller, Dave Morley, Sue Murray, Jana O'Keefe-Bazzoni, Dana Polan, Jane Root, Ron Simon, Robert Sklar, Lynn Spigel, Bill Uricchio, and John Wyver. I am also grateful to my students at Baruch College and the Graduate Center of the City University of New York for their enthusiasm and provocative suggestions in the classroom. Many of the arguments in this book have been rehearsed at a number of academic conferences, and I would like to thank the conference organizers, panel chairs, and respondents involved for their help in framing and challenging the ideas discussed. I have been lucky to have worked with a number of talented editors at Oxford University Press, especially Charlotte Brunsdon and John Caughie, the general editors of the Oxford Television Studies series, as well as Andrew Lockett, who commissioned this book, and Sophie Livingston, Sarah Hyland, and Elizabeth Prochaska, who saw it to completion.

My greatest debt is to my family, who have lived with this project longer than they might have anticipated. Evan, Tess, and Soren proved patient and understanding beyond their years, and Alison Griffiths has supported and enriched this work beyond measure at every stage.

Many of the ideas and arguments in this book are based upon material previously published in a number of publications. Portions of Chapters 2 and 5 were published as 'Archeologies of Electronic Vision and the Gendered Spectator', *Screen*, 35 (Summer 1994), 105–22; an earlier version of Chapter 3 was published as 'The Amateur, the Housewife, and the Salesroom Floor: Promoting Postwar US Television', *International Journal of Cultural Studies*, 1/1 (1998), 153–66; an earlier version of Chapter 4 was published as 'US Television Abroad: Market Power and National Introspection', *Quarterly Review of Film and Video*, 15/2 (1994), 45–55; a previous version of Chapter 6 was published as 'Weather Porn and the Battle for Eyeballs: Promoting Digital Television in the USA and UK', in J. Fullerton and A. Soderbergh-Widding (eds.), *Moving Images: From Edison to the Webcam* (Sydney: John Libbey, 2000), 133–47; a previous version of Chapter 7 was published as 'Redefining the Home Screen: Technological Convergence as Trauma and Business Plan', in D. Thorburn and H. Jenkins (eds.), *Rethinking Media Change: The Aesthetics of Transition* (Cambridge, Mass.: MIT Press, 2002), 191–200; a previous version of Chapter 8 was published as ' "Touching Content": Virtual Advertising and Digital Television's Recalcitrant Audience', in J. Fullerton (ed.), *Screen Culture: History and Textuality* (Eastleigh, UK: John Libbey, 2004), 245–62; and a previous version of Chapter 9 was published as 'Old Media as New Media: Television', in Dan Harries (ed.), *The New Media Book* (London: BFI Publishing, 2002), 242–53. I would like to thank the editors and manuscript readers involved in these earlier incarnations of the material.

W. B.

Contents

List of Figures

Introduction

THIS BOOK OFFERS a historical account of the ways in which successive media of electronic communication—radio, television, and digital media—have been anticipated, debated, and taken up in the twentieth century in the United States. The project began with the impulse to consider the cultural and economic stakes of the current transition from analogue to digital platforms for moving-image transmission, display, and interaction, a transition heralded as a decisive break with previous media forms and audience practices. Digital technologies, their various late twentieth-century proponents claimed, would overturn the business models of traditional media firms, give viewers unprecedented control over domestic media consumption, and at once enhance democratic values and international understanding while boosting American economic and political power across the globe. Over the past quarter-century, promoters of new digital moving-image technologies have celebrated technological innovation within compelling imaginary scenarios of work and leisure, identity and community. However, notwithstanding repeated claims for the unprecedented nature of technological and industrial change of our present era, the recent digital-media debates clearly drew upon notions of domesticity, gender, and national identity elaborated in the responses to radio and television much earlier in the century.

The commercial launch of any new communications technology typically combines a public rehearsal of contested and self-serving fantasies of the new product's domestic consumption with a polemical ontology of its medium and an ideological rationale for its social function. The scattered public record of these self-representations, in the ephemera of TV commercials, corporate press releases, and trade-press reporting, illuminates the larger contexts and implicit assumptions which frame both public policy and private consumption. The current era of confusion and conflict among the would-be architects of our putative post-television age offers a productive site to investigate the ways in which wider social, technological, and political changes may deform or put into crisis such calculated representations of media apparatus and artefact. The shifting boundaries between analogue and digital, cinema and television, and broadcasting and the Internet throw into question traditional critical oppositions between domestic and public media reception, active and passive modes of consumption, and authored and non-authored texts. As powerful firms within and outside the contemporary television industry improvise strategies of competition and alliance around the introduction of new digital products and services, contradictory instrumental fantasies of the medium's nature and use will undoubtedly be offered to consumers and policy makers. Despite their ephemeral nature and regardless of their predictive accuracy, these strategic fantasies of consumption can speak eloquently of the larger cultural ambivalence regarding new communications technologies.

Untangling the current disputes over the cultural implications of the technological transition to digital media involves engaging with the historiographic challenge evoked by Walter Benjamin, that of relating long-term shifts in 'the mode of human sense perception' to wider changes in 'humanity's entire mode of existence', a task that has increasingly engaged media scholars crossing traditional academic disciplines.[1] Much of the work of contemporary film and television historians has specifically addressed those historical moments marked by the dissemination of new media technologies within particular national and industrial contexts, such as the consolidation of the early motion-picture industry, the beginnings of US commercial radio broadcasting in the 1920s, the introduction of sound in the motion-picture industry, and the beginnings of commercial television. Such historical conjunctures offer privileged case studies of technological innovation, market restructuring, and changes in traditional representational practices.

The prospect of technological change within contemporary moving-image industries presents a challenge to traditional critical approaches to media innovation, approaches British cultural critic Raymond Williams characterized as 'an unholy combination of technological determinism with cultural pessimism'.[2] Conventional histories of specific communication technologies, with their fixations on the instrument and the instrumental in an imputed teleology of technological progress, threaten to consign the past to an uninformative series of failed implementations of currently prevailing media applications. Instead, media historians might profit from an initial effort to defamiliarize the everyday and common-sense assumptions presiding over contemporary media use, to 'make strange' the prosaic TV set or personal computer as object and its taken-for-granted applications and status, to contest the habit of conflating ubiquity with inevitability or 'naturalness'. The goal is to replace the traditional historiographic trope of autonomous technology with an attempt to specify the historical and cultural determinations of technological change. As Robert Romanyshyn argues:

> Technology is not just a series of events which occurs over there on the other side of the world. It is, on the contrary, the enactment of the human imagination in the world. In building a technological world, we create ourselves, and through the events which comprise this world we enact and live out our experiences of awe and wonder, our fantasies of service and control, our images of exploration and destruction, our dreams of hope and nightmares of despair.[3]

Recent film and television scholarship in the USA and elsewhere has demonstrated a new concern with the complex and ambivalent social reception of new media technologies; as film historian Tom Gunning argued in 1991, 'the new exploration of the history of technology is more than technical . . . technology can reveal the dream world of society as much as its pragmatic

---

1 Walter Benjamin, 'The Work of Art in the Age of Mechanical Reproduction', in *Illuminations* (New York: Schocken, 1973), 222.

2 Raymond Williams, *The Year 2000* (New York: Pantheon Books, 1983), 129.

3 Robert Romanyshyn, *Technology as Symptom and Dream* (London: Routledge, 1989), 10.

realization'.[4] An examination of such technological dream worlds and dead ends across the history of twentieth-century electronic communication suggests the longevity of a range of related popular fantasies and fears, and these often-forgotten responses resonate in striking ways with contemporary reactions to our own emerging digital culture.

In place of traditional historiographic metanarratives of technological progress and commercial mastery, this book investigates the relationship between technology and cultural form by examining a number of discrete historical moments associated with the public's earliest experiences of radio, television, and digital media. At such moments, the consequences of technological innovation, real and imagined, provoked both euphoria and unease within and without the communication industries. Against the traditional historiographic tropes of origins and essences, this account of media innovation approaches such episodes as privileged moments of genuine uncertainty and improvisation, where the prospect of destabilizing technological innovation served to throw into relief prevailing industry models, regulatory rationales, and consumer practices. As Raymond Williams argues, 'the moment of any new technology is a moment of choice', and historians must counter conventional teleological accounts of autonomous technological 'progress' by restoring a sense of historical agency to the social and political determinations inflecting the commercial exploitation of new media technologies.[5] Indeed, one way to access the impact of new communications technologies is to consider the ways in which their prospect unsettles prevailing textual forms, business models, and audience assumptions. The case studies examined in this book underscore both the historical tension between technological novelty and institutional and ideological continuity, as well as the power of ideas, often informal and taken for granted, to affect materially the fortunes of new communication technologies in the market place, regulatory arena, and legal system. As Williams pointed out in 1962: 'many of our communication models become, in themselves, social institutions. Certain attitudes to others, certain forms of address, certain tones and styles, become embodied in institutions which are then very powerful in social effect.'[6]

The power of ideas operating across a number of institutional contexts to shape the course of technological innovation suggests the value of considering a wide range of non-canonical historical research materials, especially those producing a 'vernacular theory' of electronic communication, where an informal set of general propositions about the nature, social role, and audience paradigms for electronic media is elaborated and contested. These diverse sites, including the trade and popular press, popular fiction and motion pictures, television commercials, industrial films, and corporate websites, collectively elaborate powerful discursive tools with which the sometimes disconcerting prospect of technological change is made sense of by policy makers and the public alike. Furthermore, the unique legal and

---

4 Tom Gunning, 'Heard over the Phone: *The Lonely Villa* and the de Lorde Tradition of the Terrors of Technology', *Screen*, 32/2 (Summer 1991), 185.

5 Williams, *The Year 2000*, 146.

6 Raymond Williams, *Communications* (Harmondsworth: Penguin, 1962), 11.

political relationship of electronic media industries to the state in the USA and elsewhere has sensitized the major corporate actors to the strategic importance of being able to define the electronic media's ontologies, audience demands, and social rationales. Such instrumentalist accounts of the nature of twentieth-century electronic media both exploit and domesticate the popular anxieties and hopes around new media elaborated in a wider imaginative horizon of popular fiction and film. The long history of popular culture's alternately fearful and euphoric representations of electronic communication in the home suggests the continuing historical relevance of such ephemeral fantasies of pleasure and terror.

While the chronological boundaries of the case studies contained in this book roughly delineate the entire twentieth century, some attention is also paid to the nineteenth-century roots of wireless communication, reaching back to the invention of the telegraph in the 1840s, the telephone in the 1870s, and cinema in the 1890s. Moreover, while the concluding case studies in the transition to digital communication largely encompass the decade of the 1990s, they also extend into the first few years of the twenty-first century, in order to capture more recent disputes among industry interests. In any event, such boundaries are always at least somewhat arbitrary, especially given the interdisciplinary nature and diverse research arenas of the study. Each case study examines a specific historical moment when the prospect of technological change threw prevailing competitive relations, business models, and consumer practices into crisis and controversy. Likewise, while the majority of the historical argument centres on the experience of electronic communication in the United States, there is an important thread of material which relates to the experience of other nations, especially the UK. This asymmetrical comparative focus echoes broadcasting's bifurcated identity between a tradition of technophilic and utopian internationalism, founded upon the technical indifference of broadcast signals to national boundaries, and broadcasting's institutional history shaped by regulatory and legal regimes resolutely national in design. As we shall see, each technological innovation in electronic media provoked new anxieties and hopes concerning the prospects for national identity in a century marked by unprecedented levels of trans-border trade and migration. Like those of the newspaper and the cinema, the institutions of broadcasting were closely linked to the new powers and constraints of the twentieth-century nation state. In particular, the opposition between American and British approaches to broadcasting has been an important structuring opposition in the rhetorical and institutional identities of media industries in both nations, from early wireless to digital television.

Throughout the twentieth century, changes in the forms and uses of electronic media in the home have served to incarnate and condense wider social tensions around the shifting definitions of public and private space, the roles of men and women inside and outside the home, and the construction of personal and national identity. A history of attempts to market new media forms for the home is thus enmeshed with wider histories of domesticity, gender, and national identity over the last century. In ways which seemed unprecedented and deeply disturbing to many in the early twentieth century, wireless communication transformed the experience of time and space and challenged the established borders between the domestic realm and public space, the individual and the market, and the citizen and the state. Electronic communication has enjoyed a long association with the magical and uncanny, and the devices which flooded the intimate spaces of the home with the sounds and images of the public and commercial worlds have served as powerful associative objects upon which personal identity and community were forged. In her discussion of the early PC hobbyist community of the early 1980s, Sherry Turkle describes the personal computer as an 'evocative object, an object that fascinates, disturbs equanimity, and precipitates thought', and other domestic media devices, from the crystal radio set in the 1920s attic, the component hi-fi system in the 1950s den, to the digital video recorder in the 1990s living room, carry the burden and thrill of this psychic investment.[7]

This book is organized around a series of historically discontinuous but thematically linked case studies in the promotion of new media technologies marketed to the twentieth-century home. The first chapter attempts to bring into dialogue the traditionally distinct historical writing on early cinema and electronic media through an examination of the popular reception of both motion pictures and wireless in the late nineteenth century and early twentieth century. Examining the scientific and popular literature from the period, the chapter analyses the ways in which wireless communication disturbed received notions of scientific rationality, national identity, and domesticity. Chapter 2 examines the transition from wireless experimentation to commercial broadcasting in the USA during the first two decades of the twentieth century, a period which saw the elaboration of the enduring figurations of the electronic media's apparatus, audience, and social function. Moving from the 1920s to the 1940s, the third chapter examines the somewhat faltering first steps in the commercial launch of American television, especially in the immediate post-Second World War period, when the viability of commercial radio as a model for the new medium was hotly debated. These disputes about the appropriate textual forms, perceptual demands, and economic models for the new television medium drew upon a repertory of established assumptions about the gendered broadcast audience and the place of electronic media within the home. Rooted in the experience of early radio broadcasting, these mid-century assumptions about the nature of the domestic audience would also play an important role in late twentieth-century debates over the place of digital media in the home.

The remaining eight chapters of the book offer a series of case studies analysing the promotion and reception of a range of late twentieth-century digital moving-image technologies, connecting the analysis of specific industry contexts to the wider issues of gender, home, and nation associated with the earlier commercial launches of radio and television. Chapter 4 juxtaposes two distinct moments of rare introspection within the US media industry—the early 1960s and the early 1990s—when economic change and geopolitical realignment brought a new self-consciousness about the relationship of US media firms to their audiences, both domestic and

---

7 Sherry Turkle, *The Second Self: Computers and the Human Spirit* (New York: Simon and Schuster, 1984), 12.

foreign. Chapter 5 examines the flurry of popular interest in the emerging technologies of virtual reality in the early 1990s, especially the manner in which the various imaginative extensions of virtual reality were united in common opposition to traditional figurations of the domestic television apparatus and viewer. Chapter 6 analyses the reaction to the near-simultaneous launches of digital television in the USA and UK in late 1998, amid the distinct market conditions, popular expectations, and political contexts of the two nations, while Chapter 7 takes up the same themes of technological innovation and national identity through an examination of the widely debated anticipated effects of the digital video recorder in the United States at the end of the 1990s. Chapter 8, 'Marketers Strike Back: Virtual Advertising', analyses one of the most remarkable technological countermeasures offered to broadcasters and advertisers fearful of the advertising-avoiding capabilities of the new digital video recorder. Chapter 9, 'How God Watches Television: Early Responses to Digital Television', examines the preliminary record of the role of the digital video recorder within the gendered household and within the wider media economy. Chapter 10 examines some of the programming and advertising implications of the introduction of a range of emerging digital television products and services in the context of the contracting advertising market and general economic recession of the first years of the twenty-first century. Finally, Chapter 11, ' "Too Easy, Too Cheap and Too Fast to Control": Intellectual Property Battles in Digital Television', analyses the powerful legislative counter-offensive led by the motion-picture studios and television networks aimed at preserving and extending their control over the distribution and consumption of copyrighted programming in the face of new digital moving-image technologies.

Drawing upon a diverse range of materials, from congressional hearings and trade reports to TV commercials and corporate websites, these eight case studies in digital media demonstrate the longevity and continued relevance of a cluster of related propositions about the nature of the electronic media, their audiences, and their place in the home and the nation. The analysis of the distinct and widely separated historical episodes of technological innovation in this book, from the earliest experiences of radio broadcasting, through post-war television, to a range of emerging digital media, illustrates how commercial, administrative, and popular voices made sense of the technological capabilities and social implications of electronic media and how these discourses connected to wider ideas about social and political life in the twentieth century. Collectively, these historical case studies suggest that the current ubiquitous claims for technological novelty and market renovation led by emerging digital technologies need to be considered alongside the manifest persistence of long-established and self-serving constructions of electronic media artefacts and audiences.

1

Cinema and Wireless in Turn of the Century Popular Imagination

Introduction

HISTORIANS OF EARLY cinema and electronic media have long operated in mutual isolation, drawing upon quite distinct historiographic assumptions, methods, and research materials. This isolation is remarkable, not only given the historical coincidence of the technological development of both cinema and the wireless at the end of the nineteenth century, but also in light of the ways in which popular responses to the anticipation and early experience of both media speak to a common set of cultural anxieties and ambitions. The new technologies of the moving image and wireless provoked a fascinating mixture of utopian and dystopian speculation arising from the new notions of time, space, and subjectivity they seemed to embody, and many contemporaneous commentators saw the technologies as emblematic of an emerging culture brought about by urbanization and industrialization. A reconsideration of the respective places of early cinema and wireless in the technological and popular imaginations of the period can suggest some of the ways in which these distinct fields of media history might inform and support one another. After offering some preliminary notes on some of the differing historiographic premises of the two fields, this chapter will explore a few common and distinctive features in the scientific and popular cultures which informed the earliest days of the two pre-eminent communications media of the twentieth century.

If cinema's recent centenary provoked widespread critical lamentation of the film medium's putative prospective demise, it also capped a quarter-century of extremely productive scholarship devoted to early cinema and pre-cinema. At the same time, the uneven but seemingly inexorable slow-motion collapse over the past two decades of the stable structures of commercial broadcast oligopolies and public service institutions of terrestrial broadcasting across the globe have thrown into crisis long-accepted scholarly and vernacular representations of broadcasting's history and nature. More recently, the introduction of the digital video recorder, with its challenge to the foundational practices of live reception and commercial underwriting, has provoked the interrogation of broadcasting's twin ontologies of simultaneity and the mass audience. For popular audiences and scholars alike, the eschatological bent of much of the current discussions of both cinema and broadcasting has foregrounded issues of origins and historical determination. Current talk of our own putative 'post-cinema' and 'post-broadcasting' era has provoked historians and journalists alike to look anew to the roots of both media in the scientific and popular cultures of the late nineteenth century and early twentieth century.

Within the academic study of electronic media, there is some justice in historian Michele Hilmes's claim that radio 'has become the "repressed" of television studies, occupying a position similar to that of the silent film era in film studies twenty years ago'.[1] As an object of formal post-secondary study, radio has been largely relegated to a few lectures in an undergraduate survey class and a handful of vocational courses in departments of communication, even as the study of television has exploded across the humanities in the past decade in North America and the UK.[2]

In support of the optimistic, perhaps wishful, implication of Hilmes's historiographic analogy between the two fields, there is at least some evidence to suggest that broadcast scholars are indeed devoting new energy to the study of the wider historical roots of broadcast culture, reflected in heightened activity in journals, monographs, and conference papers. In another temporally displaced echo across the fields of film and media studies, just as Tom Gunning once linked the historiographic turn in 1970s film studies toward the study of early cinema to what he called the 'pseudomorphs' of the cinema of attractions and the contemporaneous avant-garde film practice of North America and the UK, one could argue that recent avant-garde audio and radio work has sparked new interest in a century of experimentation by artists in recorded sound and wireless, from the Italian and Russian futurists to Antonin Artaud, John Cage, and William Burroughs.[3] Recent reconsideration of this artistic work has been accompanied by heightened attention to the rich history of recorded sound and radio theory, encompassing the writings of many figures already familiar to film studies, including Dziga Vertov, Bertolt Brecht, Rudolf Arnheim, and Theodor Adorno.[4] Indeed, even the recent debates around the emerging discipline of visual studies have served to highlight the new relevance of the historical and theoretical consideration of recorded sound and radio for the wider study of contemporary media culture. At the same time, the often-observed intellectual divide between social-science-oriented broadcast scholars and humanities-based film historians has been muted by a generation and a half of academic researchers trained in film studies who have been responsible for much of the most significant work in contemporary television and media studies.

1 Michele Hilmes, *Radio Voices: American Broadcasting, 1922–52* (Minneapolis: University of Minnesota Press, 1997), p. xv.

2 Michele Hilmes, 'Rethinking Radio', in Michele Hilmes and Jason Loviglio (eds.), *Radio Reader: Essays in the Cultural History of Radio* (New York: Routledge, 2002), 2.

3 See, for example, Douglas Kahn and Gregory Whitehead, *Wireless Imagination: Sound, Radio, and the Avant-Garde* (Cambridge, Mass.: MIT Press, 1992), and Allen S. Weiss, *Phantasmic Radio* (Durham, NC: Duke University Press, 1995).

4 See, for example, Dziga Vertov, *Kino-eye: The Writings of Dziga Vertov*, ed. with an introduction by Annette Michelson, trans. Kevin O'Brien (Berkeley and Los Angeles: University of California Press, 1984); Bertolt Brecht, *Brecht on Film and Radio*, trans. and ed. Marc Silberman (London: Methuen, 2000); Rudolf Arnheim, *Radio: An Art of Sound* (New York: Da Capo Press, 1972); Anton Kaes, Martin Jay, and Edward Dimendberg (eds.), *The Weimar Republic Sourcebook* (Berkeley and Los Angeles: University of California Press, 1994).

Meanwhile, scholars of early film have become more sensitive to the parallel genealogies of electronic media reaching back into the prehistory of motion pictures, part of a wider elaboration of the cultural and technological horizon of early cinema. As William Uricchio pointed out in 1997, the introduction of the telephone in 1876 inspired a number of speculative inventions which linked the simultaneity of the telephone to the photographic image, arguing that, 'with a few exceptions, simultaneity seems an implicit part of the pre-cinematic conception of a moving-picture medium'.[5] Uricchio linked television's prehistory in the nineteenth century's anticipated fusion of photography and the telephone to the ubiquitous 'rocks and waves' genre of early film actualities, even suggesting that such filmic evidence 'renders cinema as something like a long detour from what audiences *really* wanted', i.e. live television.[6] Similarly, Thomas Elsaesser argued that the conventional model of technological history as a series of relay-race baton-passings between successive innovations toward a foreordained goal is itself a distinctly nineteenth-century artefact. Instead, Elsaesser proposed a number of alternative media genealogies, linking serial photography, the Polaroid, the video image, the VCR, and the digital disc or, alternatively, the telegraph, the telephone, the wireless, and satellite communication.[7]

Such recent rescramblings of conventional media genealogies by film scholars suggest less a rearrangement of cast members in a familiar historical narrative than the recognition that, in historian Carolyn Marvin's words, 'media are not fixed natural objects; they have no natural edges. They are constructed complexes of habits, beliefs, and procedures embedded in elaborate cultural codes of communication.'[8] Marvin herself examines the telephone and electric light as nineteenth-century communications media, prototypes for the electronic mediation of private and public space and the provision of mass spectacle respectively, and argues that these early inventions became important tools used by audiences and critics to think about subsequent inventions and the societies that engendered them.[9] When considering the place of cinema and wireless in late nineteenth-century popular imagination, it is important to keep in mind the legacies of earlier inventions like the telegraph and telephone, which occasioned widespread popular and scientific speculation about the future of domestic communication and public spectacle. The distinct institutional and technological paths of motion pictures and electronic media in the twentieth century may obscure some of the significant common contexts and features in the nineteenth century.

At the same time, there are some fundamental methodological differences confronting historians of the two media; while film historians justly lament the loss of so much motion-picture material from the early cinema period,

---

5 William Uricchio, 'Ways of Seeing: The New Vision of Early Nonfiction Film', in Daan Hertogs and Nico De Klerk (eds.), *Uncharted Territory: Essays in Early Nonfiction Film* (Amsterdam: Netherlands Film Museum, 1997), 130.

6 Ibid.

7 Thomas Elsaesser, 'Louis Lumiere: The Cinema's First Virtualist?', in Thomas Elsaesser and Kay Hoffman (eds.), *Cinema Futures: Cain, Abel or Cable* (Amsterdam: Amsterdam University Press, 1998), 47–8.

8 Carolyn Marvin, *When Old Technologies Were New: Thinking about Electric Communication in the Late Nineteenth Century* (New York: Oxford University Press, 1988), 8.

9 Ibid. 6.

they nevertheless enjoy access to such primary texts in a way unimaginable to historians of early radio. In addition, unlike the case of the telegraph or the cinema, where the path between scientific invention and commercial diffusion was relatively brief and direct, the transition between the radio's enabling technology and its commercial application is strikingly extended and discontinuous. Thus, contrary to the straightforward periodization of 'early cinema', radio experienced the distinct stages of point-to-point Morse code transmission after 1897, amateur point-to-point voice transmission after 1907, and broadcasting proper after 1920. An imperfect analogy would be as if the first decade or two of motion-picture history consisted of amateurs fabricating their own cameras and projectors and exchanging home movies among themselves before anyone thought of opening a theatre to a paying public. As the president of RCA acknowledged in 1929, broadcasting was the 'surprise party' of radio, and it is wireless's sustained period of amateur activity and commercial uncertainty and improvisation before 1922 that marks its distinction from most pervious and subsequent media, including television.[10] Certainly, radio's successive rebirths in distinct applications makes more complicated both the preliminary historiographic task of periodization and the larger challenge of discerning the relations between technological innovation and cultural setting.

The shared contexts of cinema and wireless

Notwithstanding the complications of historical periodization and historical artefact, cinema and wireless emerged from the same rich context of scientific research and popular amusements in an era marked by modernity's massive transformations of human settlement, industrial labour, as well as the scale of business and bureaucratic organization, global commerce, and political power. One shared cultural site informing the beginnings of both media was the nineteenth-century popular exposition and world's fair, 'designed', in Tom Gunning's words, 'to bring together, in concentrated and spectacular form, the experience of modernity to masses of people'.[11] A number of film historians have eloquently laid out cinema's debt to the mass exposition as an object lesson in public spectacle, technological progress, and imperial might, and Thomas Elsaesser argues that both cinema and world's fair represent attempts to mediate a crisis of cultural self-definition.[12] In this context, it is striking to note the prominence of wireless technologies in many of the same expositions that scholars of cinema have scrutinized, including the 1900 World Exhibition in Paris and the 1904 St Louis World Exposition. The place of electrical and wireless technology in such popular expositions represents the nineteenth-century apotheosis of what historian David Nye calls the 'American technological sublime'; between 1880 and 1915, he argues, such electrical exhibitions celebrated the spectacular effects

10 J. G. Harbord, 'Commercial Uses of Radio', *Annals of the American Academy of Political and Social Science*, 142 (Mar. 1929), 57.

11 Tom Gunning, 'Re-inventing Vision: The Cinema's Radical Challenge to Representation', talk at the Guggenheim Museum, Apr. 2000, http://bboptics.com/gunning1900-1.html.

12 Elsaesser, 'The Cinema's First Virtualist?', 46.

of electric light over the scale or prowess of any specific piece of machinery.[13] Chicago's 1893 World's Fair and Columbian Exposition, visited by 27 million people, employed more lighting devices than any city in the country at the time, and featured the 82-foot Edison Tower of Light with its 5,000 electric bulbs; Buffalo's exposition of 1901, celebrating the first hydroelectric dam on Niagara Falls, used electricity as its central theme.[14] As Nye points out, for most Americans between 1880 and 1910 electrification was largely an urban, public experience; for example, at a time when only 5 per cent of US homes had electricity, Broadway was already known as the Great White Way.[15] Marvin points to the proto-broadcast nature of many of the spectacular nineteenth-century public uses of electric lighting and signage, and, more generally, the technologies of electricity and wireless were often linked in the activities of its promoters and in the popular press. Electric power and wireless pioneer Nikola Tesla would thrill his nineteenth-century audiences with displays of sparks and flames emanating from his body during public lecture-demonstrations, and his personal exhibit within Westinghouse's 1893 Columbian Exposition display included a darkened 18-foot public chamber situated between two high-frequency emitting plates, where visitors were invited to handle an assortment of autonomous phosphorescent tubes twisted into letters spelling the names of prominent inventors; as one visitor noted, 'two or three were prepared with inscriptions, like "Welcome, Electricians," and produced a beautiful effect'.[16] Marvin also notes the tension within the nineteenth-century engineering fraternity concerning the public presentation of technological innovations between a tone of scientific rationalism and the rhetoric of magic and seance, and points out that both the professional and popular presses alternately treated Tesla as scientific visionary and mystically inclined showman.[17]

It is clear that electricity, and the mysterious ether that was popularly hypothesized as its invisible medium, exerted a powerful hold on the public imagination throughout the extended anticipation of electronic communication in the nineteenth and early twentieth centuries. As historian David Nye argues, 'electricity was not merely one more commodity; rather it played a central role in the creation of a twentieth-century sensibility. Electricity seemed linked to the structure of social reality; it seemed both to underlie physical and psychic health and to guarantee economic progress.'[18] Part of the power of electricity came from its imperfectly understood nature; Ambrose Bierce's 1906 *Devil's Dictionary* defined electricity as 'the power that causes all natural phenomena not known to be caused by something else',[19] and, as

13 David Nye, *American Technological Sublime* (Cambridge, Mass.: MIT Press, 1994), 143–4.

14 Marvin, *When Old Technologies Were New*, 171.

15 David E. Nye, *Electrifying America: Social Meanings of a New Technology, 1880–1940* (Cambridge, Mass.: MIT Press, 1990), 382–3.

16 'Mr Tesla's Personal Exhibit at the World's Fair', in Thomas Commerford Martin (ed.), *The Inventions, Researches and Writings of Nikola Tesla* (2nd edn. New York: Barnes and Noble, 1992; 1st pub. 1893), n.p.

17 Marvin, *When Old Technologies Were New*, 48.

18 Nye, *Electrifying America*, 156.

19 Ibid. 152.

Jeffrey Sconce points out, by the beginning of the twentieth century, electrical communication already had a fifty-year history of association with the occult, including the intimate and sustained entanglement of the telegraph and spiritualism. As historian Daniel Czitrom notes, 'ether theory straddled the physical and the metaphysical', and popular references to the mysterious medium persisted for decades after its existence was repudiated by physicists.[20] Christoph Asendorf argues that, in the nineteenth century, imaginative ideas about electricity in popular literature preceded their technological embodiment, and notes the long-running fascination with electricity within Romantic literature and popular thought, including the spark of life in Galvani's frog's legs and Mary Shelley's *Frankenstein* of 1818, popular accounts of erotic attraction, Franz Mesmer's model of medicine, and countless late nineteenth-century therapeutic treatments and devices addressed to the new nervous and physical maladies themselves brought on by modernity.[21]

Asendorf links the Romantic fascination with electricity with a more general fascination with things that flow, including water, crowds, thoughts, libidinal energy, poetic association, money, even the visual trope of women's hair tracing the lines of a magnetic force field which permeated both Symbolist art and the trademark logos and advertisements of manufacturers of electrical equipment at the turn of the century.[22] Wolfgang Schivelbusch also notes the pervasiveness of biological metaphors of circulation in late nineteenth-century life, prevailing over ideas of transport, communication, retail design, public architecture, and the human psyche and body.[23] Tom Gunning recently linked these pervasive late nineteenth-century metaphors of flow and immersion to the serpentine dances so frequently recorded by early film-makers. The serpentine dances of the celebrated Loie Fuller, Gunning argues, themselves seen as peculiarly American and industrial in their use of the new electric light, can be linked not only to early cinema's iconography of nature's movements—the rustle of leaves, the crashing of waves, the passage of a landscape in a phantom ride film—but to the cinematic experience itself for early audiences.[24]

Wireless technology, unprecedented and imperfectly understood, provoked countless analogies to such biological metaphors of flow; as Carolyn Marvin notes, the human body, inescapable border between nature and culture, remained central to nineteenth-century attempts to understand electricity.[25] One observer in 1892 responded to a series of early wireless experiments in the UK:

> The thought in a man's brain which causes him to advance his foot, must move *something* in doing it, or how could it be transmitted down that five

20 Daniel Czitrom, *Media and the American Mind: From Morse to Marconi* (Chapel Hill: University of North Carolina Press, 1982), 64–5.

21 Christoph Asendorf, 'Nerves and Electricity', in *Batteries of Life: On the History of things and their Perception in Modernity* (Berkeley and Los Angeles: University of California Press, 1993), 153–5.

22 Ibid. 153, 164–5.

23 Wolfgang Schivelbusch, *The Railway Journey: The Industrialization of Time and Space in the 19th Century* (Berkeley and Los Angeles: University of California Press, 1986).

24 Gunning, 'Re-inventing Vision'.

25 Marvin, *When Old Technologies Were New*, 109.

or six feet of distance? If it moves a physical something, internal to the body, why should it not move also something external, a wave, as we all agree to call it, which on another mind prepared to receive it . . . will make an impact having all the effect in the conveyance of suggestion, or even of facts, of the audibility of words? Why, in fact, if one wire can talk to another without connections, save through ether . . . should not mind talk to mind without any 'wire' at all?[26]

The writer went on to argue that 'if you stir the ocean of ether, the motion so created must roll on, in some sense, for ever; for a portion of ether is displaced, and must displace another portion'.[27] Henry Parr Maskell, in his 1934 book *The Human Wireless: A Practical Guide to Telepathy and Thought Transference*, located the first scientific interest in telepathy to the founding of Societies for Psychical Research in several cities across Europe and North America in the 1870s, while tracing its popular expression back to medieval ideas of the aura.[28] Harvard professor John Trowbridge told readers of *Popular Science* in 1899 that the 'wireless telegraph is the nearest approach to telepathy that we have vouchsafed to our intelligence. . . . The nerves of the whole world are, so to speak, being bound together, so that a touch in one country is transmitted instantly to a far-distant one', and the possible utility of the wireless in communicating with the supposed inhabitants of Mars was a common topic in turn of the century scientific and popular writing.[29] The persistent association of wireless with telepathy, not surprisingly, also provoked criticism from defenders of scientific rationality during the early twentieth century; for example, a 1914 article complained that 'a great number of semi-intelligent people . . . were led by the supposition that "telepathy" was analogous to "wireless telegraphy" . . . , with a confortable assurance that their belief has somehow or another a sort of scientific basis'.[30]

As we shall see in the next chapter, for other early twentieth-century observers, the link between wireless and the occult remained both credible and disquieting. While electricity in the nineteenth-century popular imagination had long-established fearful associations with public disaster, personal trauma, and violent death, and the point-to-point media of the telegraph, telephone, and wireless were frequently linked to themes of alienation, isolation, and loss of personal agency, it is clear that the beginnings of broadcasting in the early 1920s brought new popular anxieties about the coercive and authoritarian aspects of communication technologies to the fore.[31]

26 'A Dreamy View of Mr Preece's Experiment', *Spectator* (29 Nov. 1892), 765.

27 Ibid.

28 Henry Parr Maskell, *The Human Wireless: A Practical Guide to Telepathy and Thought Transference* (London: C. A. Pearson, Ltd., 1934), 14–16.

29 John Trowbridge, 'Wireless Telegraphy', *Popular Science* (Nov. 1899), 59–73.

30 'The Analogy between Wireless Telegraphy and Waves from Brain to Brain', *Current Opinion* (Oct. 1914), 253.

31 Tom Gunning, 'Heard over the Phone: *The Lonely Villa* and the de Lorde Tradition of the Terrors of Technology', *Screen*, 32/2 (Summer 1991), 184–96; early cinema provides many examples of the association between electricity and spectacularized death as figured in the many pseudo-actuality executions by electric chair and in the filmed electrocution of a Coney Island fairground elephant before 1,500 spectators and Thomas Edison's camera in 1902; see Lisa Cartwright, *Screening the Body: Tracing Medicine's Visual Culture* (Minneapolis: University of Minnesota Press, 1995), ch. 2.

Conclusion

If wireless and early cinema are linked in the common contexts of nineteenth-century science and popular culture, there remains a seemingly irreconcilable distinction in the historiographies of cinema and wireless, that embodied in the publicness of cinema's site of reception versus the domestic setting of wireless fabrication and reception.[32] Indeed, it was cinema's creation of a new public sphere that provoked both Walter Benjamin's excitement about cinema's liberating potential and the deep anxiety among many early twentieth-century conservative critics. The popular press of the period frequently contrasted the social dangers of cinema-going (associated with the city, the street, the dance hall, and the amusement park) with the therapeutic and family-affirming qualities of radio as a hobby, especially for male adolescents. It is important to keep in mind, however, that the late nineteenth century witnessed a sustained crisis in the cultural definitions of private and public space, marked by a number of striking irreconcilable topographies conflating the domestic and the public, including Schivelbusch's public railway carriage appointed in the deeply upholstered style of the bourgeois living room, Benjamin's urban arcade presenting the street as furnished interior, and the domestic living room itself penetrated by the new industrial artefacts of the telephone, the stereopticon, and the magic lantern.[33] Likewise, while radio clearly participated in a 200-year-old anti-urban vision of demographic dispersal and domestic self-sufficiency going back to the use of electric power in factories, the nature of domesticity that wireless helped to bring about was itself deeply contradictory.[34] A Maine newspaper article in 1898, foreseeing the widespread electrical transmission of live events into the home, predicted that 'one's own family and neighborhood would then be the stable center of the universe—beyond it would be margin and chaos'.[35] At the same time, broadcasting also represented an unprecedented integration of the home with the time values and economic imperatives of large-scale capitalism.[36] Thus, the prominent claims for a new technologically achieved domesticity in the early twentieth century seem less like observations about the empirical role of wireless in the home and more like yet another reaction formation to modernity's assault on subjectivity which film scholars and social historians have been describing for decades. The longevity of such reactionary appeals to an imagined domesticity restored by electronic communication is apparent in the promotion of contemporary digital media in our post-cinema and post-broadcasting era. The widely predicted disruptive effects of a range of new public and domestic

---

32 This opposition is belied to some degree by both the early use of motion pictures within the home (although the institutionalization of the 'home movies' arrives only in the 1920s) and the collective nature of much early wireless activity, including equipment fabrication, group listening outside the home, proliferating amateur radio clubs, and widespread socializing in radio shops.

33 Tom Gunning, talk at Deutsches Haus, Columbia University, 19 Apr. 2002.

34 'Removing the Last Objection to Living in the Country', *Country Life* (London) (Feb. 1922), 63.

35 Quoted in Marvin, *When Old Technologies Were New*, 200.

36 Raymond Williams, *Television: Technology and Cultural Form* (New York: Schocken, 1975); also see William Boddy, 'The Rhetoric and the Economic Roots of the American Broadcasting Industry', *Cinetracts*, 6 (Spring 1979), 37–54.

moving-image platforms, including the digital video recorder, video on demand, and electronic cinema, suggest the usefulness of a historical reconsideration of earlier periods of technological innovation for unravelling the meaning of our own era's prospects and choices. Such a reconsideration is offered in the following chapters.

2

Wireless Nation: Defining Radio as a Domestic Technology

DESPITE UBIQUITOUS CLAIMS for the revolutionary nature of the changes associated with the current transition from analogue to digital moving-image media, there is little doubt that the public's first experiences with wireless communication 100 years ago represent a period of more traumatic uncertainty and improvisation than our own. Moreover, the fundamental economic models, institutions, programme forms, and audience practices which emerged from the first two decades of radio in the twentieth century have proven to be remarkably durable across the decades of successive technological innovations. Older media technologies, especially those like the telegraph, telephone, and wireless, which inspired widespread public and scientific speculation and anxiety, function as powerful templates through which subsequent media forms are understood and promoted. Many of the controversies associated with the recent introduction of a range of digital products and services, from virtual reality to high-definition television, from the digital video recorder to virtual advertising, echo debates which accompanied the rise of radio broadcasting in the first quarter of the twentieth century. These persistent themes include the role of electronic media in mediating public and private space, in accommodating the gendered routines of domestic life, and in constructing a public sense of national identity. The first two decades of wireless activity in the United States precipitated these questions in their starkest form, anticipating many of the ways the same topics would be taken up in subsequent controversies.

The wireless nation

Early radio broadcasting gained a powerful hold on popular imagination in part because it was widely seen as the culmination of a series of marvellous inventions in transportation and communication—the railway, the telegraph and telephone, the electric light, the photograph, the cinema —of what one rapturous 1920s commentator called 'the last decade of that great, forward-striding century, the nineteenth', when 'the Western world—particularly among its northern races—was on the very verge of that complete individual mastery of nature towards which its creative minds had been working since the revival of learning some four centuries earlier'.[1] Not surprisingly, wireless became enmeshed in the nationalist and geopolitical issues of the day. The recurring triumphantist allegory of technologically enabled racial and geopolitical ascendancy was offered as early as 1858, when H. L. Wayland argued in the *New Englander* that the new telegraph 'gives the preponderance of power to the nations representing the highest elements of humanity . . . It is the civilized and Christian nations, who, though weak comparatively in numbers, are by these means of communication made more than a match for the hordes of barbarism.'[2] Pointing to the projected linguistic consequences of rapid development of radio broadcasting in the USA and UK in a 1924 article, 'The Social Destiny of Radio', Waldemar Kaempffert (former editor of *Scientific American*) offered the general historical proposition that 'the more powerful commercial and military nations have forced their languages upon the weaker'. Kaempffert went on to argue that the new communications medium would bring about a hegemony of the English language over the other languages of Europe:

> who will deny that radio will bring about a more pronounced unification of speech? . . . It so happens that the United States and Great Britain have taken the lead in broadcasting. If that lead is maintained it follows that English must become the dominant tongue. . . . In a generation radio can do more toward making English the language of the world than would be possible in a century of international railroading, telegraphing, and cabling. The most numerous and powerful broadcasting stations are now American; the most captivating programs are those of American stations; the foremost political orators, preachers, actors, editors, authors, and artists have addressed hundreds of thousands in English. Compared with our radio efforts at mass entertainment and mass education, European competition is pathetic. All ears may eventually be cocked to hear what the United States and Great Britain have to say. Europe will find it desirable, even necessary, to learn English.[3]

In the same article, Kaempffert offered similarly reassuring forecasts of radio's role in preserving global empire, dismissing fears of 'a few pessimistic students of English history [who] assume that the British Empire, sprawling over large areas in the East and West, must ultimately collapse'. Instead, Kaempffert insisted that

> they forget that time and not distance is the controlling factor in communication, that this is the age of electricity and not of the frigate and the horse . . . Communication means organization, and radio, particularly in its broadcasting aspect, will prove the most potent unifying influence that has appeared since the railway and the

1 Paul Schubert, *The Electric Word: The Rise of Radio* (New York: Macmillan, 1928), 3, 6.

2 Quoted in Daniel Czitrom, *Media and the American Mind: From Morse to Marconi* (Chapel Hill: University of North Carolina Press, 1982), 10. For an examination of the discourses of electrical communication in the late 19th century, see Carolyn Marvin, *When Old Technologies Were New* (New York: Oxford University Press, 1988), ch. 5.

3 Waldemar Kaempffert, 'The Social Destiny of Radio', *Forum* (June 1924), 770–1.

telegraph were invented. It must knit the dominions of Great Britain more closely together than ever.[4]

Just as some early twentieth-century commentators saw the emerging electronic media serving to shore up Western ascendancy and imperial power across the globe, others viewed wireless as a way to enhance national identity and state power in the United States. Underlying many initial reactions to radio in the USA were the often fearful implications of the demographic changes that unprecedented industrialization and immigration had brought to early twentieth-century America, changes that, many worried, threatened the viability of the nation state itself. In 1924, Waldemar Kaempffert offered a lyrical and paternalistic vision of the new radio medium as agent of national identity:

> Look at a map of the United States and try to conjure up a picture of what home radio will eventually bring. Here are hundreds of little towns set down in type so small that it can hardly be read. How unrelated they seem! Then picture the tens of thousands of farmhouses on the prairies, in the valleys, along the rivers—houses that cannot be noted. It is only an idea that holds them together—the idea that they form part of the United States. One of them might as well be in China and another in Labrador were it not for this binding sense of a common nationality. All these disconnected communities and houses will be united through radio as they were never united by the telegraph and telephone. The President of the United States delivers important messages in every home, not in cold, impersonal type, but in living speech; he is transformed from what is almost a political abstraction, a personification of the nation's dignity and power, into a kindly father, talking to his children.[5]

As we shall see in Chapter 4, the figuration of the broadcast audience as childlike, part of what media scholar John Hartley calls broadcasting's 'paedocratic regime', has enjoyed remarkable longevity in twentieth-century American critical and policy debates.[6] In more martial terms than Kaempffert's, a writer in *Radio Dealer* in 1923 also lauded broadcasting's unique mobilizing power, another recurring theme in post-Second World War discussions of American media:

> No longer will the roll of drums or the blare of bugles be needed to rouse the nation to arms. A single voice, spoken in Washington but heard throughout the length and breadth of the land, a voice vibrant with emotion, staunch with courage and ringing with authority will summon

4 Kaempffert, 'The Social Destiny of Radio', 769–70; for a discussion of electronic communication and empire, see Stephen Kern, *The Culture of Time and Space, 1880–1918* (Cambridge, Mass.: Harvard University Press, 1983), ch. 8.

5 Waldemar Kaempffert, *Modern Wonder Works: A Popular History of American Invention* (New York: Blue Ribbon Books, 1924), 378. Kaempffert went on to argue: 'The telegraph and telephone have been called "space annihilators" in their day. Space annihilation indeed! We never really knew what the term meant until the time came when thousands listened at the same time to the voice broadcast through the ether just as if they were all in the same room.'

6 John Hartley, 'Invisible Fictions: Television, Audiences, Paedocracy, Pleasure', in Gary Burns and Robert Thompson (eds.), *Television Studies: Textual Analysis* (New York: Praeger, 1989), 223–43.

the nation to action, will weld a hundred million people into a solidarity such as the world has never known before.[7]

Many other early observers endorsed the vision of radio as political and cultural unifier. Broadcasting provided, according to NBC's president in 1930, a perfect means 'to preserve our now vast population from disintegrating into classes. . . . We must know and honor the same heroes, love the same songs, enjoy the same sports, realize our common interest in our national problems,' he argued.[8] In a more alarmist tone, J. M. McKibbin Jr., in a 1923 trade magazine article entitled 'New Ways to Make Americans', hailed radio as an invaluable instrument of national unity in an increasingly multicultural America:

> Today this nation of ours is slowly but surely being conquered, not by a single enemy in open warfare, but by a dozen insidious (though often unconscious) enemies in peace. . . . Millions of foreigners were received into the country, with little or no thought given to their assimilation. . . . Each [ethnic community] is a parasite living upon the natural resources and under the protection offered by America, yet giving little or nothing in return. It is this process of nationality isolation within one country which is ruinous.
>
> Until recently we have given little thought to the assimilation of the foreign element within our shores, But now the crisis is upon us; and we must face it without a great leader. Perhaps no man could mold the 120 million people into a harmonious whole, bound together by a strong national consciousness: but in the place of a superhuman individual, the genius of the last decade has provided a force—*and that force is radio.*[9]

The belief in broadcasting as an authoritarian and paternalistic agent of national unity had many supporters in the early twentieth century, including A. N. Goldsmith, RCA's director of research, who told a journalist in May 1922: 'At last we shall have a "voice of the government." The government will be a living thing to its citizens instead of an abstract and unseen force . . . it will elicit a new national loyalty and produce a more contented citizenry.'[10] Similarly, Stanley Frost, in a 1922 *Colliers* article entitled 'Radio Dreams that Can Come True', argued that radio 'can do more than any other agency in spreading mutual understanding to all sections of the country, to unify our thoughts, ideals and purposes, to making us a strong and well-knit people'.[11]

Not surprisingly, there were dissenters to such rosy visions of radio as agent of the centralization of language, culture, and political power. Joseph K. Hart, in a 1922 article, 'Radiating Culture', challenged the optimistic predictions of electronic media as instruments of global harmony already

---

7 A. H. Corwin, 'Bright Future for the Dealer is Assured', *Radio Dealer* (Mar. 1923), 18.

8 Merlin Aylesworth, 'Report of the President', in *Reports on Advisory Council* (New York: NBC, 1930), n.p.

9 J. M. McKibbin Jr., 'New Way to Make Americans', *Radio Broadcast* (Jan. 1923), 238. Emphasis in original.

10 E. H. Felix, 'A. N. Goldsmith on the Future of Wireless Telephony', *Radio Broadcast* (May 1922), 44.

11 Stanley Frost, 'Radio Dreams that Can Come True', *Colliers* 10 (June 1922), 18.

familiar from both popular scientific writing and utopian fiction since the last third of the nineteenth century. Hart warned that 'a means of instantaneous communication to all the peoples of the earth ought to usher in the day of universal understanding, sympathy and peace. But it is not likely to do so. It is more likely to usher in the day of domination and control, with all the struggles implied in such attempts.'[12] The long-imagined perfection of electronic communication, rooted in what historian James Carey calls the nineteenth-century 'electrical sublime', for Hart might lead instead to the aggrandizement of a single powerful individual in control of the new broadcast technology:

> That mind will 'bestride the earth like a colossus.' Speaking through his radiophone, he will command the world and the obedient minds of men. He will tell men what to think and say and how to act. He will shape them to a common, uniform, subservient mediocrity.[13]

While noting the contributions of motion pictures to popular education, Hart declared that radio would made such visual education antiquated; the 'all-pervasive ether', declared Hart, 'has been pressed into the service of an all-pervasive culture, near-culture and pseudo-culture. If any one remains uncultured, today, it will be against the combined efforts of the world.'[14] Bruce Blevin, also writing in 1922, displayed similar foreboding about the centralizing effects of broadcasting when he imagined the nature of broadcasting in 1930, when, he forecast,

> there will be only one orchestra left on earth, giving nightly world-wide concerts; when all universities will be combined into one super-institution, conducting courses by radio for students in Zanzibar, Kamchatka and Oskaloosa; when, instead of newspapers, trained orators will dictate the news of the world day and night, and the bed-time story will be told every evening from Paris to the sleepy children of a weary world; when every person will be instantly accessible day or night to all the bores he knows, and will know them all; when the last vestiges of privacy, solitude and contemplation will have vanished into limbo.[15]

These fears of a centrally administered wireless culture undoubtedly resonated in an era whose popular and elite cultures were preoccupied with the widely feared invidious implications of the new 'mass mind' brought about by traumatic urbanization and the explosion of mass commercial leisure of the late nineteenth and early twentieth centuries. Jenny Irene Mix, in a 1923 *Radio Broadcast* article entitled 'Is Radio Standardizing the American Mind?', cited recent complaints from Brown University president William Herber Perry Faunce that radio was creating a 'mob mind', as millions listening to the same programme were 'brought down to the level of mass intelligence'.[16]

---

12 Joseph K. Hart, 'Radiating Culture', *Survey* (18 Mar. 1922), 949.

13 Ibid.

14 Ibid. 948.

15 Bruce Blevin, 'The Ether Will Now Oblige', *New Republic* (15 Feb. 1922), 330.

16 Jenny Irene Mix, 'Is Radio Standardizing the American Mind?', *Radio Broadcast* (Oct. 1923), n.p.

Radio and the uncanny

Such misgivings suggest that the confident and instrumentalist visions of radio as a conservative force for national unity and global power coexisted with more ambivalent and anxious responses to the medium in the early twentieth century. Likewise, while the otherworldly qualities of wireless communication were appropriated by some commentators in support of mainstream Christianity, for many others the mysterious nature of wireless communication was less reassuring. A commentator in 1892 expressed hope that radio science would 'make possible for men to conceive of what spiritual existence may be like', and C. N. Broadhurst, a Methodist minister from Missouri, in 1910 published a book, *Wireless Messages: Possibilities through Prayer*, which consisted entirely of brief sermon excerpts and anecdotes built around an exhaustive catalogue of analogies between wireless communication and prayer.[17] A 1922 article in *Radio Broadcast* alluded to the loftier aspects of the new radio hobby, arguing that 'all the fascination of a link between the physical and the spiritual is here, and it is far from easy to rid ourselves of the feeling that we are on the threshold of fundamental truths which have baffled humanity through the centuries'.[18] Mark Casper, editor of the *Masonic Review*, writing in *Radio Dealer* in 1922, argued flatly that:

> radio proves the truth of the omnipotence of the Almighty. When the Bible tells us God is omnipresent and sees all we do and knows all our thoughts—we can now better realize that if we, mere humans, can 'listen in' and hear people talk all over the earth with a radio set, a foot or two long, what power must we ascribe to the Almighty? Can we longer doubt his omnipresence and omnipotence? Behold, the all-seeing eye![19]

A Baptist minister from Maine writing in *Radio Broadcast* in 1923 offered the following pious reaction to his first on-air exposure to the chatter of distant amateur wireless messages: 'Such, I thought, is the spirit of America, the spirit of Christianity, the spirit and goodwill the world needs. Moreover, broadcasting is glorified as it scatters this cordial good feeling to the ends of the earth.'[20] Howard Vincent O'Brien, writing in *Colliers* in 1924, argued that radio might bridge the prominent contemporary schism between Fundamentalism and Modernism, and religion and science generally, among the legion of new wireless fans:

---

17 'A Dreamy View of Mr Preece's Experiment', *Spectator* (29 Nov. 1892), 765; C. N. Broadhurst, *Wireless Messages: Possibilities through Prayer* (London: Fleming H. Revell, 1910). Indicating the pervasiveness and looseness of the popular association between wireless and telepathy, a 1915 book describing a spiritualist's communication with beings from Mars, Neptune, Jupiter, Mercury, and Saturn entitled *Wireless Messages from Other Worlds* makes no other direct reference to wireless technology beyond its title; see Eva Harrison, *Wireless Messages from Other Worlds* (London: L. N. Fowler and Company, 1915). For a discussion of the links between early radio and the spiritual, see Susan Douglas, *Listening In: Radio and the American Imagination* (New York: Times Books, 1999), ch. 2.

18 W. H. Worrel, 'Do Brains or Dollars Operate your Set?', *Radio Broadcast* (Nov. 1922), n.p.

19 Mark Casper, 'Radio Broadcasting', *Radio Dealer* (June 1922), 62.

20 Revd H. F. Huse, 'Radio Angling and Fisherman's Luck', *Radio Broadcast* (Aug. 1923), 318.

As they move interleaved aluminum plates a fraction of an inch, and in space multiply that movement to thousands of miles, the dullest of them cannot fail to wonder and inquire. And thus, in some measure, they will learn obedience to the Sovereign of the world and acquire confidence in His declarations. For the end of inquiry is wisdom. And the end of wisdom is faith.[21]

Former ad-man and best-selling religious writer Bruce Barton described his experience of early wireless in 1922 in similar spiritual terms:

I thought of the first telegraph message flashed over the Baltimore–Washington line seventy-eight years ago last spring—the pious exclamation of a reverent soul: 'What hath God wrought!' And it seemed to me that every program from a broadcasting station might well be prefaced by a modification of that solemn message: 'What *is* God working', and 'What *will* God work?'[22]

Expressions of this putative teleology of faith and scientific progress pervade the record of conservative responses to electronic communications, from popular reports of the first telegraph message in 1846 to the prognostications of conservative digital-media pundits in the 1990s, as we shall see in Chapter 6.

However, in contrast to those who discerned a reassuring divine plan in early radio's technological progress, other observers viewed the otherworldly aspects of wireless communication with disquiet, including Joseph K. Hart, who warned in 1922 that 'the most occult goings-on are about us. Man has his fingers on the triggers of the universe. He doesn't understand all he is doing. He can turn strange energies loose. He may turn loose more than he has figured on; more than he can control.'[23] In much of the early commentary and popular fiction devoted to wireless, such technological anxieties were enacted around the trope of static, that mysterious and arbitrary ocean of noise which provided both the background to and frequent interruption of early wireless messages. A writer in the *New York Times* in February 1922 cited the shock of his first exposure to what amateurs called 'Old Man Static': 'You are fascinated, though a trifle awestruck, to realize that you are listening to sounds that, surely, were never intended to be heard by a human being. The delicate mechanism of the radio has caught and brought to the ears of us earth dwellers the noises that roar in the space between the worlds.'[24] Historian Jeffrey Sconce has noted the ways in which early twentieth-century fiction insistently figured radio's ethereal medium as an ocean which threatened to swallow up and disperse human consciousness.[25] Wireless's ethereal ocean was a recurring trope for writers of imaginative fiction in the early twentieth century; Don Marquis, in a 1906 poem entitled 'Wireless

21 Howard Vincent O'Brien, 'It's Great to be a Radio Maniac', *Colliers* (13 Sept. 1924), 16.

22 Bruce Barton, 'This Magic Called Radio', *American Magazine* (June 1922), 12.

23 Hart, 'Radiating Culture', 948.

24 A. Leonard Smith, Jr., 'Broadcasting to Millions: Radio Telephony's Extraordinary Growth—200,000 Stations Installed in Last Three Months', *New York Times* (19 Feb. 1922), 6.

25 Jeffrey Sconce, *Haunted Media: Electronic Presence from Telegraphy to Television* (Durham, NC: Duke University Press, 2000), 69.

Telegraph', saw the myth of Mercury 'born anew in the death of time and space' via the new invention: 'Man has stolen the wings of the deathless Things that range where spirit is lord,' he wrote.[26] Similarly, Henry Anderson Lafler's 1910 poem 'Wireless' linked the image of a towering radio antenna against a starry night bringing word of distant men to the winds, storms, and darkness of unsettled seas:

Wilt thou garner by thy mystic might
Some word to still our ancient long despair?
Some whisper from the infinite?—A breath
Caught from the far unfathomed gulf of death?[27]

John Fleming Wilson's 1911 short story 'Sparks' tells the story of an obsessed radio operator who constructs an ultra-long-wavelength receiver to decipher the mysterious roar of static recently troubling operators across the seas. The operator eventually extracts from the inchoate roar a message addressed to his own wireless station from his dead girlfriend, and after replying that he is joining her, suddenly falls dead himself at his equipment, whereupon the uncanny static ceases.[28] Rudyard Kipling's 1902 short story 'Wireless' also links the new wireless technology to themes of isolation, the occult, and death.[29] These works of popular fiction suggest that while radio's links to the uncanny provided comforting confirmation of the workings of a benign deity for some, others viewed its mysterious operation with trepidation. As Catherine Covert points out, the distant coded messages and disembodied voices of wireless were both Godlike and terrifying, the legacy of several decades of associations between electronic communication and the occult.[30]

If the links between wireless and the themes of alienation, despair, and death recur in early wireless literature, the medium's oceanic resonances could also be linked to the heroic virtues of adventure and male agency. Walter S. Hiatt, in a 1914 *Scribner's* essay, 'Sparks of the Wireless', after lamenting that 'going to sea' had lost its adventure for young men, associated the career of shipboard wireless operator with new scenarios of romantic adventure. Addressing the reader as a hypothetical young male wireless operator, Hiatt offered readers two lyrical fantasies of technologically enabled heterosexual attraction:

Always curious maidens of wondrous beauty come aboard to see the wireless wonder. You let one such put on your earphones, you guide her hand and the sending key. How good and sweet she seems, how her presence adorns and purifies that staid, dingy old craft! You are invited

26 Don Marquis, 'Wireless Telegraph', *American Magazine* (June 1906), 144–5.

27 Henry Anderson Lafler, 'Wireless', *Sunset Magazine* (June 1910), 597.

28 John Fleming Wilson, 'Sparks', *McClure's Magazine* (June 1911), 149–54.

29 Rudyard Kipling, 'Wireless', in *Traffics and Discoveries* (London: Penguin, 1987), 181–99; see also Sconce, *Haunted Media*, 69–70.

30 Catherine L. Covert, ' "We May Hear Too Much": American Sensibility and the Response to Radio, 1919–24', in Catherine L. Covert and John D. Stevens (eds.), *Mass Media between the Wars: Perceptions of Cultural Tension, 1918–1941* (Syracuse, NY: Syracuse University Press, 1984), 199–220.

ashore to church, to dinner. There are songs at the piano, the air is all sentiment. She seems yet more good and sweet. You tell her so—and there you are.

Such matters fall out even more frequently at sea aboard the passenger-ships. Mothers and giggling daughters come trouping merrily along the boat-deck. . . . you note the quiet, brown-eyed one by the door who doesn't ask a single question. She's the kind of girl that makes your heart jump. When the others leave, you manage to ask her if she really would like to stay and watch the wireless work. You exchange names, you write each other after the voyage is over. Finally, you decide to give up this wandering over the seas like a sodden derelict. You get a job ashore and settle down and live like the other fellows.[31]

Even Hiatt's happy scenarios of heterosexual wireless romance were tinged with death, however, as his hypothetical second-person hero, the wireless operator Sparks, drowns in his heroic efforts to rescue a foundering ship's passengers. Hiatt concludes his narrative with the familiar oceanic collapse of ether and afterlife: 'You are then gone—as say mother and sweetheart—free to wander at large, further, in the more mysterious ports of the ether ocean.'[32] Supporting the shipboard wireless operator's heroic image, other writers pointed to the number of lives saved at sea through the intervention of such operators, including Francis A. Collins, who estimated in 1912 that 10,000 lives had been saved by the actions of wireless operators.[33] The role of wireless in the First World War provided narratives of heroic male action; a *Literary Digest* article near the beginning of the conflict noted the US government's need for radio operators, and pragmatically urged amateurs to keep their wireless skills sharp: 'It's up to you if you prefer the trench to the radio tent behind the lines. You can be heroic and manly in either. Which do you choose?'[34] The heroic associations of wartime wireless persisted after the end of the conflict. In 1920 *Woman's Home Companion* told its readers that 'America's wireless men may always recall their record in the war with pride', and the *New York Times* in 1922 stressed the positive aspects of wireless in the midst of the war's trauma: 'Under the stress of the nation's need, the toy became the mighty machine, recompensing the universe, as it were, for the years of sickness and sorrow, devastation and death.'[35] Like its associations with shipboard disaster, early radio's links to the battlefields of the First World War provided reassuring narratives of heroic male adventure without completely escaping the medium's connection to the horrors of alienation and death.

---

31 Walter S. Hiatt, 'Sparks of the Wireless', *Scribner's Magazine* (Apr. 1914), 502, 511. Radio was depicted as an instrument of long-distance courtship in George Allan England's short story 'Wooed by Wireless', *Cosmopolitan* (Apr. 1908), 497–501.

32 Hiatt, 'Sparks of the Wireless', 511.

33 Francis A. Collins, *The Wireless Man: His Work and Adventures on Land and Sea* (New York: The Century Company, 1912), 104.

34 'Work for Wireless Amateurs', *Literary Digest* (18 Aug. 1917), 24.

35 F. A. Collins, 'Boys and the Wireless', *Woman's Home Companion* (Apr. 1920), 44; Smith, 'Broadcasting to Millions', 6; for recollections of a British First World War wireless operator, see E. W. G. Gill, *War, Wireless and Wangles* (London: Basil Blackwell, 1934), ch. 4.

The culture of the early radio amateur

Early popular literature concerning wireless had roots not only in American scientific literature and experimentation going back to the founding of *Popular Science* in 1872, but also in an equally long-lived tradition of science-themed utopian fiction beginning with the novels of Jules Verne in the 1860s and Edward Bellamy's 1888 *Looking Backward*. The two discursive strands, along with the entrepreneurial enthusiasm of a pioneer radio retailer, coalesced in the career of tireless electronics dealer, publisher, and author Hugo Gernsback. His dual literary and marketing legacies are suggested by his status as the founder of American science fiction and his posthumous induction into the Consumer Electronics Association's Hall of Fame in 2001.[36] Nurtured as a student in Germany on Jules Verne and American pulp fiction, Gernsback came to the USA in 1904, opened an electrical parts shop in New York City in 1906, and began selling mail-order radio kits in 1908, the same year he organized the Wireless Association of America (with no dues or obligations, it quickly gained 10,000 members) and began the first of his many magazines, *Modern Electrics*, chiefly as a promotional vehicle for his radio parts business.[37] In 1909 the magazine included a brief Gernsback speculative discussion of 'television', which he later claimed was the term's first use in print; in 1911 *Modern Electrics* published Gernsback's first serialized science fiction novel, *Ralph*.[38] Broadcast historian Susan Douglas describes Gernsback as the 'most avid promoter' of the new radio hobby, and, evoking themes that would be widely echoed in the amateur radio boom a decade later, Gernsback wrote to the *New York Times* in 1912 in praise of radio as a socially sanctioned hobby: 'This new art does much toward keeping the boy at home, where other diversions usually, sooner or later, lead him to questionable resorts; and for this reason well-informed parents are only too willing to allow their sons to become interested in wireless.'[39]

Just as early radio broadcasting was seen by some observers as a bridge across the national cleavages of class and ethnicity, as Gernsback's letter suggests, radio as a hobby was viewed as a way to integrate young men into a domestic life under siege from the trauma of modernity. A 1908 article by Charles Barnard in the juvenile magazine *St Nicholas* lamented that 'even to-day there are young folks who make the same mistake in thinking that all the great things that are worth doing have been done: all the great discoveries made: all the strange countries have been visited: all the great inventions finished, and all that is worth finding out has all been printed in books.'[40] Barnard offered a portrait of the young wireless fan as refutation of such

---

36 For a discussion of this utopian literary tradition, see Joseph J. Corn and Brian Horrigan, *Yesterday's Tomorrows: Past Visions of the American Future* (New York: Summit Books, 1984); regarding Gernsback's Hall of Fame award, see www.ce.org/publications/vision/2001/janfeb/p28.asp.

37 George H. Douglas, *The Early Days of Radio Broadcasting* (Jefferson, NC: McFarland, 1987), 389; Jesse Walker, *Rebels on the Air: An Alternative History of Radio in America* (New York: New York University Press, 2001), 16–17.

38 Hugo Gernsback, ' "Television" Coined in 1909', *Television News* (Mar.–Apr. 1932), 11.

39 Hugo Gernsback, letter to the *New York Times* (29 Mar. 1912); quoted in Susan J. Douglas, *Inventing American Broadcasting, 1899–1922* (Baltimore: Johns Hopkins University Press, 1987), 199–200.

40 Charles Barnard, 'A Young Expert in Wireless Telegraphy', *St Nicholas* (Apr. 1908), 530.

fears: 'we find him a rather quiet young man with a pleasant face, simple and natural manners, and when he speaks we find he talks like a man of science. We go up-stairs to the very top of the house and sit down in a little room filled in every side with electrical appliances of various kinds and sizes.' After this early evocation of 'the boy in the attic', a fixture of popular depictions of the twentieth-century electronics enthusiast, Barnard concludes: 'Think of it! Only twenty and yet a man of science, an inventor and skillful operator in this new art. Could anything be more inspiring to every boy and young man?'[41]

Scenarios of wireless as an all-powerful tool of intelligence and control at a distance recurs in early twentieth-century popular adolescent literature, including the popular Tom Swift series as far back as *Tom Swift and his Wireless Message* of 1911. Writer and business consultant Christine Frederick told the young readers of *St Nicholas* magazine in 1922 that 'not only should the owner of a radio set be constantly watching for some new kink or discovery, but he can also regard himself as a sort of self-appointed *Sherlock Holmes* of the air!'[42] Frederick explained:

> Rainy days or winter evenings won't seem dull and lonely if you have Ralphie Radio to talk to you. There's something always exciting and mysterious about operating a radio set. Perhaps that's its chief fascination. You never know what to expect! . . . Yes, radio is a real 'sport', because the results always have an element of uncertainty—you don't know absolutely what you're going to catch! . . . The more distant and more doubtful, the more delight and fun in landing your man or your station! And after trying to catch one station or message, you never feel satisfied until you have caught another![43]

In the same year *Radio Broadcast* initiated a regular short-story feature in the magazine, 'Adventures in Radio', arguing that 'perhaps no other branch of science enjoys the romance and spirit of adventure ever present in Radio'.[44] After evoking the possible adventures of the 'Radio Reporter, Radio Detective, Radio Doctor, and Radio Actor', the editor continued:

> Then we have radio as the leading factor in lives of the gunrunner, the smuggler, the arch criminal, the Central American revolutionist, the international spy, the cast-away sailor, and so we might go on indefinitely, for the exploits of radio are legion; some of which stand out as moments of scientific achievements; others are ignominious ones with which this noble art has been unwittingly subjected. All these nevertheless are intensely interesting, breathing of the very spirit of adventure and romance.[45]

Informing this imaginative landscape for the cultural reception of early radio were enormous changes in the American economy and living habits.

---

41 Charles Barnard, 'A Young Expert in Wireless Telegraphy', *St Nicholas* (Apr. 1908), 530–1, 532.

42 Christine Frederick, 'Radio: The New Aladdin's Lamp', *St Nicholas* (Nov. 1922), 4.

43 Ibid. 8.

44 'Adventures in Radio', *Radio Broadcast* (May 1922), 72.

45 Ibid. 74.

The early years of wireless experimentation coincide with a period of massive change in both the industrial and white-collar workplaces, altering the value and uses of leisure time and the cultural definitions of masculinity. As historian Michael Kimmel argues, the closing of the American frontier, the growing scale of industrial organization, and the time regimentation and deskilling brought about by the assembly line, coupled with new labour competition from both immigrants and internal migrants from the rural Southern states, all contributed to new tensions in the traditional constructions of masculinity.[46] The radio hobby was seen as a palliative for the new stresses of contemporary American industrial and urban life; as the author of the 1922 *The Book of Radio* put it, 'Many neurologists are prescribing for their patients' "hobbies." "Acquire a hobby and you won't require medicine," a prominent neurologist told a patient recently. No hobby is more suitable in general than radio.'[47] Paul Nystrom in his 1929 *Economics of Consumption* related the new importance of male hobbies to the changes in the blue-collar and white-collar workplaces in stark terms:

> Activities quite naturally taken up during leisure times generally stimulate and satisfy instincts or human hungers that do not find adequate exercise in the activities connected with the practical and necessary sides of living. The routine worker confined to machine or desk, performing standardized operations, directed by unrelenting supervision, seeks an outlet for surplus energies in leisure activities, in freedom from control, in opportunity for creative effort, for self-expression and in exertion for the mastery and perhaps even the tyranny over others, compensating for the grind and humiliation of the regular work.[48]

In its compensatory and socially positive effects, the radio hobby was seen in contrast to the contemporary leisure innovations of the automobile and the motion picture, which were frequently decried for taking young people out of their homes and introducing them to new vices. As such, the hobby of radio in the early twentieth century helped set up the gender and domestic associations of the electronic media which still resonate a century later. For example, a high school teacher advised readers of *Radio Age* in 1922:

> How many even consider the possibility of keeping the boy home at nights by giving him even the simplest of radio sets to play with? . . . If you are up against the problem of keeping boys in at nights, keeping them off the streets, just get a radio set as one for your home; it is

46 Michael Kimmel, *Manhood in America: A Cultural History* (New York: Free Press, 1996), 81–5; on the changes electricity brought to the industrial workplace, see David E. Nye, *Electrifying America: Social Meanings of a New Technology, 1880–1940* (Cambridge, Mass.: MIT Press, 1990), ch. 5. For a discussion of radio and the changing images of masculinity in early 20th-century America, see Douglas, *Listening In*, 'Introduction'.

47 C. W. Taussig, *The Book of Radio* (New York: Appleton, 1922), 9.

48 Paul Nystrom, *Economic Principles of Consumption* (New York: Ronald Press, 1929), 440. As discussed in Chapter 5, Sherry Turkle argues a similar link between a changing workplace and the rise of the personal computer user in the 1970s and 1980s; see Sherry Turkle, *The Second Self: Computers and the Human Spirit* (New York: Simon and Schuster, 1984), especially ch. 5.

inexpensive, and actually the expense is absolutely negligible if taken into account at all in comparison with the good it does to your boy.[49]

Parallel to its function as an instrument of national unity, radio was celebrated at a more intimate level for promoting family unity and providing a socially sanctioned male adolescent activity, albeit one that provoked occasional paternal anxiety. For example, amateur radio was linked to the rapidly growing Boy Scout movement, which was founded in the USA in 1910 and reached a membership of 500,000 by 1923.[50] The Boy Scout's radio-related activities of learning Morse code, logging distant stations, and passing on wireless messages were celebrated in 1923 by Armstrong Perry (trade press editor and 'Sea Scout Radio Commodore' of the Boy Scouts of America), all in the service, he argued, of keeping 'boys busy, useful, and self-respecting'.[51] The early twentieth century also saw the growth of the children's summer camp movement and the professionalization of the study of recreation; Elon Jessup in *Radio Broadcast* pointed to the 500,000 children enrolled in summer camps by 1921 and argued that both summer camps and the radio hobby were uniquely associated with 'progressive tendencies of the day'.[52] Arthur H. Lynch's article in *Radio Broadcast* in 1923, 'What Radio Holds for Boy Scouts', lauded Scouts' efforts in building receiving sets for patients in hospitals and in quarantine.[53] In an era marked by both traumatic rural emigration and the unprecedented massification of urban leisure in the forms of spectator sports, amusement parks, and motion-picture palaces, radio as a domestic hobby appealed to many commentators who looked back to the nation's rural, pre-industrial past as moral model.

In the context of early twentieth-century movements for civic reform and public recreation, radio was celebrated as a means both of building local and national communities and of cementing familial bonds within the household. Michael Kimmel points to widespread efforts at the time to enlarge the role of the father within domestic life, a response, he argues, to restricted social mobility and the increased routinization of the workplace.[54] Helen Sedgewick Jones, writing in the *Annals of the American Academy of Social Science* in 1923, reported the recent professional emphasis upon 'home play', especially the need for boys and fathers to 'get acquainted', and noted with approval the ascendancy of inventor Thomas Edison over boxer Jack Dempsey as masculine ideal.[55] Many commentators in the 1920s saw the radio hobby as a way to bring old and young together. Howard Vincent O'Brien told *Colliers* readers in 1924 that his 10-year-old son 'has picked up more pure and applied electricity than engineering graduates were able

49 Elizabeth Bergner, 'Woman's Part in Radio', *Radio Age* (July–Aug. 1922), 10.

50 Kimmel, *Manhood in America*, 81–5; Armstrong Perry, 'The Boy Scout's Place in the Radio Game', *Radio Broadcast* (Feb. 1923), 277.

51 Perry, 'The Boy Scout's Place', 279.

52 Elon Jessup, 'Radio in Summer Camps', *Radio Broadcast* (June 1923), 102.

53 Arthur H. Lynch, 'What Radio Holds for Boy Scouts', *Radio Broadcast* (July 1923), n.p.

54 Kimmel, *Manhood in America*, 202.

55 Helen Sedgewick Jones, 'Recreation Tendencies in America', *Annals of the American Academy of Social Science*, 105 (Jan. 1923), 248.

to dig out of their books when I left college. . . . As a practical man I wish my children to have as much of that kind of education as they can get.'[56] Revd H. F. Huse wrote in *Radio Broadcast* in 1923: 'I taught my boy fishing and he has taught me radio. When the fifteen-year-old came home and said: "Dad, we are behind the times. We have got to have a radio set," then it was time for the boy's best chum to sit up and take notice.'[57] The radio hobby could unite the generations outside the family circle as well; 'The Young Heart', a 1924 article in *Radio Broadcast*, quotes an elderly radio fan who shared his hobby with neighbourhood boys: 'Now, I forget I am old. I am always busy. I sing at my work bench. My heart is young. The boys come to me and we have good times, splendid times together. We speak the same language, a language of enthusiasm and happiness.'[58]

Just as it was seen as an agent of inter-generational harmony, radio as both medium and hobby was also looked upon to ameliorate the disparities of class in early twentieth-century America. Radio broadcasting 'can tend strongly to level the class distinctions, which depend so largely on the difference in opportunity for information and culture', argued a 1922 *Colliers* article, 'Radio Dreams that Can Come True'.[59] The author quotes a misspelled letter of gratitude to a radio operator from a listener in a 'dingy house in a dreary street in a little factory town, where a miracle is working'. The author argues that 'there are others, hundreds of letters a day of appreciation and delight from illiterate or broken people who are for the first time in touch with the world around them'.[60] Similarly, radio as a hobby was lauded for bridging the boundaries of class on an interpersonal level, via the exchange of disembodied wireless messages, the operation of hundreds of radio clubs, and the lively social interaction among customers in shops selling radio parts. *Radio Broadcast* in June 1922 reported from the streets of lower Manhattan that 'office boys now congregate daily to exchange the parts of radio apparatus they don't want for others that they do'.[61] A 1923 comic essay in *Radio Broadcast* by R. O. Jasperson, 'Confessions of an Unmade Man', described the new bonds of a shared hobby—the radio 'addiction'—between the middle-aged professional worker and a young office assistant: 'The office boy, also an addict, discovered my secret. . . . Now, the office boy and I sneak off to the seclusion of the stock room to exchange hook-ups. We are companions in crime. Once the office boy's opinions on any subject were of no interest to me. Now I eagerly seek his advice.'[62] In central business districts across the nation, shops selling electrical parts were deluged by a diverse collection of radio-fan customers at midday, including Jasperson, who complained that 'even without taking time to eat lunch, I find that I have difficulty in getting back to the office at

---

56 O'Brien, 'It's Great to be a Radio Maniac', 16.

57 Huse, 'Radio Angling and Fisherman's Luck', 317.

58 Robert Oliver, 'The Young Heart', *Radio Broadcast* (Feb. 1924), 322.

59 Frost, 'Radio Dreams that Can Come True', 18.

60 Ibid. 9.

61 'The March of Radio', *Radio Broadcast* (June 1922), 95.

62 R. O. Jasperson, 'Confessions of an Unmade Man', *Radio Broadcast* (June 1923), 21.

noon'. He offered a facetious lament concerning the inter-generational lure of the radio parts retailer:

> There ought to be a law against exposing radio parts for sale. It is putting temptation into the way of the slave to radio. No effort is made to screen the shops where radio addicts congregate. The traffic goes on openly in full view of the young and impressionable.
>
> Even mere boys are among the worst cases. I have seen mere babes of no more than nine or ten rush wildly into a radio shop and demand three honeycomb coils and a vernier rheostat, throwing the money madly at the clerk and dashing away with the parts clasped to their eager breasts. It's a sad commentary on our American institutions.[63]

Given the heterogeneous and highly interactive community of radio fans at the height of the radio craze, *Radio Broadcast* in May 1922 suggested that the parts dealer 'should not only join a radio club . . . he should be an active member' and set up a club room within his retail establishment: 'This is especially true in the business sections of large cities because it permits prominent radio amateurs and professional men to get together for a short time during their lunch hour,' the magazine advised.[64] The store's club room should be equipped with table, chairs, and blackboard, and 'patrons should be permitted to borrow equipment from stock for the purpose of making special tests or demonstrations'. The author also advised that 'whenever possible, sales folk should take an active interest in fostering this club room, helping to make prominent amateurs known to each other and settling some of the technical discussions which are bound to arise'.[65] As we shall see, this model of the technically informed, amateur-centred retailer was soon to be challenged within the radio trade press.

Despite radio's inter-generational appeal, it is clear that most US commentators considered the hobby chiefly the province of boys and young men, and often viewed their prominence within radio as a peculiarly American phenomenon. An article in *Radio Broadcast* in 1922 argued that

> in no other country has the boy taken such a prominent part in the development of radio, partly because of the severe governmental restrictions in other lands, but largely owing to a different attitude here. A new application of science has an excellent chance for rapid development in a country which is itself new and rapidly developing. . . . If the boy of today should suddenly lose interest in radio, it would mean the loss of millions in business in the coming year alone. But he won't.[66]

US Secretary of Commerce Herbert Hoover, radio's chief regulator until the 1927 Radio Act, told an industry group in 1925 that 'radio . . . has found a part in the fine development of the American boy, and I do not believe

---

63 R. O. Jasperson, 'Confessions of an Unmade Man', *Radio Broadcast* (June 1923), 21–2.

64 A. Henry, 'Merchandising Radio', *Radio Broadcast* (May 1922), 84.

65 Ibid. 86.

66 'The American Boy in Radio', *Radio Broadcast* (Dec. 1922), 91–2.

anyone will wish to diminish his part in American life'.[67] Christine Frederick told the young readers of *St Nicholas* in 1922 that 'the chief reason why America leads the world today in radio progress is just because Uncle Sam is a wise old person and allows the radio amateurs to remain unmolested by hampering government restrictions'. Contrasting the situation for amateurs in the USA to that in the UK or France, Frederick told her readers to 'be thankful, then, that the United States is the land of the wireless amateur'.[68] It is important to keep in mind that the ubiquitous construction of the early radio amateur as childlike or adolescent had important policy implications for the gathering controversies which pitted amateur radio operators against a new group of emerging commercial broadcasters.[69] Robert F. Gowan complained in the trade press in early 1923 that

> a 'ham' is not a small boy using a spark coil, jamming up the ether with noises sounding like a boiler factory in action, but a young man of the average age of twenty years who has enthusiastically studied radio both theoretically and practically and whose idea is to better the art in any way he can by unselfish application. He has solved many problems that have confronted him, not for financial gain, but for the love of the thing.[70]

While Secretary of Commerce Hoover reassured trade press readers in 1922 that 'it is my belief that it will be possible to accommodate the most proper demands of broadcasting and at the same time to protect that precious thing—the American small boy, to whom so much of this rapid expansion of interest in radio is due', official attitudes toward the radio amateur would cool considerably over the next few years.[71]

The ambivalent paternal reaction to the enthusiasm of young radio hobbyists was underscored by the nationally celebrated case of Eric Palmer, Jr., whose father wrote the Federal Radio Commission (FRC) in 1924 to request that his 12-year-old son's radio licence be withdrawn until he was 16. 'If Junior's license is not suspended', the father complained, 'I believe the boy will die of under nourishment and lack of sleep and his mother fall victim to a nervous breakdown. I do not believe he has seen the sunlight in three months.' Young Palmer's case was picked up by the national press, led by a front-page story in the *New York Times*, after the FRC suspended his licence with the following official advice: 'We believe with your father that you need a good rest. . . . This is a marvelous field for the American boy, and such enthusiasm as you have displayed should as a rule be commended rather than discouraged, but in order to develop into a big, strong healthy boy you must have regular meals and your full quota of sleep.' In an introduction to Palmer's 1930 book about his radio adventures, FRC Chairman Ira Robinson wrote in heroic terms of the male adolescent radio enthusiast:

---

67 Herbert Hoover, 'A Statement by Secretary Hoover on Radio Progress and Problems', Fourth National Radio Congress, Washington, DC (9 Nov. 1925), 11.

68 Frederick, 'Radio', 3.

69 See Michele Hilmes, *Radio Voices: American Broadcasting 1922–52* (Minneapolis: University of Minnesota Press, 1997), 39.

70 Robert F. Gowen, 'The "Ham" What Am', *Radio Broadcast* (Feb. 1923), 304.

71 Frederick, 'Radio', 3–4.

'Marconi opened the way in wireless but the amateurs found out much more. They were like those who followed the discovery of Columbus. . . . All hail to the boy in the attic.'[72] This mixed expression of paternalistic pride and concern regarding the adolescent electronics enthusiast has been echoed in more recent discursive constructions of the ham radio operator, computer hacker, video game user, and virtual reality fan.

The assembly of radio sets from inexpensive parts purchased separately or fabricated by the hobbyist was only part of the image of radio as an active, adventurous male leisure activity in the early 1920s. In 1922 an article by Christine Frederick described home-made umbrella-antennas, radio-equipped bicycles, and radios in the forms of tie-clips and dice, all of which could be made cheaply; 'indeed, many of the sets made by young boys cost but a couple of dollars for materials which may often be rescued from the junk heap or family tool-chest', she noted.[73] Sociologists Robert and Helen Lynd described the radio hobby in their study of the town of Muncie, Indiana, in 1924:

> Here skill and ingenuity can in part offset money as an open sesame
> to swift sharing of the enjoyments of the wealthy. With but little
> equipment one can call the life of the rest of the world from the air, and
> the equipment can be purchased piecemeal from the ten cent store. Far
> from being simply one more means of passive enjoyment, the radio has
> given rise to much ingenious manipulative activity.[74]

The roots of wireless as a hobby go back to at least 1907, before the era of vacuum tubes, loudspeakers, and organized broadcasting. Carl Dreher, writing in *Radio Broadcast* in 1924, recalled the situation seventeen years earlier, when wireless enthusiasts

> suffered from loneliness and hardships, self-inflicted, to be sure, but
> none the less poignant. Signals were few and we were ignorant as to the
> proper procedure to follow in receiving those few, so that an amateur
> would sometimes listen for weeks without hearing anything. Yet he
> would listen for hours every day holding his breath a good part of the
> time, in the hope of hearing a few dots and dashes.[75]

However, by 1912, when Francis A. Collins published his book *The Wireless Man*, the author could point to an audience of radio amateurs already consisting of 'a hundred thousand boys all over the United States . . . beyond doubt . . . the largest audience in the world'; Collins estimated that 40 per cent of the amateurs operated transmitting as well as receiving stations.[76] In 1923 writer Robert F. Gowen credited the Radio Act of 1912, which set up a national system of transmitting-station call letters, for spurring the growth of radio clubs across the USA. Evoking the novel mixture of isolation and

---

72 Eric Palmer Jr., *Riding the Airwaves with Eric Palmer Jr.* (New York: Horace Liveright, 1930), 115–17, introduction.

73 Frederick, 'Radio', 9.

74 Robert S. and Helen Merrell Lynd, *Middletown* (New York: Harcourt Brace and World, 1956), 269.

75 Carl Dreher, 'Is the Amateur at Fault?', *Radio Broadcast* (Feb. 1924), 293.

76 Collins, *The Wireless Man*, 26, 29.

camaraderie which marked the early radio hobby, Gowan pointed to the 1912 legislation:

> With it came the birth of the radio club. It came from the natural tendency to gather together and exchange experiences, information and knowledge. In this way the radio club became the meeting ground of the amateurs and presently there came into being a wonderful spirit of fraternity. One felt a queer little thrill at these early radio club meetings when he came face to face with a fellow he knew well in the air but whom he had never met. To one who has never sat in his little back room late at night and conversed with another fellow seated in *his* little back room away over in some remote town, and then finally come to grasp the hand of this fellow, can never come this peculiar thrill.[77]

The sustained radio boom which began in the USA in 1922, however, expanded the radio audience far beyond its original group of enthusiasts, creating a tension in the goals and modes of radio listening between the single-minded fan and the more casual broadcast listener. In a 1922 *Radio Broadcast* article, 'Do Brains or Dollars Operate your Set?', W. H. Worrel described the differences between the two types of radio listeners and their devices, opposing the image of the radio set as musical instrument versus mere wind-up record player:

> The first of these [listeners] recognizes in radio a fad which he would feel ashamed not to appear interested in; he does what he does because it is 'done'. Radio to him is also an easy means of entertainment, and a source of free music—especially jazz. Where the music comes from doesn't concern him much, if it is only strong enough—regardless of weather conditions—and always on draught. He wants to be able to turn a spigot and just let 'er pour forth. In short, such a man isn't a very good sport. He's the kind that generally doesn't like fishing unless he can get a boy to hang the worms on his hook and take off the fish. . . . He will not survive the first summer of static, nor the first week of experimenting with his receiving set. He will discover that radio is a game in which a certain amount of patience and skill are demanded, and that a vacuum tube is more like a violin than a victoria.[78]

Worrel's antipodes of fashion-followers versus dedicated initiates, unreflective ease versus focused expertise, and passive entertainment versus dedicated sportsmanship anticipate figures in debates accompaning the introduction into the home of many subsequent twentieth-century electronic communication technologies. In distinction to this new, more casual, radio listener, Worrel offered a lyrical description of the values shared by the traditional radio enthusiast, whatever his age and social class:

> The other type of person is fascinated by radio as by anything that seems to be above or beyond common experience. . . . He seizes upon the apparently supernatural, or at least the unusual, as affording a change

---

77 Gowen, 'The "Ham" What Am', 306–7.
78 Worrel, 'Do Brains or Dollars Operate your Set?', n.p.

from the regularity of nature and of ordinary human experience. . . . His unconscious purpose is to render space and time, and all that limits and thwarts human existence, as completely amenable to the will of man as in a fairy tale. This is the real radio devotee, whether he is a lawyer spending his evenings in the attic with his home-made set, or a boy tuning in at midnight for the signals of some distant comrade.[79]

The ubiquitous contemporary metaphor for early radio listening was fishing, as men and boys intently teased out distant stations with battery-powered sets in attics and basements, using headphones which isolated them from other household activities. Describing distant listening, or 'DXing', as 'rare sport', O. E. McNeals told the readers of *Scribner's* in 1923 that the radio loudspeaker 'must be regarded as only a poor substitute for the far more perfect head-receiver set. . . . If you would know what radio receiving really means, put on the "ear-muffs." '[80] Howard Vincent O'Brien, in a 1924 *Colliers* article, 'It's Great to be a Radio Maniac', evoked the distinctive listening style of the DX fan: 'Some day, perhaps, I shall take an interest in radio programs. But at my present stage they are merely the tedium between call letters. To me no sounds are sweeter than "this is Station Soandso." ' He explained that 'in radio, it is not the *substance* of communication without wires, but the *fact* of it that enthralls. It is a sport, in which your wits, learning, and resourceful-ness are matched against the endless perversity of the elements.' [81] Echoing Worrel's opposition of violin versus Victoria, O'Brien argued that 'radio is *not* perfected . . . and therein lies its greatest fascination. When it is perfected there will be no more fascination in it than there is in a phonograph or a washing machine. Meanwhile there is open to you all the zestful entertain-ment of scientific research—without the very tedious necessity of learning, beforehand, any extremely difficult science.'[82] The psychic investment in domestic communication devices by the early electronics enthusiast and the ensuing distinctive patterns of media use and social and gender distinctions are themes of continued relevance in the study of subsequent twentieth-century media.

Selling radio to the housewife

However, the centrality of the male hobbyist as radio listener and set buyer in the USA began to change in 1923 as RCA, which controlled the major US patents in radio receivers, undertook to redefine and expand the radio set market, moving away from the sale of single parts to hobbyists to more profitable sales of complete loudspeaker-equipped receiving sets in fine cabinets to a wider public. This shift had important and lasting effects upon

79 Worrel, 'Do Brains or Dollars Operate your Set?', n.p.

80 O. E. McNeals, 'Great Audience Invisible', *Scribner's* (Apr. 1923), 412. For more on listening styles in early radio, see Ray Barfield, *Listening to Radio: 1920–1950* (Westport, Conn.: Praeger, 1996); for a discussion of the DX listening style in the 1920s, see Douglas, *Listening In,* ch. 3.

81 O'Brien, 'It's Great to be a Radio Maniac', 16. Like many other commentators, O'Brien compares the activity of distant listening to big-game fishing; likewise, Revd H. F. Huse offers an extending analogy to trout fishing in 'Radio Angling and Fisherman's Luck', n.p

82 O'Brien, 'It's Great to be a Radio Maniac', 16.

the definitions of radio's consumer, listener, and programme forms. Writing in the trade journal *Radio Dealer* in 1923, Ralph Jayres noted the change in targeted consumer from the 'parts buying fan' and advised radio retailers how to reach the new consumer: 'And, by all means, don't talk circuits. Don't talk in electrical terms. . . . You must convince every one of these prospects that radio will fit into the well appointed home.'[83] A 1930s broadcast historian described the new radio receiver design as a 'bold psychological move in the struggle to bring radio out of the attic and into the living room. And it worked.'[84] As the two comments suggest, the move away from the amateur market had implications for the design of both the salesroom floor and the domestic space in order to accommodate radio's new status as a mass consumer product.

Radio's marketing shift involved new physical layouts, decor, and sales tactics within the radio salesroom. Between 1922 and 1925 a debate was staged in the radio trade press about the most appropriate retail outlet for radio, principally between the electrical parts dealer already familiar with the amateur wireless market and the phonograph showroom staffed with non-technical personnel paid on commission. However, both sides of the debate recognized the economic appeal for the radio manufacturer and dealer of moving from the market for radio parts to that of complete sets. For example, George J. Eltz, Jr., sales manager of the Manhattan Electrical Supply Company, told readers of *Radio Broadcast* in November 1923 that 'unquestionably, from the angle of the public, manufacturer and dealer, it would be far better to have radio sales confined entirely to complete sets'.[85] Likewise, the head of a phonograph firm in January 1924, noting the 'tapering down' of the radio parts business in favour of complete sets, predicted that 'the dealer in radio will of course follow the lines of least resistance. Complete radio sets offer more profit, less trouble, less stock investment than radio parts.'[86]

The early 1920s shift in radio retailing from that of parts to complete sets had implications for where radios would be sold, how, and to whom. Defending the electrical parts merchant as radio dealer, A. Henry, in a May 1922 *Radio Broadcast* article, 'Merchandising Radio', advised radio retailers to set up radio club facilities within their stores, lend parts for informal club demonstrations, and be prepared to adjudicate technical disputes among customers. Henry also suggested that a 'modern transmitting station should be installed in the dealer's home as well as his store, and he should avail himself of every opportunity to carry on communication with his customers'.[87] George J. Eltz, in his *Radio Broadcast* article 'Why the Electrical Dealer is the Proper Outlet for Radio', contrasted the retail practices of the radio industry, dominated by amateur experimenters buying parts, to those of the phonograph dealer, where the sales of parts were insignificant, despite what he

83 Ralph Jayres, 'Putting Radio in the Parlor', *Radio Dealer* (July 1923), 17.

84 Gleason L. Archer, *The History of Radio to 1926* (New York: American Historical Society, 1938), 209.

85 George J. Eltz, Jr., 'Why the Electrical Dealer is the Proper Outlet for Radio', *Radio Broadcast* (Nov. 1923), 54.

86 T. M. Pletcher, 'Music Dealers: Logical Salesmen of Radio Sets', *Radio Broadcast* (Jan. 1924), 226.

87 Henry, 'Merchandising Radio', 86. Henry also told his readers that 'in order to make certain of a permanent standing in the radio business, it is necessary for the dealer to be able to discuss amateur radio conditions with his customers' (84).

judged to be the relative technical simplicity of building a phonograph versus a radio receiver. 'As far as can be learned', Eltz noted, 'there has never been a class of amateur phonograph constructors'.[88] In defence of the electrical parts dealer as radio sales venue, Eltz pointed to twenty years of experience selling parts to amateur radio operators, a group he estimated totalled 150,000 by 1920.[89] At the same time, Eltz admitted that the need for technical expertise in radio retailing was changing: 'In selling complete sets the problem is of course much simpler than when selling parts. The sale of parts requires the service of a man who is fully familiar in every particular with radio circuits and radio construction work.'[90]

On the other side of radio's retail-venue debate, T. M. Pletcher, president of the QRS Music Roll Company, argued in *Radio Broadcast* in January 1924 that the 'development of the business depends more on selling than on technical ability', favouring the non-technical 'salesman' over the skilled 'radio expert':

> The average salesman . . . is burdened with no more knowledge about construction than to answer the usual questions of a layman. . . . The radio expert talks glibly in the radio vernacular about things which are mysterious to the average man, who upon hearing the highly technical explanation becomes even more befogged than ever. The salesman's gift is to understand the importance of selling the results rather than the means . . . and he also realizes the importance of keeping technical and mechanical questions in the background. I should rather have . . . good salesmen who learned a little something about radio, than expert radio men who had learned a little something about selling.[91]

Pletcher also argued that the phonograph dealer was more likely than the electrical parts dealer to have a 'well-appointed' shop suitable for product demonstrations, greater experience with advertising, and established lines of credit with bankers in the community; in sum, the phonograph dealer was, Pletcher argued, better skilled at 'the art of selling, the art of advertising, the art of effective shop display, the art of financing, the art of successfully selling on the installment plan, the art of giving service'.[92]

As we will see in the travails of marketing post-war US television, competing visions of the role of technical expertise on the showroom floor often turned on assumptions about the gendered consumer of domestic media devices. The RCA-initiated marketing shift from the sale of radio parts to that of complete sets, and the associated debates over the proper venue for radio sales, were both tied to larger issues of gender and modes of reception. RCA executive Harry Grawler told *Radio Broadcast* readers in 1923 that 'to sell to the home, you must sell to the woman', urging retailers to redesign showrooms to resemble middle-class living rooms.[93] A January 1924 *Radio*

88 Eltz, 'Why the Electrical Dealer is the Proper Outlet for Radio', 54.

89 Ibid. 53.

90 Ibid. 55.

91 Pletcher, 'Music Dealers', 228.

92 Ibid. 229.

93 Harry Grawler, 'Radio in the Home', *Radio Dealer* (June 1923), 20.

Broadcast article entitled 'Making Radio Attractive to Women' lauded Donald Stevens, a Washington, DC, radio retailer who outfitted his shop 'not like a store at all; he got away from shelves and counters, replacing these with furniture in the fashion of a parlor or a drawing room'.[94] Explained Stevens: 'I have tried to make it so that the prospective customers who come in here, especially the women, do not have to use their imaginations.'[95] In a 1923 article in *Radio Dealer*, 'Putting Radio in the Parlor', a radio executive called the housewife 'the great American purchasing agent', responsible for 85 per cent of the household's consumption decisions.[96] In a 1925 trade-press article, 'Ten Suggestions to Help Dealers Sell Radio to Women', business consultant Christine Frederick urged radio retailers to 'take a leaf out of the book of washing machine, gas range, vacuum cleaner and other makers and sellers of household equipment' and link the radio set to the status needs of the well-appointed home.[97] Crucial in the shift in the radio market was the transition from headphone-equipped sets to those with loudspeakers, a change, RCA executive Harry Grawler argued, which was spurred by the fact that women would not tolerate headphones spoiling their hairstyles.[98]

The introduction of radio into the living room stirred simmering tensions regarding the gendered spaces and routines of the early twentieth-century home. Indeed, the physical spaces and domestic routines of the middle-class household into which radio was to be inserted were themselves under unique strains at the time. The decline of domestic servants, the growth of streetcar- and automobile-based suburbs, and the application of scientific management principles in the home all repudiated the traditional ideology of the self-sufficient home and underscored the links between the individual household and the rising consumer economy of the 1920s. This change was part of a larger economic shift: in 1920, only one of the top twenty US manufacturing firms was engaged in producing consumer products; by 1930 nine of the twenty largest manufacturers sold consumer products.[99] Behind the new consumer economy was an expanding advertising industry, rising levels of consumer debt, and a sustained boom in home construction. While the average new home shrank in size over the decade of the 1920s, and the amount of money spent on furnishings for every room except the living room declined, the growing expenditures on living-room furnishings were enough to offset declines elsewhere in the home.[100] Such macroeconomic and demographic changes provided the context for the marketing of increasingly expensive and lavishly designed radio receivers in the 1920s. The growth in home-owning was also linked to the psychological effects of changes in the industrial and white-collar workplaces, as efficiency expert

94 Lewis Wood, 'Making Radio Attractive to Women', *Radio Broadcast* (Jan. 1924), 221.

95 Ibid.

96 Jayres, 'Putting Radio in the Parlor', 61.

97 Christine Frederick, 'Ten Suggestions to Help Dealers Sell Radio to Women', *Radio Industry* (Jan. 1925), 11; Jayres, 'Putting Radio in the Parlor', 61.

98 Grawler, 'Radio in the Home', 20.

99 George E. Mowry, *The Urban Nation, 1920–1960* (New York: Hill and Wang, 1969), 11.

100 For discussion of changes in domestic spending, see George Soule, *Prosperity Decade: From War to Depression, 1917–29* (New York: Rinehart, 1947), 148 and Nystrom, *Economic Principles of Consumption*, 385.

Lilian Gilbreth wrote in 1927: 'If we don't own our own business or control our day work, we need especially to own our own home.'[101]

Debates over the design and ideology of domestic space in the early twentieth century also inevitably involved what historian Michael Kimmel describes as new efforts by men 'to find a small corner that could be unmistakably "his"' within the home, including the den, a room associated with wall-mounted big-game trophies and austere oak and leather furniture.[102] A literalization of such efforts of gendered domestic design is elaborated in 'Decorating the Radio Room', a 1923 article in *House and Garden* by Alwyn Covell, which sets out 'to develop a room dedicated to the secluded pursuit and enjoyment of wireless', complete with detailed floor plans and elevations.[103] According to Covell, radio, 'a thing of great distance and far horizons', demands 'a special radio room, developed in an attic wing, and furnished in a manner befitting its purpose'. He elaborates: 'A room of masculine character, obviously. No frills or trimmings. The first thought, for some psychological reason (perhaps the primary use of radio at sea) is of a room with a nautical air.'[104] The twelve-by-sixteen-foot attic space Covell describes is a riot of masculine iconography, from the two-tone nautical grey linoleum flooring through the bookshelves, drop-leaf desk, folding divan, and smoking cabinet, to the bric-a-brac of model ships, celestial and terrestrial spheres, clocks, world maps, and model cannons.[105]

The possible domestic tensions arising from the pursuit of amateur radio were not limited to battles over domestic space, however. Robert Oliver's 1923 *Radio Broadcast* article 'Radio is Expensive for the Married Man' offered tongue-in-cheek advice for the married radio fan, describing one husband who felt the need to buy his wife furs and jewellery after turning the family basement into a 'one-man radio factory'.[106] Describing another radio-fan acquaintance who 'had to get his wife a new car and teach her to drive it', Oliver explained that 'when he came home at night with his arms full of parts he could pretty safely bank on his wife's being out with the car'.[107] Oliver's article offered readers a final suggestion to relieve a wife's discontent over her husband's time-consuming radio hobby: inviting the wife to take a solo automobile trip to California, in order 'to thaw out the frigidity resulting from such a schedule'. Oliver elaborated, in the symptomatic language of psychopathology: 'The only way is to search out some of the wife's repressed desires. See if she hasn't a complex centering around a trip to California. Every woman has such a complex, something that comes to the surface every now and then, under stress.'[108] Such common apocryphal tales

---

101 Lilian Gilbreth, *The Homemaker and her Job* (New York: D. Appleton, 1927), 5.

102 Kimmel, *Manhood in America*, 111, 158; for a discussion of the distinctive spaces and rituals of 19th-century boyhood, see E. Anthony Rotundo, *American Manhood: Transformation in Masculinity from the Revolution to the Modern Era* (New York: Basic Books, 1993), ch. 2.

103 Alwyn Covell, 'Decorating the Radio Room', *House and Garden* (Aug. 1923), 50.

104 Ibid. 51.

105 Ibid. 50.

106 Robert Oliver, 'Radio is Expensive for the Married Man', *Radio Broadcast* (July 1923), 203.

107 Ibid. 202.

108 Ibid. 204.

of radio-induced domestic discord were echoed in a 1924 front-page *New York Times* account of a Bridgeport, Connecticut, woman who sued for child custody after leaving her husband 'because he cared more for his radio set than he did for her'.[109] While the judge refused her custody petition, he noted that 'the husband was wrapped up in his radio set', and warned that 'a husband should remember he owes duties to his wife . . . [who] naturally had to seek pleasures elsewhere'.[110]

Not surprisingly, the shift in radio set design and marketing strategy around 1923 provoked sharp objections from many radio amateurs, who saw it as part of a larger change in the nature of radio broadcasting and listening. Contemporary historian Gleason Archer described the 'personal scorn' the new living-room style receiving set provoked from amateur radio enthusiasts and the 'virtual feud [which] speedily developed'.[111] Coincident with the metamorphosis of the amateur radio set into parlour furniture were the efforts of AT&T and other large broadcasters to exploit broadcasting for direct advertising messages aimed at the same housewife-consumer to whom radio retailers were directing their new marketing efforts. Describing these programming shifts, an assistant editor of *Radio Journal* warned in 1922 that 'many amateurs are looking with grave concern at the invasion of what they consider their own field by business concerns'.[112] A 1922 editorial in *Radio Dealer* warned: 'The first result of any real attempts by advertisers to control the air will be and should be met by firm resistance. . . . When it comes to monopolizing the air for mercenary (advertising) purposes a real man-sized vocal rebellion can be expected.'[113] In 1922 Joseph H. Jackson warned *Radio Broadcast* readers of the incipient practice of radio advertising, likely to become a 'very troublesome pest . . . unless something is done, and that quickly':

> The very thought of such a thing growing to be common practice is sufficient to give any true radio enthusiast the cold shakes. And he doesn't need to be a dyed-in-the-shellac radio man to see the point, either; the veriest tyro with his brand-new crystal set can realize, if he has listened in only once, what it would mean to have the air filled with advertising matter in and out of season: to have his ears bombarded with advertisers' eulogies every time he dons a pair of head phones.[114]

Jackson called on his reader as 'a radio enthusiast, not above getting up on your hind legs now and then, as every liberty-loving citizen and taxpayer should, and yelling loudly for what's coming to you'.[115] Responding to press

109 'Wife Leaves Radio Fan; Judge Says He's Right', *New York Times* (10 Feb. 1924), 1.

110 Ibid.

111 Archer, *The History of Radio to 1926*, 209.

112 W. L. Pollard, 'Possibilities of Radio', *Radio Journal* (July 1922), 64; for discussions of the shift from amateur to commercial broadcasting, see Walker, *Rebels on the Air*, ch. 2, and Susan Smulyan, *Selling Radio: The Commercialization of American Broadcasting 1920–1934* (Washington, DC: Smithsonian Institution Press, 1994), ch. 1.

113 'Editorial', *Radio Dealer* (Apr. 1922), 30.

114 Joseph H. Jackson, 'Should Radio be Used for Advertising?', *Radio Broadcast* (Nov. 1922), 70.

115 Ibid. 74–5.

reports of AT&T's plans to initiate advertising over its New York City station, a 1922 editorial in *Radio Dealer* lamented that 'it is a matter of regret for most of those who realize that the radio art is in its infancy, to learn that the commercial minds of the community are already prepared to take advantage of a condition developed for them—not by them'. Arguing that the 'government can have no legal or moral right to permit the monopolistic use of the air for direct advertising', the magazine warned: 'The broadcasting stations themselves can expect interference from the thousands of amateurs who are licensed to send messages. . . . Trouble is bound to develop, not only for the broadcasting station, but for the trade itself.'[116] Some defenders of broadcast advertising cast the debate in equally stark terms; a 1925 book characterized radio amateurs as 'in general made up of boys in their teens who regard a transmitter as a toy befitting their age and social importance'. The authors complained of a surfeit of amateur broadcasters and warned: 'There is no altruism in broadcasting. It is a cold, commercial thing squirming under the unmerciful heel of exploitation. . . . Broadcasting must throw off the embarrassing yoke of universality and common ownership.'[117]

As early as late 1922 some amateurs were expressing pessimism about maintaining their prominence in the face of the growth of broadcast advertising and casual listeners. In November 1922 a *Radio Broadcast* article, 'Too Many Cooks are Spoiling our Broth', complained of the rapid growth of new stations on the air and warned that 'many of them will merely send out advertising noise'.[118] Armstrong Perry, amateur radio pioneer and editor of *Radio News*, lamented in December 1922 that

> the novice, who wishes merely to listen to broadcast programs and news reports, has become so abundant and so insatiate that he threatens to crowd the experimental amateur out of the field that only a few months ago he occupied quite unchallenged. . . . The amateur, once alone in his fascinating field, finds himself jostled and trampled by a horde of common folks who want to hear a concert or something—that's all.[119]

Proposals from amateur operators for time sharing between commercial broadcasters and amateurs or for local late-night blackouts by commercial stations to permit distant reception went unheeded, as did pleas for federal legislation to restrict the practice of broadcast advertising. By early 1924 Carl Dreher was counselling *Radio Broadcast* readers: 'If the amateur is wise, he will read the handwriting on the wall, adjust himself quietly to new conditions and superior forces, save what he can—which is considerable—and so keep a reasonably prominent place in the radio game.'[120]

The outcome of these battles over the design, domestic location, and function of the radio set, like those over the propriety of broadcast advertising, was clear by the late 1920s, when commercial radio assumed

---

116 'Mistake to Broadcast Advertising', *Radio Dealer* (Nov. 1922), 55.

117 Samuel L. Rothefel and Raymond F. Yates, *Broadcasting: Its New Day* (New York: Century, 1925), 139, 15.

118 'Too Many Cooks are Spoiling our Broth', *Radio Broadcast* (Nov. 1922), 3.

119 'Is the Radio Amateur Doomed?', *Literary Digest* (2 Dec. 1922), 28.

120 Dreher, 'Is the Amateur at Fault?', 294.

its now-familiar place in the American home and commerce. As disgruntled amateur radio enthusiast Eric Palmer Jr. wrote in 1930 from his now-marginalized perch in the attic:

> Modern broadcasting receivers are pretty much fool-proof. Even a baby can start 'em up.
>
> We've got to what my dad calls the parlor stage of radio. What he means is that radio has gone ritzy, with fancy cabinets, to roost in the drawing room along with the curio cabinet and grandpa's picture. The idea is that radio has ascended from the attic era, or descended, rather, from the top floor corner to a position of state for the visitors to gape at.
>
> But I'm still up in the attic. There are thousands more like me, all over the world.[121]

Sociologists Robert and Helen Lynd noted the changing place of radio in the home in their 1924 Indiana study; 'As it becomes more perfected, cheaper and a more accepted part of life', the Lynds predicted, 'it may cease to call forth so much active, constructive ingenuity and become one more form of passive enjoyment.'[122] Writer Christine Frederick in 1928 argued that 'for a long time women tolerated radio as a man's and boy's toy. But to-day radio is far more to women than a lot of messy machinery with which men and boys love to play and clutter up the house.'[123] One industry observer noted the 'thrill of conquering time and space' enjoyed by amateurs intent on pulling in distant stations, but, writing in 1933, admitted that 'this thrill is decidedly less than it was in the early days of broadcasting when it probably constituted the principal reason for listening'.[124] The characteristics of radio listening as an activity of adolescent male hobbyists—isolation and intensity, the fabrication of the technical apparatus itself, an interactive role as broadcaster or letter-writer to distant stations received—were increasing marginalized by the emerging US industry's construction of the radio listener as distracted housewife. As we shall see, these early discursive oppositions of the gendered media consumer have been repeatedly invoked in popular discussions accompanying the launch of subsequent electronic media in the home.

The distracted style of listening encouraged by loudspeaker-equipped sets in the parlour struck many early observers of American radio as novel; as one journalist noted, 'a majority of housewives turn on the radio in the morning "just for company" and let it rattle away with whatever comes . . . merely taking comfort in the human voice breaking the loneliness'.[125] As early as 1923 Christine Frederick argued in *Good Housekeeping* that 'the radiophone, it seems to me, is primarily an invention for the benefit of woman. Its greatest achievement is banishing isolation.'[126] Frederick elaborated: 'Isolation!

121 Palmer, *Riding the Airwaves*, 16.

122 Lynd and Lynd, *Middletown*, 271.

123 Harvard University, Graduate School of Business Administration, *The Radio Industry: The Story of its Development, as Told by Leaders of the Industry* (Chicago: A. W. Shaw, 1928), 11.

124 Herman J. Hettinger, *A Decade of Radio Advertising* (1933; repr. New York: Arno Press, 1971), 18.

125 Edmund de S. Brummer, *Radio and the Farmer* (New York: Radio Institute for the Audible Art, n.d.), 24.

126 Reprinted in Christine Frederick, 'Radio for the Housekeeper', *Literary Digest* (9 Sept. 1923), 28.

Who better than a woman can understand the full meaning of this dreaded word?' After noting the appeal of radio for geographically dispersed rural women, Frederick argued that 'housekeepers, also, as a class, have felt that they were imprisoned within the four walls of the house, that they were "tied down" to the monotony of household tasks, and that they were often deprived of participation in cultural pleasures because they had to stay at home and take care of young children'.[127] Outlining a hypothetical daytime broadcast schedule containing an exercise programme and a talk on domestic science, Frederick argued that

> such a short morning talk would do much to give the housekeeper a stimulus in her work and make her feel that she is not engaged in degrading tasks, but is following an occupation which is worthy of professional interest and public recognition. Further, she will no longer feel that she is isolated and deprived of the extremely valuable group stimulus of working with others, because she will realize that at the same moment thousands of other housekeepers are also being trained, thus supplying her with the incentive she has always needed.[128]

Similarly, in 1926 the president of the General Federation of Women's Clubs and an NBC radio programming adviser pointed to radio's 'importance among the facilities without which family isolation and stagnation are inevitable under modern conditions of life'.[129]

The radio industry's model of the distracted housewife-listener also had significant implications for broadcast programming. Commercial broadcasters were advised to keep programmes simple, since the attention of listeners in the home was likely to be divided; 'besides', one industry executive argued, 'the average woman listener is neither cosmopolitan nor sophisticated. Nor does she have much imagination.' On the other hand, another early radio advertising executive optimistically suggested that 'literacy does not figure. Mental effort is reduced to that involved in the reception of the oral message.'[130] By the end of the 1920s, commercial radio broadcasters, armed with such ideological assumptions of their imagined domestic audience, rarely designed programming to elicit or repay full attention; instead, as the author of the monograph *Women and Radio Music* argued, radio, like furniture or wallpaper, 'creates an atmosphere'.[131] At least in the United States, by the end of the decade, radio was firmly committed to the twin ideological projects identified by a scornful Bertolt Brecht in 1932 as those of 'prettifying public life' and 'bringing back coziness to the home and making family life bearable again'.[132]

127 Reprinted in Frederick, 'Radio for the Housekeeper', 28.

128 Ibid. 29.

129 National Broadcasting Company, *Reports of the Advisory Council* (New York: National Broadcasting Company, 1927), 37.

130 Frank Presbrey, *The History and Development of Advertising* (New York: Doubleday, 1929), 581.

131 Peter W. Dykema, *Women and Radio Music* (New York: Radio Institute for the Audible Art, n.d.), n.p. For a discussion of these changes in the 1920s radio industry, see William Boddy, 'The Rhetoric and Economic Roots of the American Broadcast Industry', *Cinetracts*, 2/2 (Spring 1979), 37–54.

132 Bertolt Brecht, 'Radio as a Means of Communication', reprinted in John Hanhardt (ed.), *Video Culture: A Critical Investigation* (New York: Visual Studies Workshop, 1986), 53.

If this chapter has taken some pains to locate the emerging popular tropes which defined the radio apparatus, listener, and programme within the specific historical circumstances of the early twentieth century, it is also clear that such notions enjoyed a remarkable longevity across a century of technological innovation in the American home. In this regard, 100 years of historical experience of electronic communication in the home repeatedly rehearse a series of gendered and normative oppositions between the active and passive domestic audience, from the male wireless amateur versus distracted housewife in the 1920s to the degraded couch potato versus heroic Internet surfer of the 1990s. As we shall see, such persistent figurations helped define the role of electronic media in the intimate spaces and gendered routines of everyday life.

3

The Amateur, the Housewife, and the Salesroom Floor: Promoting Post-war US Television

IF THE PREVIOUS chapter on early radio pointed to a set of remarkably enduring images of domestic media users, this chapter will examine how such constructions of the media audience were deployed in the commercial rivalries associated with the launch of US commercial television after the Second World War. An analysis of the public and trade debates over the nature, uses, and even economic viability of commercial television in the 1940s suggests the value for the historian of a heuristic refusal of the inevitability of the medium's subsequent spectacular success. Tracing the historical path which leads to the current and prospective place of television in domestic life requires a defamiliarization of the prosaic and over-familiar living-room TV set as both an artefact of domestic technology and a medium of popular culture. This tactic is part of a larger effort to consider the history of communication technologies and the complex popular reactions to them beyond the secure contemporary vantage point of their current applications and our habituated and largely unexamined ways of thinking about them. The historian's task becomes one of recovering the sense of novelty, improvisation, euphoria, and terror at a time when 'old technologies were new'.[1] A technological and social archaeology of television would insist upon the importance of specific historical determinations and contingencies, especially regarding a medium whose ubiquity is often mistaken for 'naturalness' and inevitability. This effort is especially appropriate at the present moment, when a new generation of information technologies seems ready to redefine domestic spaces and the gender and family roles within them.

Alongside the ethnographic research into contemporary TV audiences by scholars in cultural studies, it is also important to begin to trace a history of

---

1 This effort can be seen in a number of works, including Carolyn Marvin, *When Old Technologies Were New* (New York: Oxford University Press, 1988); Susan J. Douglas, *Inventing American Broadcasting, 1899–1922* (Baltimore: Johns Hopkins University Press, 1987); Cecelia Tichi, *Electronic Hearth: Creating an American Television Culture* (New York: Oxford University Press, 1991); and Lynn Spigel, *Make Room for TV: Television and the Family Ideal in Postwar America* (Chicago: University of Chicago Press, 1992).

television spectatorship, to interrogate the complex constituents of the prosaic act of watching television, to examine how spectatorship and, more broadly, the public reaction to television relate to the social histories of technological innovation, domesticity, and gender. This attempt to consider domestic communications technologies, in this chapter the case of post-war US television, from the 'bottom up'—from accounts of viewers and buyers of TV sets, from the public discourses of magazine advertisements and popular TV fictions—reveals a more complicated and ambivalent relation between the American public and commercial television in its early years than most traditional institutional histories offer. While the conspicuous and highly profitable position of US commercial television by the mid-1950s may make its 'fit' within American post-war culture and ideology seem seamless and complete, it is important to note that the industry's post-war success was not without conflict, resistance, and self-doubt. This sense of the historically contingent and contested underscores the fact that communications technologies have no 'natural' place in our homes or our culture, a lesson especially appropriate at a time when powerful economic interests are attempting to propose and naturalize a new set of domestic media technologies and uses, to frame the public debate in ways that make some important questions impossible to raise.

In light of these larger issues, this chapter considers some of the anxieties and conflicts which accompanied the post-war launch of commercial television in the United States. These conflicts were rehearsed in the reporting of the popular press, in the prescriptive writings of a new generation of mass-mediated experts offering advice to baby-boom parents, in the glossy advertisements of television manufacturers, and in the programming efforts of the early television industry. The post-war debates reveal a profound cultural ambivalence about the television set as an object, television viewing as an activity, and about television's relation to the ideals of post-war domesticity. Similar themes characterize popular reactions to a long trajectory of domestic media technologies, from early wireless to the Internet, and are inextricably enmeshed in larger histories of gender inside and outside the home. Thus the ubiquitous and unimposing television set in the corner of the living room condenses a number of complex and conflicted attitudes toward the private and the public, the technological, and the gendered domestic routines of everyday life.

Post-war television's hesitations

While by 1950 US TV-set manufacturers were selling 7.5 million units a year, television's commercial success in the immediate post-war period was by no means assured, at least in the eyes of many observers at the time.[2] The rapid growth in TV-set sales did not begin until the last quarter of 1947, after nearly two decades of popular and financial speculation regarding the medium and several unsuccessful attempts to launch it commercially. Although it is

---

2 Alfred R. Oxenfeldt, *Marketing Practices in the TV Set Industry* (New York: Columbia University Press, 1964), 12. For the next fifteen years, the 1950 set production figure of 7.5 million was only exceeded in 1955 and 1963.

unsurprising to find a TV industry leader boasting that 'no other invention has ever had so much advance publicity as television . . . before [it] was made available to the public', the fact that this confident statement by C. F. Jenkins was made in 1929 may be unexpected.[3] A decade later, a substantial television set marketing and direct-sales effort by RCA before the US entry into the Second World War resulted in the sale of only 10,000 sets, almost all in New York City. Even after the Second World War, only 6,500 sets were sold in 1946, mostly for use in taverns and the homes of media professionals.[4] An executive at Zenith Radio Corporation told a group of security analysts in early 1945 that 'television broadcasting began in 1928, but in seventeen years television has made less progress than radio did in its first year'.[5] Another Zenith executive told a Chicago advertising group in January 1947 that television had been launched commercially at least four times in the previous fifteen years and concluded: 'we are very dubious about the success of today's television boom.'[6] Writing in an investment journal in August 1947, a CBS executive estimated that there were still no more than 45,000 sets in use nationwide, fully two-thirds of them in New York City, and argued that 'it is currently recognized in the industry that television will not have an easy time in establishing itself as a large-scale, profitable enterprise'.[7]

While both Zenith and CBS had specific business motives behind their public scepticism, the uncertainty about TV's immediate post-war success was widely felt across the industry.[8] A March 1946 *Fortune* magazine article entitled 'Television: A Case of War Neurosis' warned that 'television could conceivably turn into the biggest and costliest flop in US industrial history'.[9] According to the 1946 *Annual Report* of the Federal Communications Commission (FCC), 80 of the 158 post-war applications for television stations had been withdrawn by the end of 1946; in May 1947 there were still only ten stations on the air in eight cities, and a year later *Fortune* reported that cancellations of television advertising contracts exceeded new advertising time sales through most of 1947.[10] Even the head of the Radio

3 Charles Francis Jenkins, *Radiomovies, Radiovision, Television* (Washington, DC: National Capital Press, 1929), 9.

4 US Congress, Senate Committee on Interstate and Foreign Commerce, *Hearings: Development of Television*, 76th Cong., 3d. sess. (Washington, DC: Government Printing Office, 1940), 11; Donald Horton, 'Television Problems and Prospects', *Dun's Review* (Aug. 1947), 20.

5 J. J. Nance, 'Future Problems of the Radionics Industry', *Commercial and Financial Chronicle* (1 Feb. 1945), 1.

6 H. C. Bonfig, 'Television Prospects', *Commercial and Financial Chronicle*, (23 Jan. 1947), 403, 477.

7 Horton, 'Television Problems and Prospects', 20.

8 Zenith was then promoting Phonevision, a pay-television system, arguing that commercial sponsorship could not provide adequate programme budgets in the medium's early years; CBS petitioned the Federal Communications Commission to scrap the existing VHF black and white service in favour of colour broadcasts in higher frequencies. Many in the industry viewed the petition as a CBS attempt to delay commercial television altogether; CBS executive Worthington Miner later indicated that he believed this was the case ('Television: A Case of War Neurosis', *Fortune* (Mar. 1946), 107–8; Franklin Schaffner, *Worthington Miner* (Metuchen, NJ: Scarecrow Press, 1985), 179). For material on Zenith's television strategy, see Robert W. Bellamy, 'Zenith's Phonevision: An Historical Case Study of the First Pay Television System' (Ph.D. dissertation, University of Iowa, 1985).

9 'Television: A Case of War Neurosis', 104.

10 US Federal Communications Commission, *Annual Report* (Washington, DC: US Government Printing Office, 1946), 17; Horton, 'Television Problems and Prospects', 19; 'Television! Boom!', *Fortune* (May 1948), 191.

Manufacturers' Association admitted to a trade journal in March 1947 that 'television has had more starts and stops than a horse-drawn milk wagon'.[11]

Lessons from radio: the hobbyist and the homemaker

This surprising period of uncertainty about the immediate prospects for post-war commercial television was marked by an unusual degree of intro-spection and contention within the television industry in the mid- and late-1940s. The debates over the viability of commercial television waged within the trade and popular presses of the period are dominated by the recurrent rhetorical figures of the hobbyist and the homemaker. As the previous chapter suggested, this opposition was established at the beginnings of com-mercial radio broadcasting in the early 1920s, as commercial broadcasting became the dominant application of wireless, which had earlier been fre-quently figured as a quasi-interpersonal communications medium for men and boys, listening on headphones to distant stations on home-made receivers located in the peripheral domestic spaces of attics and basements. The shift in radio set design and listening styles accompanied and supported the introduction of advertising in radio, a move strongly opposed by many amateurs. However, it was precisely commercial radio's ability to provide background accompaniment for women working in the home during the day that was hailed by industry leaders as the defining feature of American radio and the key to its profitability, which remained undisputed through the Depression.[12] The figure of the female homemaker as consumer of daytime radio programming would provide an important rhetorical marker in the post-war debates over commercial television.

As a result of these marketing and programming shifts in the radio indus-try, by the late 1920s and early 1930s many hobbyists shifted their attention from standard AM radio into the new fields of short-wave radio and mech-anical television. This shift took place within a electronics hobbyist sub-culture going back at least as far as publisher Hugo Gernsback's first popular electronics magazine, the 1908 *Modern Electrics*. In a series of sometimes short-lived magazines, including *Television* (launched in 1928), *Short-Wave Craft* (1930), and *Television News* (1932), Gernsback, as publisher, editor, and author, brought speculative and technical material on television to the mostly male electronics hobbyist, alongside articles on space travel, 'tele-kinetics', and other technological discoveries, including 'beneficial radio fevers which actually cure a number of diseases ranging from pneumonia to certain forms of insanity' (Fig. 3.1).[13] Gernsback told his readers in 1930 that AM radio is now 'highly standardized . . . which has tended more and more to reduce radio to automatic reception of local stations' and argued that the excitement of the 1920–2 era of wireless experimentation was now to be found in short wave and television.[14]

---

11 'Radio Today', *Radio and Television Retailing* (Mar. 1947), 34.

12 Thomas W. Volek, 'Examining Radio Receiver Technology through Magazine Advertising in the 1920s and 1930s' (Ph.D. diss., University of Minnesota, 1990), 117–28.

13 Hugo Gernsback, 'The Future of Radio', *Short-Wave Craft* (Apr.–May 1931), 447.

14 Hugo Gernsback, 'The Short Wave Field', *Short-Wave Craft* (June–July 1930), 5.

Fig. 3.1 Representing the male electronics enthusiast: 'Dream of a short wave fiend', cover of *Short-Wave Craft*, edited by Hugo Gernsback, 1932

Limited to 48–60 lines of resolution and broadcasting in the short-wave portion of the spectrum, early experimental television broadcasts, including those from CBS's New York City transmitter, could reach 'lookers in' as far away as Canada and the American Midwest. One amateur enthusiast in Michigan wrote to the manager of the CBS New York City station in 1931:

> Last night I succeeded in bringing in the picture of a partially bald-headed man on my television machine. The image was quite clear, but I could not hold it long. There was some fading. The man moved his head quite often. The lips could be seen to move. I did not hear the sound.

This is the only station I have succeeded in framing and I hope you can verify reception of this partially bald-headed person.[15]

A. Frederick Collins (author of *The Boy Astronomer*, *The Boy Chemist*, and *The Boy Scientist*) defended the limitations of early mechanical television in his 1932 amateur handbook *Experimental Television*:

> Now, while *television is here*, I would not have you believe that the received images are perfect; nay, they are not even good, but it is this very fact that gives the television experimenter a thrill, for, like wireless telegraphy and telephony of yore, he has a practically unlimited field in which to exercise his inventive ability.[16]

In a similar allusion to radio's lost era of unfettered amateur activity, Hugo Gernsback told readers of the inaugural issue of *Television News* in 1932 that 'television promises to be a real paradise for the experimenter who will "make his own," just as he built his radio sets between 1921 and 1927. History in this case is sure to repeat itself.'[17]

Despite Gernsback's optimism, it is clear that history did not repeat itself, and the role of the amateur in early radio was very different from the amateur's role in television, especially after the early 1930s era of low-resolution mechanical television. The competing architects of post-war commercial television were unanimous in their wish to avoid what they uniformly saw as the mistakes of the early radio industry, including the development of organized resistance among a community of radio amateurs to the use of broadcast advertising. As the radio trade publishers Caldwell-Clements put in their 1944 book *Get Ready Now to Sell Television: A Guidebook for Merchants Who Recognize an Extraordinary Opportunity*: 'Fortunately, television has never been a gadget, except in the laboratory. It has already reached a degree of perfection before release to the public, that is unparalleled in our economic history.'[18] Similarly, the Television Broadcasters Association's 1945 newsletter, while recalling the 'romanticism that accompanied the spread of radio entertainment across the continent in the early 1920s', nevertheless had no words of encouragement for the would-be television amateur.[19]

If the radio amateur was marginalized in the trade press of the early television industry, the figure of the daytime female radio listener seems ubiquitous. Promoters of post-war television echoed many of commercial radio's discursive constructions of its audience, as well as its financial imperatives and programming strategies. As the vice-president of Philco remarked in 1945: 'Probably never before has a product of a great new industry been so

15 Orrin E. Dunlap, 'Television's Mail', *New York Times* (7 Aug. 1932), n.p. For a discussion of the activities of CBS in early mechanical television, see William Boddy, ' "Spread Like a Monster Blanket All Over the Country": CBS and Television', in Annette Kuhn and Jackie Stacey (eds.), *Screen Histories* (Oxford: Oxford University Press, 1998); reprinted from *Screen*, 32 (Summer 1991), 39–48.

16 A. Frederick Collins, *Experimental Television* (Boston: Lothrop, Lee & Shepard, 1932), p. xiii.

17 Hugo Gernsback, 'Editorial', *Television News* (Mar.–Apr. 1932), 7.

18 Caldwell-Clements, Inc., Publishers, *Get Ready Now to Sell Television: A Guidebook for Merchants Who Recognize an Extraordinary Opportunity* (New York: Caldwell-Clements, Inc., 1944), 5.

19 Television Broadcasters Association, *Weekly Newsletter on Television* (16 Mar. 1945), 1.

completely planned and highly developed before it was offered to the public as has television.'[20] The would-be leaders of the new TV industry, while forming the Television Broadcasters Association in 1944, asserted that the organization's 'prime objective . . . is to avoid any repetition of the errors that marked radio's beginnings in the roaring '20s'.[21] In 1950 NBC network head and television pioneer Sylvester (Pat) Weaver wrote in an internal memorandum that 'whereas in radio we had to find our way through hit or miss methods, we now have a pattern we believe will enable us, with great economy, to do a tremendous job in television without too much experimentation'.[22]

Despite the confidence of some industry officials about the expected continuities between the two media, the more attention-consuming and intrusive activity of watching a TV broadcast in place of listening to a radio programme provoked new gender-bound anxieties within the leadership of the young television industry. One industry official worried that television in the home might undermine patriarchal authority, wondering, for example, if 'the father of the house would be willing to have the lights turned out in the living room when he wants to read because his children want to watch a television broadcast of no interest to him'.[23] Industry anxieties around the new TV audience often centred on the figure of the housewife, and although one industry executive fretted that 'retuning a television set is far more difficult than a standard broadcast set. Women may not like the mechanics of television tuning,' the larger concern about the female homemaker was founded on the fundamental perceptual demands of the new visual medium.[24] Given what were presumed to be television's unique demands on audience attention, the central question became, according to the executive, 'the degree to which housewives would drop their housework to watch television during the daytime'.[25] A 1949 *Sales Management* article, 'Who Will Watch Daytime Television?', called the housewife 'the heart and backbone of America's vast daytime radio audience', but many in the industry worried that what they believed to be television's demand for undivided audience attention would weaken its value as an advertising medium during the lucrative daytime hours, when programme costs were low and audiences relatively high.[26] The general manager of DuMont's New York City television station laid out the problem at an industry conference in May 1946:

---

20 Quoted in Lyndon O. Brown, 'What the Public Expects of Television', in John Gray Peatman (ed.), *Radio and Business 1945: Proceedings of the First Annual Conference on Radio and Business* (New York: City College of New York, 1945), 136. For a discussion of the continuities between commercial radio and the early television industry, see William Boddy, *Fifties Television: The Industry and its Critics* (Urbana: University of Illinois Press, 1990), ch. 1.

21 Television Broadcasters Association, *Television* (Spring 1944), 9. In 1944, an executive of the newly formed TBA contrasted the industry's careful plans for television with the earlier radio industry where 'stations mushroomed indiscriminately across the nation', and 'broke out like a rash'. Will Baltin, 'Television Chaos Avoided', *Televiser* (Fall 1944), 52.

22 Pat Weaver, 'Television's Destiny' (1950), 5, collection of the NBC Records Administration Library, New York.

23 Brown, 'What the Public Expects of Television', 137.

24 Ibid. 139.

25 Ibid. 137.

26 Jules Nathan, 'Who'll Watch Daytime Television?', *Sales Management* (1 Apr. 1949), 46.

There are certain people who have maintained that the American housewife would turn television on early in the morning just as she does the radio, and leave it on throughout the day and most of the night. . . . That, of course, is hardly so, because the benefits of television can be derived only when you are looking at it directly and not doing anything else. The housewife will not very long remain a housewife who attempts to watch television programs all afternoon and evening instead of cooking or darning socks.[27]

The female homemaker-listener constructed in the industry trade press was criticized as both perceptually distracted and psychologically over-identified in relation to daytime radio programming. As one advertising executive argued in 1949:

Radio is an unqualified success during the daytime hours. To a large extent its popularity rests squarely on those factors which may be an insuperable obstacle to video. Women can clean, cook, bake, and engage in all the varied mystic rites of the homemaker while keeping a sharp ear out for the latest agonies of the radio dramas. Television, alas for the business side of the enterprise, will share the spotlight with no other activities.[28]

Such offhand and disdainful references to daytime radio soap opera listening in defining the female audience run through widely disparate writings on post-war American broadcasting. For example, Charles A. Siepmann's 1946 reformist manifesto *Radio's Second Chance* casually offers a gendered opposition between the thoughtful (and potentially reform-minded) male radio amateur and the pathological housewife listener. On the one hand, Siepmann calls for the creation of a new journal of radio criticism aimed at elevating public taste in broadcasting; the journal itself might attract a popular readership, Siepmann argues, by appealing to electronics amateurs with 'articles on the technical side of radio'. Evoking the lost paradise of the 1920s radio amateur, Siepmann argued that 'FM and television provide a fresh fillip to the amateur radio fan's enthusiasm of earlier days. Adult and high school children alike provide a market for such articles. We are all born mechanics.'[29] While Siepmann links amateurs to a project of public enlightenment and programme taste elevation, elsewhere in the book the author calls for the creation of a foundation-supported Critical Radio Research Institute, citing one example of its possible scientific work: 'For sociologists, soap operas provide revealing case histories of maladjustment and escapist daydreaming among millions of women.'[30] Thus the alleged pathology of female soap listeners was associated with the commercial constraints and programme mediocrity that Siepmann and other broadcast reformers saw as central to the cultural and civic shortcomings of US broadcasting. Paul

27 Samuel Cuff, General Manager, WABD, quoted in D. E. Moser (ed.), *Radio and Business: Proceedings of the Second Annual Conference on Radio and Business* (New York: City College of New York, School of Business and Civic Administration, 1946), 121.

28 Nathan, 'Who'll Watch Daytime Television?', 46.

29 Charles A. Siepmann, *Radio's Second Chance* (Boston: Little, Brown and Company, 1946), 254.

30 Ibid. 264.

Lazarsfeld and Frank Stanton, in the introduction to their edited volume *Radio Research, 1942–1943*, pointed to the 'special importance' of the daytime serial as subject of critical controversy. Their volume featured Herta Herzog's pioneering audience study, 'What do we Really Know about Daytime Serial Listeners?', which attempted to refute some of the more extreme claims made for the psychopathology of female soap opera fans.[31]

In terms more hyperbolic than Siepmann's, Philip Wylie's 1942 best-seller *A Generation of Vipers* placed the female radio listener at the centre of a cultural and moral crisis. Wylie wrote of the soap opera: 'This filthy and indecent abomination, this trash with which, until lately, only moron servant girls could dull their credulous minds in the tawdry privacy of their cubicles, is now the national saga.'[32] After invoking the class- and gender-bound rhetoric of domestic contamination, Wylie attacked what he saw as the conspiracy of female radio listeners ('moms') and Madison Avenue advertising executives: 'The radio is mom's final tool, for it stamps everyone who listens to it with the matriarchal brand . . . our land is a living representation of the . . . fact worked out in matriarchal sentimentality, goo, slop, hidden cruelty, and the foreshadow of national death.'[33]

In the context of such extravagant expressions of concern over the cultural implications of radio soap opera listening among housewives, some mid-century observers began to worry about the effect of post-war TV viewing on American men. One advertising executive writing in *Sales Management* in 1949 predicted that television viewing would cause a decline in traditional male leisure activities, including pleasure driving, barbecuing, home repair, and 'such hobby pursuits as stamp-collecting, wood-working, oil-painting, golf, tennis, photography, and gardening'.[34] He predicted that the new TV-watching male, being sedentary and stress free,

> may live longer. But, just to be sure that this doesn't hurt TV sales, let me hasten to point out, girls, that while your men may, therefore, be around longer, they'll be little bother. Just put them in the corner, leave them alone, let them look and listen, they'll be no trouble at all. What more could you ask?[35]

As we will see in a subsequent chapter, these representations of the role of gender in spectatorship, commercialization, and technology around the time of television's post-war launch are part of a larger and persistent set of beliefs about the place of masculinity in post-war mass culture, a position elaborated as antipode to the contemporaneous heroic male artist in modernist high culture. The converse gendering of American mass culture as feminine and feminizing arguably reached an apotheosis in mid-century, the era of 'Momism'. Shaped by these larger cultural frames, television viewing

---

31 Paul Lazarsfeld and Frank Stanton (eds.), *Radio Research, 1942–1943* (New York: Essential Books/Duell, Sloan and Pearce, 1944).

32 Philip Wylie, *A Generation of Vipers* (New York: Holt, Rinehart and Winston, 1955), 214–15, quoted in Spigel, *Make Room for TV*, 62.

33 Wylie, *A Generation of Vipers*, 215.

34 J. David Cathcart, 'Will TV Play Hob with our Design for Living?', *Sales Management* (1 Mar. 1949), 52.

35 Ibid. 54.

in post-war America has persistently been figured as a pacifying, emasculating, and feminizing activity. These cultural polarities, I would argue, owe a great deal to the gendered history of radio listening going back to the 1920s and have continued relevance to the promotion and social meanings of domestic communications technologies today.

Early battles on the television sales floor

The gender issues in play in the post-war television industry can also be discerned in contemporaneous accounts of the interpersonal encounters of customer and salesperson in the television showroom. As in the other sectors of the television industry, the immediate post-war era was an unsettled period for TV manufacturers and retailers; one historian of the television manufacturing industry noted that between 1946 and 1951 'beauty parlors, gasoline stations, hardware stores, and cleaners and pressers were retailers of television sets for a while in some communities', and the uncertainties brought about by post-war changes in consumer taste and demographics, as well as the technological novelty of television itself, all made the TV retail trade press unusually introspective about the proper sales methods and targets.[36]

In the years immediately after the Second World War, the trade journal *Radio and Television Retailing* offered the would-be television dealer stern advice on many topics, including assuring 'that your windows are well-lighted, free from dead flies and dust' and advising the dealer to ' "get shed" of the weak sisters, gripers and goldbricks both in his sales and service departments'.[37] Elsewhere, the journal coached retailers on how to deal with undesirable clients, including 'plain out-and-out bores, cynical-appearing starers, and meddlers who "participate" in sales discussions between other customers and the salesman'.[38] A 1946 article, 'Let the Seller Beware', alerted dealers to the schemes of con artists and other 'unscrupulous buyers', including

> the honest housewife who possesses an adaptable conscience when it comes to dealing with a merchant. She may go to church every Sunday and teach her children the difference between right and wrong, but when it comes to her dealings with a retail merchant, her motives are not only selfish, but often palpably dishonest.[39]

In addition to such hard-nosed prescriptions for television retailers, industry leaders and the trade press also offered dealers more general guidance about introducing television's technological powers to the public. Television manufacturer Allan B. DuMont instructed the company's dealers in 1948:

> Remember that the selling of television receivers is still in the pioneering stage. You are not only selling a DuMont set, you are selling Television

36 Oxenfeldt, *Marketing Practices in the TV Set Industry*, 14.

37 'Cash in on a Great New Trend!', *Radio and Television Retailing* (July 1946), 107; 'Sell the Modern Way!', *Radio and Television Retailing* (Feb. 1947), 42.

38 'Superstition in Selling', *Radio and Television Retailing* (Aug. 1946), 112.

39 'Let the Seller Beware', *Radio and Television Retailing* (Dec. 1946), 122.

itself. . . . Sell television on what it can do for the customer. You are selling more than just a gadget—you are selling a new outlook on life.[40]

Allan DuMont's worries about salespersons presenting the TV set as a technological gadget to customers were widely echoed in the business press. The 1944 trade handbook *Get Ready Now to Sell Television* advised dealers to avoid attempting to sell specific features of the apparatus which might be of interest only to technically minded amateurs. Instead, the book urged 'selling the wonders of television', quoting with approval DuMont's print advertisements aimed at readers even before the end of the war and relaunch of TV sales: 'You'll be an armchair Columbus on ten-thousand and one thrilling voyages of discovery!' (see Fig. 9.3).[41] However, while the technical aspects of the new medium were played down in television's early promotional literature, the rhetoric of mobility, omnipotence, and adventure familiar in the established literature of amateur radio was quickly enlisted to serve the consumer imperatives of post-war commercial television. Business consultant Carle A. Christiansen explained in a 1949 trade-press article, 'DON'T Sell "Nuts and Bolts" ':

> In selling to the average person, there is very little in the way of cold, hard thinking that enters into the process. True, you may explain how the article you sell operates, but it will be helpful *only insofar as it appeals to or awakens one or more of the prospect's desires to possess it.* Technical explanations that go beyond this do not help the sale, and if the prospect is not able to understand or appreciate your explanation, it may 'kill' the sale.[42]

Christiansen continued: 'It is especially important that the salesman with a technical background keep this in mind, because many of the sales that he loses . . . are forfeited because he sells "nuts and bolts," or should we say "coils and condensers," instead of what his product could do to fulfill the desires of the prospect.'[43]

In another article the same year Christiansen offered additional advice to the technically inclined salesperson, attempting to translate the language of electronic technology into showroom salesmanship: according to Christiansen, 'selling, like any other science, is subject to analysis and can be taught. . . . In many ways, the science of selling and the science of radio are parallel . . . in selling we must reach the prospect on a "frequency" of thought and feeling to which he will respond.' Expanding upon the electronics analogy, Christiansen identified seven basic buying motives, using a technical schematic diagram to indicate 'EMF' as emotional motive force, an electrical resistor as the prospective customer's sales resistance, the useful load as the customer's buying action, and a sales meter which is designed to measure 'the "Yes" potential'. He summed up the lesson for sales personnel:

40 Allan B. DuMont, *DuMont Dealer's Book of Television* (DuMont, 1948), DuMont Collection, Smithsonian, Series 4, Box 42, Folder 71, 15–16.

41 Caldwell-Clements, Inc., *Get Ready Now to Sell Television*, 41–2.

42 Carle A. Christiansen, 'DON'T Sell "Nuts and Bolts" ', *Radio and Television News* (Dec. 1949), 40. Emphasis in original.

43 Ibid.

'Basically, our job is to increase the *emotional motive force* and reduce the *buying resistance* of the prospect, so that a sufficient amount of *emotional motive force* will flow through the circuit to obtain a "Yes" reading on our *sales meter*.'[44]

While Christiansen's articles may represent an unusually explicit and elaborate attempt to translate the language of the electronic hobbyist into the instrumental terms of the TV receiver showroom, the early television industry clearly made great efforts to present the television set as a fully domesticated, if still marvellous, technological artefact. From the heights of the industry's 'great men' to the hard-nosed lessons of the salesroom floor, the tropes associated with the radio amateur were instrumentalized in the service of selling complete television sets to post-war families. At the same time, the potentially disruptive legacy of amateurs as opponents to the introduction of broadcast advertising was repressed in the early television literature, and the alternatives to the commercial network radio model for post-war television were almost completely absent from public discussion.

These instrumental post-war constructions of the TV set customer and television viewer retained enormous power through the following decades of industry growth and technological innovation. As we will see, they are also crucial in understanding the contemporary consumer electronics industry, animated at the prospect of an immense new market of American households whose television sets will be made obsolete with the introduction of high-definition television. The regulatory approval for high-definition television initiated a new set of discursive contests over the redefinition of the television set and its place in the home, including a clash between the consumer electronics industry eager to reach consumers sated with CDs, VCRs, camcorders, and second and third TV sets and the computer industry frustrated by low penetration rates of home computers. Meanwhile, the computer's transformation from a calculating device to a communications medium has already provoked new moral panics about electronic reconfigurations of public and private spaces within and beyond the home. As the rhetorical and commercial struggles begin over the would-be convergence of computer monitor and TV screen, there is more at stake than who will manufacture and sell the new hardware. As we will see, the move to digital television, besides bringing some broadcasters and electronics manufacturers enormous revenues, will also put into play new social scenarios of domesticity, gender, the nature of work, and the lure and panic of electronic presence, what RCA president David Sarnoff in 1928 predicted as television's eventual merging of 'reality and its electrical counterpart'.[45] In this context, attending to the persistent discursive conventions which have marked the reception of new media technologies can illuminate the deeper continuities and discontinuities which underlie both the seemingly inevitable and monolithic position of American post-war television as well as the widely touted 'revolutionary' changes on offer by the contemporary corporate champions of the new digital media.

---

44 Carle A. Christiansen, 'The Buying Motives: Key to More Sales', *Radio and Television News* (Aug. 1949), 38–9. Emphasis in original.

45 David Sarnoff, 'David Sarnoff Previsions Television', *Television: America's First Television Journal* (June 1928), 100.

4

US Television Abroad, 1960/1990: Market Power and National Introspection

Introduction

FOLLOWING THE TRAUMATIC post-war debates over the viability and nature of commercial television in the American home, the TV industry settled into a half-century of remarkable economic growth and institutional stability. However, after decades of steady expansion and stable industry structures, the early 1990s marked—in both the USA and Europe, in both public service and commercial television systems—a moment of crisis in political and economic legitimization for broadcast institutions and a reconfiguration of the long-established institutional representations of the national audience. Parallel to the crisis in the three-network TV oligopoly in the USA, a distinct era of public service broadcasting seemed to be coming to an end in many Western European nations by the end of the 1980s.[1] The upheaval on both sides of the Atlantic can perhaps most acutely be read as a crisis in the manner in which the respective television institutions have constructed what John Hartley has called the twin 'imaginary communities' of nation and audience.[2]

The unsettled conditions in international television at the start of the 1990s suggest an intriguing parallel to the position of the American TV industry during the undisputed boom years of early global television programming trade in the early 1960s, an era which defined US network hegemony in both

---

1 For contemporary material on the crisis in European public service broadcasting, see Dennis McQuail, 'Western Europe: "Mixed Model" under Threat?', in John Downing, Ali Mohammadi, and Annabelle Sreberny-Mohammadi (eds.), *Questioning the Media: A Critical Introduction* (Newbury Park, Calif.: Sage, 1990), 125–38; Willard D. Rowland and Michael Tracey, 'Worldwide Challenges to Public Service Broadcasting', *Journal of Communication*, 40/2 (Spring 1990), 8–27; Steven S. Wildman and Stephen E. Siwek, 'The Privatization of European Television: Effects on International Markets for Programs', *Columbia Journal of World Business* (Fall 1987), 71–6; Ien Ang, *Desperately Seeking the Audience* (London: Routledge, 1991), 99–152; Edward Buscombe, 'Coca-Cola Satellites? Hollywood and the Deregulation of European Television', in Tino Balio (ed.), *Hollywood in the Age of Television* (Cambridge, Mass.: Unwin and Hyman, 1990), 393–415; Jay Blumer and T. J. Nossiter (eds.), *Broadcasting Finance in Transition: A Comparative Handbook* (New York: Oxford University Press, 1991); Kenneth Dyson and Peter Humphreys (eds.), *The Political Economy of Communications: International and European Dimensions* (London: Routledge, 1990); Kenneth Dyson, Peter Humphreys, Ralph Negrin, and Jean-Paul Simon (eds.), *Broadcasting and New Media Policies in Western Europe* (London: Routledge, 1988); Preben Sepstrup, *Transnationalization of Television in Western Europe* (London: John Libbey, 1990); R. Negrin and S. Papathanassopoulos, *The Internationalization of Television* (London: Pinter Publishers, 1990).

2 John Hartley, *Tele-ology: Studies in Television* (London: Routledge, 1992), 101–18; also see Benedict Anderson, *Imaginary Communities: Reflections on the Origins and Spread of Nationalism* (2nd edn. London: Verso, 1991).

international and domestic markets. These two moments which bracket the 'network era' of US television can be analyzed via the shifting public and trade discourses addressing television, especially in the way in which such discourses have proposed new definitions of the television audience. In each case, a period of sustained growth in American market power in the international media market, combined with a crisis in a consensus vision of the US government's global political and military roles, created unusual national introspection as media industry and political leaders redefined the stakes and meaning of US media around the globe. It is ironic, though not entirely unexpected, that the nature of the 'network era' of American television has become clearer to scholars only after the networks' tight-fisted grip on their domestic audience had slipped. Likewise, the contrasting moments of American self-consciousness as an actor on the international media stage during the periods of crisis in market power and public relations of the early 1960s on the one hand and the late 1980s and early 1990s on the other may suggest wider issues of the economic and ideological constructions of the nation in contemporary film and television studies. There is an urgent need for contemporary media historians to address the US film and television industries as part of a global market, sensitive not only to transnational economic forces but also to the power of representations of the national audience themselves produced by media institutions around the world. As the other case studies in media innovation in this volume suggest, changes in media technology and market structure inevitably throw such representations of the nation and audience into crisis.

Broadcast culture has long inhabited a curious contradictory context, where broadcast signals, themselves technologically indifferent to national boundaries, have, since the beginnings of radio broadcasting, triggered utopian visions of international understanding, even a withering away of the nation state in a kind of one-world oral and image community, while at the same time the legal, economic, and discursive constructions of broadcast institutions and audiences have been resolutely national in design. This chapter will trace the playing out of these tensions of nation and other under the distinct economic, political, and technological conditions of two significant periods for the global media industry.

Pax Americana redux?   The US media's role in the 1991 USA–Iraq War crystallized some of the perennial issues of nation and broadcast audience. Joshua Muravchik, a resident scholar at the conservative American Enterprise Institute, wrote euphorically in the *New York Times* in January 1991 about what he saw as the happy fallout of the military success of Operation Desert Storm on chastised Democrats at home, on Arab malcontents who mistakenly 'believed that . . . the humiliations of colonialism and underdevelopment could be redeemed', and on all those around the globe who would doubt America's new willingness to use force in a (post) post-Vietnam syndrome era. Most optimistically, however, Muravchik saw in the ashes of the lopsided Gulf War the long-sought fulfilment of the post-war US dream of a Pax Americana, now sovereign in a new unipolar world. Muravchik proclaimed:

This Pax Americana will rest not on domination but on persuasion and example as well as power. It will consist not of empire but of having won over a large and growing part of the world not only to the joys of jeans and rock and Big Macs but also to our concept of how nations ought to be governed and to behave.[3]

But just as the US military's carefully managed image repertory of smart-bomb nose cone footage and uniformed talking heads could not entirely erase the presence of the war's actual victims, the technological muscle-flexing of CNN's new global reach during the 1991 Gulf War showcasing the carrots and sticks of a new Pax Americana failed to assuage recent US anxieties about its role in the new global media system. The Gulf War, along with recent economic changes in the international landscape of television, a crucial part of what *Fortune* magazine in 1990 called 'a one-world pop-tech civilization', has brought anxious new institutional configurations of the nation and the TV audience, at a time when television serves a predominant role as both a product and producer of the nation around the world.[4]

By the late 1980s, the implications of the long-heralded 'technological revolution' in the electronic media were made manifest in distinct ways in the United States and Western Europe, and an examination of the trade and popular discourses which anticipated and accompanied the technological and market changes in TV broadcasting can illuminate larger cultural processes involved in constructing national identities on both sides of the Atlantic. The new TV delivery systems of cable and direct broadcast satellites, the ongoing consolidation of the telecommunications and computer industries, the international trend toward broadcast deregulation, and the growth of significant new transnational entrepreneurs all point to the late 1980s as the beginning of a period of the greatest change in global television since the decisive growth of international television in the second half of the 1950s.

The changes in the global market place of television by the early 1990s also affected the ways in which scholars and others considered the medium. The study of international television increasingly presented challenges of responding not only to a rapidly changing economic environment but also to major shifts within the premises and methods of critical media research, in part reflecting a clash of generations, disciplines, ideologies, and national contexts. By the early 1990s, there had been twenty years of sustained critical scrutiny of the massive export of US television programming, long enough for some of the fundamental assumptions about the implications of international programme flows to be challenged during a time when European nations have undergone a decade of significant changes in their own institutions of national broadcasting. Ongoing European debates in television studies in turn began to inform US critics increasingly sensitive to the

3 Joshua Muravchik, 'At Last, Pax Americana', *New York Times* (24 Jan. 1991), A23.

4 John Huey, 'America's Hottest Export: Pop Culture', *Fortune* (31 Dec. 1990), 50; for a discussion of the media's role in the Gulf War, see Kevin Robins and Les Levidow, 'The Eye of the Storm', *Screen*, 32/3 (Autumn 1991), 324–8.

domestic implications of the altered international TV landscape in the 1990s.[5]

One striking contrast between the discussions of television policy in the USA and Western Europe is the degree to which such debates abroad, in contrast to their general insularity in the USA, have spilled into the popular press and into wider debates over national identity and public policy. The early 1980s, for example, saw across Europe a scattered panic at the prospect of what one British TV critic called *TV Today and Tomorrow: Wall to Wall Dallas*, invoking the American prime-time serial that French Cultural Minister Jack Lang called 'the symbol of American cultural imperialism'.[6] The ensuing debates among European media scholars usefully re-examined received notions of public service broadcasting, the national, the politics of popular pleasure, and the functions of television melodrama.[7] In the USA, by contrast, nearly an entire earlier generation of TV critics and intellectuals saw their polemical investment in television's 'golden age' of live drama dashed at the end of the 1950s in the trauma of the quiz show scandals and a rising tide of filmed action-adventure shows. Until well into the 1990s, the post-1960 interventions of American intellectuals and academicians into popular discourses on television were too often limited to drop-dead broadsides, rudimentary content analysis, and the perennial hot-button topics of TV sex and violence.

Thinking globally

At the same time that many New York-based TV critics were lamenting the death of live drama at the hands of filmed action-adventure shows and abandoning what they viewed as a disloyal and corrupted medium, the American television industry began to exploit the booming world market for the same easily exported telefilms. In 1961 for the first time there were more TV sets in use outside the USA than inside the country, and the three American networks eagerly looked abroad for new programme markets, foreign partnerships, and direct investments. ABC, for example, used a newly created international division to acquire a majority interest in a private TV network

---

5 On changing international scholarship as represented by papers from the International Television Studies Conferences organized by the British Film Institute, see Philip Drummond and Richard Paterson (eds.), *Television in Transition* (London: BFI, 1986); Drummond and Paterson (eds.), *Television and its Audience: International Research Perspectives* (London: BFI, 1988).

6 Chris Dunkley, *TV Today and Tomorrow: Wall to Wall Dallas* (London: Penguin, 1985); Lang is quoted in Ien Ang, *Watching 'Dallas': Soap Opera and the Melodramatic Imagination* (New York: Methuen, 1985), 2.

7 See, for example, David Morley, 'Changing Paradigms in Audience Studies', in Ellen Seiter, Hans Borchers, Gabriele Kreutzner, and Eva-Maria Warth (eds.), *Remote Control: Television, Audiences and Cultural Power* (London: Routledge, Chapman and Hall, 1989), 16–43; Nicholas Garnham, 'Public Service Versus the Market', *Screen*, 23/2 (July–Aug. 1983), 6–27; Ian Connell, 'Commercial Broadcasting and the British Left', *Screen*, 24/6 (Nov.–Dec. 1983), 70–80; Ian Connell and Lydia Curti, 'Popular Broadcasting in Italy and Britain: Some Issues and Problems', in Drummond and Paterson (eds.), *Television in Transition*, 87–111; Richard Collins, 'Wall to Wall Dallas? The US–UK Trade in Television', in Cynthia Schneider and Brian Wallis (eds.), *Global Television* (Cambridge, Mass.: MIT Press, 1988), 79–94; Richard Collins, *Culture, Communication and National Identity: The Case of Canadian Television* (Toronto: University of Toronto Press, 1990); John Tomlinson, *Cultural Imperialism* (Baltimore: Johns Hopkins University Press, 1991); John Caughie, 'Playing at Being American: Games and Tactics', in Patricia Mellencamp (ed.), *Logics of Television: Essays in Cultural Criticism* (Bloomington: Indiana University Press, 1990), 44–58.

in Central America as well as minority interests in Australian and Latin American stations.[8] But the most lucrative international sector for the US television industry quickly became the export of television programming; by 1960 the three networks' telefilm arms had become the world's three largest TV programme traders. The head of ABC told the *Saturday Evening Post* in 1961:

> Television has a great future. ABC is out in front on the international front. We have acquired a minority interest in twenty-two stations abroad. *The Untouchables, 77 Sunset Strip, Maverick* are the most popular programs in Australia. In Bangkok they watch *Wyatt Earp*. Half the people in the world are illiterate. Television can penetrate that barrier . . . Television is a worldwide medium. You have to think globally. If you own a show, you own it worldwide.[9]

By 1963 CBS's film sales division had become the world's largest exporter of TV programming, and that year for the first time its foreign sales exceeded the company's revenues from domestic syndication.[10] CBS's experience with the Japanese market is illustrative. The network began supplying news film to Japan in 1955; between 1955 and 1961 CBS sold over 2,700 different TV programmes in Japan, and by 1961 50 per cent of network prime-time programming in Japan (then the world's largest TV market after the USA) was supplied by American firms, a 'direct result', CBS chairman Frank Stanton argued at the time, 'of the removal of restrictions on how much programming the Japanese networks could accept, and how much they were permitted to pay for it'. In 1964 CBS set up CBS Japan, Inc. to distribute TV programming; in 1967 CBS Records entered a fifty-fifty joint venture with Sony Corporation to manufacture and market records in Japan and elsewhere.[11]

At the same time, however, the global penetration of US programming in the early 1960s brought to US media industry leaders, politicians, and cultural commentators a new anxiety and self-consciousness about the image of America abroad, the fear, as CBS chairman Frank Stanton told a Japanese-American group in 1961 (speaking in place of an ailing Edward R. Murrow), 'that what entertains us at home may embarrass us abroad'.[12] As film critic J. Hoberman argued in 1991, 'a dozen years after the end of World War II, the United States was suffering from an new sort of malady, namely an "image

---

8 'Income and Earnings Reach Record High', *Broadcasting* (4 Apr. 1960), 76–7.

9 John Bartlow Martin, 'Television USA: Part 1: Wasteland or Wonderland?', *Saturday Evening Post* (21 Oct. 1961), 24.

10 Columbia Broadcasting System, *Annual Report* for year ending 28 Dec. 1963 (New York: Columbia Broadcasting System, 1964), 4, 19; for contemporary accounts of American telefilm exports, see 'World Laps up US TV Fare', *Business Week* (23 Apr. 1960), 129; 'TV Abroad Thrives on US Ways', *Business Week* (3 Sept. 1960), 105–7; Robert Lewis Shayon, 'Breakthrough in International TV', *Saturday Review of Literature* (14 Jan. 1961), 35.

11 Columbia Broadcasting System, *Annual Report* for year ending 2 Jan. 1965 (New York: Columbia Broadcasting System, 1965), 4; Columbia Broadcasting System, *Annual Report* for year ending 30 Dec. 1967 (New York: Columbia Broadcasting System, 1968), 3. The percentage of US-produced programming on Japanese television fell significantly after the early 1960s, for a variety of reasons.

12 Frank Stanton, Keynote Address, Second United States–Japan Conference on Cultural and Educational Interchange, Washington, DC (16 Oct. 1963), 3. Collection of the CBS Reference Library.

problem," ' as works such as the 1959 best-selling novel *The Ugly American* adopted the domestic introspection of 1950s popular fiction and non-fiction and 'took this self-doubt global'. *The Ugly American*, according to Hoberman, struck a responsive chord in the US public and was used by Democrats to promote a New Frontier foreign policy, perhaps the high point of Joshua Muravchik's original post-war Pax Americana.[13]

The high-profile congressional hearings in 1961 and 1962 into sex and violence in prime-time TV programming led by Senator Thomas Dodd also exposed widespread anxieties about the detrimental effects of such programming on the US image abroad. Clara Logan, president of the National Association for Better Radio and Television, complained to the subcommittee: 'Worst of all, the Communists the world over use gangsterism in American telefilms for their own political ends, propagandizing that this TV gangsterism and violence really is America.' Several witnesses before Dodd's committee expressed concern about the harmful effects of American television programming on what they viewed as especially impressionable foreign audiences.[14]

A 1961 *Broadcasting* magazine article entitled 'TV, Movies Cast as Villains of Delinquency' reflected the dual moral panics about impressionable television audiences at home and abroad. The magazine reported one Congressman's insertion into the *Congressional Record* of TV critic John Crosby's charge that 'we teach juvenile delinquency on television', and the magazine also noted official concern about the harmful effects of American television programme exports on the US image abroad displayed in the confirmation hearings for Edward R. Murrow as United States Information Agency (USIA) director. Could Murrow 'persuade' leaders of the industry to stop exporting them, one Senator asked; Murrow said he would try.[15] In a potent symbol of both the new political sensitivity about American TV exports and the industry–government alliances typical of the New Frontier, in 1961 President John F. Kennedy first offered the directorship of the USIA to CBS's Frank Stanton, only offering the post to Murrow after Stanton declined. One of Murrow's first official acts as USIA director involved an attempt to prevent the BBC from airing his own *CBS Reports: Harvest of Shame*; Murrow later removed the unflattering documentary from all USIA programmes circulating abroad.[16]

Nevertheless, what is striking in these expressions of official anxiety as the USA moved to predominance in world image markets in the early 1960s is the general confidence in the structural role of the USA as programme exporter, with the occasional misgivings reflecting either partisan disputes or the muted ambivalence of a delicate imperialist sensibility. Historian

13 J. Hoberman, 'Believe it or Not: J. Hoberman on *The Ugly American*', *Artforum* (Apr. 1991), 27–8; see also J. Hoberman, *The Dream Life: Movies, Media, and the Mythology of the Sixties* (New York: The New Press, 2003).

14 US Congress, Senate, Committee on the Judiciary, Subcommittee to Investigate Juvenile Delinquency, *Hearings Part 10 Effects on Young People of Violence and Crime Portrayed on Television*, 87th Cong., June–July 1961; Jan., May 1962, 1678–81, 1883; also see Val Adams, 'Stanton Defends TV Sent Overseas', *New York Times* (4 May 1962), 67.

15 'TV, Movies Cast as Villains of Delinquency', *Broadcasting* (20 Mar. 1961), 76.

16 James L. Baughman, *Television's Guardians: The FCC and the Politics of Programming 1958–1967* (Knoxville: University of Tennessee Press, 1985), 56.

Herbert Schiller has identified the early 1960s as the high point of the confident Cold War consensus of government officials, media industry leaders, and academic researchers about the constructive role of US media exports in what one communication scholar at the time called 'the persuasive transmission of enlightenment ... [as] the modern paradigm of international communication'.[17]

The early 1960s also witnessed the emphatic institutional construction of the domestic US television audience along the lines of what John Hartley has termed a paedocratic regime (built around an audience imagined as having childlike qualities and needs), a notion constructed simultaneously from the good-parent, bad-parent discourses of CBS network head James Aubrey's widely reported programme directive of 'broads, bosoms and fun' on the one hand and the paternalistic inquisitions into TV and juvenile delinquency by ex-seminarian, ex-Nuremberg prosecutor, and ex-FBI agent Senator Thomas Dodd on the other.[18] Both Hartley and Ien Ang have noted the colonialist and orientalist quality of the institutional discourse of the American TV industry concerning knowledge about and address to its audience, a discourse which helped to create an objectified, dominated, and often childlike 'other' as audience. This regime of knowledge, functional to the network industry's need for profit maximization and self-preservation, was characteristic of an ascendant US television industry supremely confident of its domestic and international hegemony.[19]

National culture in a one-world pop-tech civilization

The American television industry grew, prospered, and remained structurally unchanged through the 1960s and 1970s. At the same time, the unequal growth rates of the domestic and foreign programme markets widened in the 1970s and 1980s; between 1970 and 1988, the number of TV households worldwide grew from 80 million to 500 million, a rate of growth the mature US market could not match. Nevertheless, in the late 1980s the USA remained the predominant supplier in the international programming market; with less than 5 per cent of the global TV audience, the US television industry represented one-third of the world's total TV programme expenditures in 1989. This extended period of profitable stability in the network television industry from the late 1950s to the 1970s, along with the continued marginalization of public television and the virtual absence of foreign programming on American commercial TV, made domestic evidence of US television's reciprocal links to the rest of the TV world nearly invisible. Large US audiences, cosily divided among three network firms, a high proportion

---

17 Daniel Lerner quoted in Herbert Schiller, *Culture, Inc.* (New York: Oxford University Press, 1989), 139.

18 Hartley, *Tele-ology*, 108; for a discussion of Aubrey's alleged dictum, see 'Networks Offer Definitions of Sex', *New York Times* (12 May 1962), 51; Aubrey told Dodd's subcommittee: 'I do not believe I have ever used the term "broads, bosoms, and fun" in connection with a CBS television network program. But I believe it is quite easy for people who work in this particular business to interpret a request for attractive girls, wholesome, attractive girls, rather than neurotic, unhappy, unattractive women as "broads", and also, because you want them attractive, I believe you use the word "bosoms." ' *Hearings*, 2481–2.

19 Hartley, *Tele-ology*, 105; Ang, *Desperately Seeking the Audience*, 22–3.

of US gross national product spent on advertising (2.4 per cent in 1986, the highest in the world), nearly double-digit annual growth rates in advertising expenditures (from $5 billion to $100 billion between 1948 and 1988, with nearly a quarter of the total spending going to television), and the one-way nature of the US trade in TV programmes (the US imported about 2 per cent of its programming in 1983) all contributed to an international profile for the US television industry which recalls the boastful sign along the rusting New Jersey industrial corridor of an earlier era: 'Trenton Makes, The World Takes.'[20]

Despite the continued dominance of US firms in world image markets, as the 1990s began there was a noticeable shift in the popular and industry view of the relation of US television to the rest of the world.[21] In the early 1990s US context of sustained economic recession and growing anxiety about the nation's ability to compete successfully in changing global markets, American media pundits, industry executives, and government leaders recast the domestic stakes of the new international media landscape. These trade and public policy discourses reconfigured the US media business in industrial policy terms as a rare success story of American ingenuity and market appeal, but one increasingly threatened by international intellectual property piracy on the one hand and by a Japanese financial takeover of US media firms on the other.[22] In 1990 US trade surpluses from media exports were outpaced only by the aerospace sector in an otherwise bleak balance of trade picture; when combined with the export of the high-profile mass consumer goods of Joshua Muravchik's new Pax Americana (Ninja Turtles, Coke, Big Macs, and Levi's), whose demand is in large part driven by American media exports, the combined pop culture sector represents the largest single contributor to US exports.[23]

By the early 1990s, the construction of the US media industry along industrial policy terms, often combined with more or less explicit nationalist appeals, brought a new reciprocal consciousness of America's place in the international media market among leaders of the US film and television industries. The infamous 1991 'leaked' memorandum from Disney head Jeffrey Katzenberg argued:

> In a way, there is something quite noble in what we do. Our potential impact can not be minimized and should never be trivialized. At the same time that America has lost its dominance of the world's economy, it has become a pre-eminent force in the world's culture. And this is largely

---

20 The data in this paragraph are found in Peter Dunnett, *The World Television Industry* (London: Routledge, 1990), 1, 4, 6, 25, 41.

21 The early roots of this anxiety can be sensed in CBS chairman Frank Stanton's 1961 speech to the United States–Japan Conference on Cultural and Educational Interchange, when he noted prophetically: 'it is true, and I would be the first to concede the point, that for the moment at least the exchange is lopsided: we export far more than we import. But I also believe that Japanese television film product will increasingly find its way into the world market. . . . Recall, if you will, that only a little over a decade ago world manufacturers of optical and electronic components and devices never dreamed what Japanese inventiveness and industry would mean to them competitively in an astoundingly short time. . . . Habits, no matter how deeply entrenched, have a way of changing'; Stanton, Keynote Address, 4, 5–6.

22 See Huey, 'America's Hottest Export', 51, 58; also see David Morley and Kevin Robins, 'Techno-Orientalism: Foreigners, Phobias and Futures', *New Formations*, 19 (Spring 1992), 136–56.

23 Huey, 'America's Hottest Export', 50.

because of what we do. People around the world may no longer drive in American cars, build with American steel, or listen to American radios. But they do go see American films. They share our hopes and dreams and values when they experience the joy of a *Pretty Woman*, the enchantment of a *Little Mermaid* or the inspiration of a *Dead Poet's Society*.[24]

Notwithstanding Katzenberg's lyrical evocation of national pride, a fearful and defensive tone within the US media industry of the early 1990s was rarely far from the surface. Several significant purchases by foreign-based multinationals of major US media producers (by 1992, four of the eight major motion-picture studios were owned by firms based outside the USA, as were four of the five major record labels), culminating in Sony's purchase of Columbia Pictures and CBS Records and Matsushita's $7 billion buyout of MCA, the largest acquisition ever of a US company by a Japanese firm, provoked new discursive configurations of 'nation' and 'other' within the US media industry.[25] Conservative pundit George Gilder in 1990 warned that

as the 1980s roared and tumbled to a close, sirens wailed and moods darkened in Japanese–America relations. . . . For the first time since World War II, the underpinnings of friendship and prosperity between the US and Asia appeared to be in serious jeopardy. . . . A consensus emerged that the US was a graying and gullible nation, slipping into churlish senility, and that Japan was a mercantilist shyster, seizing power by unfair trade.[26]

Media industry observers related the new Japanese media acquisitions to the desire of Japanese hardware manufacturers to exploit horizontal integration via control or ownership of movie studios, record labels, and TV production companies. Michael Schulhof, president of Sony USA, citing the lessons of the VCR and the audio CD, told *Fortune*: 'Unless you have software to support your hardware, you can't have a successful industry.' But the move by Japanese firms into software production provoked a new self-consciousness in Hollywood of American cultural identity as insistently defined against a cultural and racial other. The CEO of Coca-Cola, which sold Columbia Pictures to Sony for $3.4 million, told the magazine: 'Hollywood, unlike Detroit, has found a product that the Japanese can't improve upon.'[27] Disney's Katzenberg warned in his 1991 memo that Sony and Matsushita were getting into a business 'out of their cultural context' in acquiring Hollywood studios, explaining:

Filmmaking in its essence is about the conveyance of emotion. Not coincidentally, filmmakers by their nature are an emotional group— from the actors on the screen to the dealmakers behind the scenes. It is said to be a crazy business and most of its practitioners admittedly are, by normal standards, a bit eccentric.

24 'The Teachings of Chairman Jeff', *Variety* (21 Jan. 1991), 5.

25 Huey, 'America's Hottest Export', 51.

26 George Gilder, *Life after Television: The Coming Transformation of Media and American Life* (Knoxville, Tenn.: Whittle, 1990).

27 Huey, 'America's Hottest Export', 51.

The Japanese, on the other hand, culturally err on the side of withholding emotion. In saying this, I am not simply offering an American perspective. The Japanese are the first to tell you this about themselves.[28]

Meanwhile, the economic and institutional boundaries between the US motion-picture and television industries, long effaced by converging financial, ownership, and textual structures and practices, have become further blurred in the new international media landscape. Despite the financial success of 'character-driven' sleeper hits in 1990, for example, the US domestic theatrical box office continued to represent a diminishing share of total studio revenues. As *Variety* pointed out, the US domestic box office represented 80 per cent of a typical Hollywood film's total global revenues in the early 1980s; ten years later, it represented only about 30 per cent. Notwithstanding disingenuous proclamations by studio heads of the new centrality of character and story, studio management remains focused on what are seen as the star-, action-, and special effects-driven demands of home video and the foreign box office; as one studio executive told *Variety* in 1991: 'It's almost like theatrical distribution is your loss leader.'[29]

Some of the implications of such shifts in the figuration of 'nation' and 'other' in the contemporary US media industry are worth noting. As David Morley and Kevin Robins argue, the new media technologies are deeply transgressive of traditional discursive boundaries of the national and the audience, disaggregating 'fixed national audiences and communities and creating new ones across national boundaries'.[30] In *Fortune*'s 'one-world pop-tech civilization', media firms have constructed a new global media culture as transnational youth market. Bill Roedy, the CEO of MTV Europe, which captured 20 million viewers in its first three years with the support of major advertisers such as Coke, Levi's, Nike, and the Hollywood studios, explained: 'An 18-year-old in Denmark has more in common with an 18-year-old in France than either has with elders in their own country.' Roedy continued: 'The programming has been so regulated over here, we're like an oasis in the desert. And our idea is so simple: English language music programming works regardless of the culture or the language. It's an international art form.'[31] Similarly, Coca-Cola CEO Roberto Goizueta explained his company's international marketing strategy:

> Our message has been consistent since 1923, and it's been a very emotional one: family, friends, good times. What they're buying is the good things in life. Americans may say, well, that's the American way, but it's not really. There's a thirst out there everywhere to have a good time. It's *everybody's* way.[32]

The recent growth of the international TV programme market, besides creating new opportunities for US-based (if no longer US-owned)

28 'The Teachings of Chairman Jeff', 5.

29 Ibid.

30 David Morley and Kevin Robins, 'Spaces of Identity', *Screen*, 30/4 (1989), 11–12.

31 Huey, 'America's Hottest Export', 52.

32 Ibid. 58. Emphasis added.

programme producers, has also had significant implications for European broadcasters and audiences. The 1980s and early 1990s brought not only new financial and competitive pressures on European public service broadcasters, but also a new crisis of political legitimacy for established broadcast institutions. As Ien Ang has argued, European public service broadcasting's traditional forms of institutional knowledge about television audiences, based on the philosophical certainties of paternalism and an imputed public sphere, have been gradually replaced by the bureaucratic self-validating values of professionalism and balance, and, as a result, public service broadcasters have increasingly relied upon the market-oriented empiricist constructions of the TV audience common to commercial broadcasting. In the face of newly contested audience representations for European public service broadcasters, the political challenge for defenders of public service broadcasting became, as Nicholas Garnham wrote in 1983, that of addressing

> a crisis in imagination—an inability to conceive of an alternative to broadcasting controlled by profit-seeking private capital other than as centralized, bureaucratic, inefficient, arrogantly insensitive to the people's needs, politically subservient to the holders of state power.[33]

At the same time, the US television industry in the 1980s began a wrenching discursive reconstruction of its audience accompanied by industry hostility to what it viewed as the new fickle and irresponsible multi-channel viewer.[34] As several contemporary media critics have noted, the commodification of commercial television's audience brought with it the structural imperative for continuous audience surveillance and quantification. Far from achieving the panopticon ideal of audience surveillance and control, the improved technologies of spectator visibility have instead only underscored the hopelessly vague and slippery nature of audience activity. While contemporary commentators such as John Fiske, Ian Connell, and Lidia Curti have opted, with varying degrees of explicitness and commitment, to endorse commercial television as promising fuller satisfaction of popular pleasures than public service broadcasting, Ien Ang sees a wider complicity between the two systems in their institutional constructions of the TV audience.[35]

Despite the increasingly globally integrated marketing campaigns of the multinational consumer goods industry and the transnational media networks they support, issues of the nation have gained new urgency in the debates over television policy around the globe since the early 1990s. As David Morley and Kevin Robins point out, notions of national identity—themselves constructed in part by specific cultural technologies—are always ideologically defined against an other: the USA and Japan, Europe and the USA.[36] As multinational media firms reach audiences in an ever more

---

33 Garnham, 'Public Service Versus the Market', 21.

34 For a discussion of the new viewing practices, see Carrie Heeter and Bradley S. Greenberg, *Cableviewing* (Norwood, NJ: Ablex, 1988).

35 John Fiske, 'TV: Re-situating the Popular in the People', *Continvim* 1/2 (1987), n.p.; Connell, 'Commercial Broadcasting and the British Left'; Connell and Curti, 'Popular Broadcasting in Italy and Britain'.

36 Morley and Robins, 'Spaces of Identity', 10.

intimate and global fashion, such issues would only grow more pressing, even in the United States, where questions of cultural production and national identity had long seemed so nearly isomorphic as to be axiomatic. The secure bravado of an earlier, and extinct, US industrial era reflected in 'Trenton Makes, The World Takes', which served so long as the implicit paradigm for the US communication industry in relation to its domestic and international audiences, seemed by the early 1990s to enter into increasing crisis, notwithstanding rosy visions by some of a resuscitated consumerist Pax Americana in a putative one-world pop-tech civilization.

5

'Mission Number One is to Kill TV': Remaking the Domestic Television Apparatus in the 1990s

Introduction

THE PROLIFERATION OF DIGITAL imaging technologies in the early 1990s, with virtual reality (VR) as their most technically elaborate and high-profile application, inspired new scholarly attention to the relations between the histories of communication technologies and those of cultural forms. Part of the challenge in addressing the range of technologies and discourses constituting the field of virtual reality in American culture is an almost wilful slipperiness of the object. This is a problem less in fixing a denotative meaning to 'virtual reality' (a computer-generated environment with which users interact via a range of human senses) than in the seamless way in which popular and trade press discussions of virtual reality frequently slipped from technical accounts of the rudimentary state of the art into hypothetical phenomenological descriptions of yet-unrealized electronic environments. As film scholar Vivian Sobchack noted, even the most ardent VR boosters admitted that it is more compelling to talk about what VR might someday become than to describe the current impoverished devices; the most vivid description of the VR experience, she and others have argued, remains the fictional prose of cyberpunk novelist William Gibson.[1] However, rather than viewing this semantic slippage as a problem to be policed, it may be more useful to consider how these diverse new digital technologies were made sense of in united opposition to the ubiquitous and prosaic domestic television set.

Virtual reality was represented in the early 1990s as merely the most compelling imaginative extension of an entire complex of technologies of electronic imaging. Critic Andy Darley, comparing the emergence of VR with that of cinema a century earlier, points out that 'computer imaging' is itself a complex term, its processes deployed in diverse contexts in design, advertising, cinema, television, and video, as well as in the military.[2] As Darley argues, digital imaging developed largely through a process of infiltrating existing signifying practices which are already embedded in a diverse set of highly developed cultural forms. Such media hybrids have collapsed the boundaries between electronic and photographic, static and

1 Vivian Sobchack, 'New Age Mutant Ninja Hackers', *Artforum* (Apr. 1991), 25.

2 Andy Darley, 'Big Screen, Little Screen: The Archeology of Technology', *Ten.8.* 2/2 (Autumn 1991), 82.

moving, real and unreal. These transgressions have served to destabilize conventional photographic, cinematic, and televisual ontologies and professional codes, provoking, for example, new ethical debates over the use of digitally created and manipulated images in 'truth-telling' indexically coded image contexts such as journalism or the legal system.[3] The institutional complexities of the uneven adoption of the various technologies of electronic imaging suggest the value of a widely conceived approach to their forebears and ideological determinants.

Film theorist Peter Wollen distinguishes the essentially nineteenth-century communication technology Walter Benjamin addressed in his essay 'The Work of Art in the Age of Mechanical Reproduction' from our own technological and cultural era which, Wollen argues, can best be understood as 'not so much [that] of "mechanical reproduction" as "electronic intertextuality" '.[4] The shift has enormous implications for the rehearsal of notions of gender in contemporary American culture. Bill Nichols contrasts the regimes of power and knowledge associated with mechanical reproduction with those characteristic of an era of computer imaging, arguing that 'a (predominantly masculine) fascination with *control* of simulated interactions replaces a (predominantly masculine) fascination with the to-be-looked-at-ness of a projected image'.[5] Pursuing these extensions of Benjamin's speculations into new 'modes of human sense perception', this chapter will explore the social inscription of gender in early 1990s discussions of enhanced television systems, computer imaging, and virtual reality. Its aim is to consider VR, along with its associated technologies, imaginative landscapes, and social genealogies, in the twin contexts of what Claudia Springer has identified as a contemporary crisis in masculinity and a widespread social anxiety about technology.[6] As the publicity poster for the 1992 feature film *Lawnmower Man*, whose VR-enhanced hero condensed the themes of masculinity, sexual violence, and technophilia, put it: 'God Made Him Simple. Science Made Him a God.'

| 'Already the soggy buzzword of the '90s' | Underscoring the centrality of Nichols's identification of 'a (predominantly masculine) fascination with *control* of simulated interactions' in our era, the diverse set of contemporary media technologies—some actual, some envisioned for the future—in applications ranging from high-definition and interactive television to amusement park attractions and virtual reality, are united by little more than their shared debt to various notions of 'interactivity', a term identified by one sceptical critic in 1990 as 'already the soggy buzzword of the '90s'.[7] What is striking across the diverse discourses traversing the range of new electronic imaging technologies which emerged |

---

3 On the ethical issues raised by computer imaging in electronic journalism, see Daniel Sheriden, 'The Trouble with Harry', *Columbia Journalism Review* (Jan.–Feb. 1990), 4, 6.

4 Peter Wollen, 'Cinema/Americanism/The Robot', *New Formations*, 8 (Summer 1989), 28–9.

5 Bill Nichols, 'The Work of Art in the Age of Cybernetic Systems', *Screen* (Winter 1988), 31–2.

6 Claudia Springer, 'The Pleasures of the Interface', *Screen*, 32/3 (Autumn 1991), 318.

7 Erik Davis, 'TV's Fascinating, Frightening Future', *Utne Reader*, 48 (July–Aug. 1990), 86–7; also see the cover story by Bill Powell, 'Interactive: The Future is Here', *Newsweek* (31 May 1993), 34–7.

in the 1990s is the common claim that they promise to remake or destroy conventional television, to transform the scorned and degraded domestic TV set into a good cultural object, to reinvest the pacifying, even feminizing (in)activity of consuming television with fantasies of (masculine) agency and power, even to reinvigorate American national will and global industrial potency in the process.

As historians Lynn Spigel and Cecelia Tichi have argued, television viewing in the USA has persistently been figured as a pacifying, emasculating, and feminizing activity.[8] As we have seen in previous chapters, the industrial architects of post-war US television drew upon the audience assumptions and programme formats of commercial radio and quickly devised programme formats differentiated by day part and imputed gendered audience, tailoring low-visual-involvement, highly segmented programme styles to hours when the housewife was the presumed primary audience.[9] Spigel quotes Philip Wylie's 1942 best-seller, *A Generation of Vipers*, which attacked the supposed alliance of female radio listeners ('moms') and Madison Avenue advertising executives for creating radio as 'mom's final tool'.[10] In the twentieth printing of Wylie's book in 1955, the author added a footnote on the continuity between radio and television, arguing that 'in place of, "radio," of course, the alert reader will now automatically substitute "TV" '. Wylie warned that '[Mom] will not rest until every electronic moment has been bought to sell suds and every program censored to the last decibel and syllable according to her self-adulation—along with that . . . of her de-sexed, de-souled, de-celebrated mate.'[11]

Such mid-twentieth-century attacks on television viewing as emasculating echo long-running discursive constructions of popular culture as feminine, often in opposition to a valorized and masculinized traditional high culture.[12] Central to such constructions is a persistent gender-inflected opposition between passivity and activity; Patrice Petro quotes the French theorist Hélène Cixous: 'Every theory of society, the whole conglomeration of symbolic systems . . . is all ordered around hierarchical oppositions that can only be sustained by means of a difference posed by cultural discourses as "natural", the difference between activity and passivity.'[13]

---

8 See Lynn Spigel, *Make Room for TV: Television and the Family Ideal in Postwar America* (Chicago: University of Chicago Press, 1992), ch. 2; Cecelia Tichi, *Electronic Hearth: Creating an American Television Culture* (New York: Oxford University Press, 1991), especially chs. 1 and 3.

9 For recent analyses of the operation of such gendered programme assumptions, see Tania Modleski, 'The Rhythms of Reception: Daytime Television and Women's Work', in E. Ann Kaplan (ed.), *Regarding Television: Critical Approaches: An Anthology* (Frederick, Md.: University Publications of America/ American Film Institute, 1983), 67–75; Rick Altman, 'Television/Sound', in Tania Modleski (ed.), *Studies in Entertainment* (Indianapolis: Indiana University Press, 1986), 39–54.

10 Philip Wylie, *A Generation of Vipers* (New York: Holt, Rinehart and Winston, 1955), 214–15, quoted in Spigel, *Make Room for TV*, 62.

11 Wylie, *A Generation of Vipers*, 213–14.

12 Andreas Huyssen, *After the Great Divide: Modernism, Mass Culture, Postmodernism* (Bloomington: Indiana University Press, 1986), ch. 3; Tania Modleski, 'Femininity as Mas[s]querade: A Feminist Approach to Popular Culture', in Colin MacCabe (ed.), *High Theory/Low Culture: Analysing Popular Television and Film* (Manchester: Manchester University Press, 1986), 37–52; Patrice Petro, 'Mass Culture and the Feminine: The "Place" of Television in Film Studies', *Cinema Journal*, 25/3 (Spring 1986), 5–21.

13 Hélène Cixous, 'Castration or Decapitation', *Signs*, 7/1 (Autumn 1981), 44, quoted in Petro, 'Mass Culture and the Feminine', 6.

Television's
second chance

This gendered cultural positioning of domestic television as object and activity has served as a remarkably consistent foil for contemporary enthusiasts of the range of advanced electronic vision systems, including virtual reality, what a chorus of diverse commentators have called 'television's second chance'. *Newsweek* magazine's April 1992 *Wayne's World* cover story on new television technologies quoted Apple Computer CEO John Sculley: 'Television's going to get a second chance, and there's a chance to do it right this time.'[14] The 31-year-old virtual reality pioneer Jaron Lanier told *US News and World Report*: 'The best thing about VR is that it will kill TV.'[15] Lanier told a group of VR fans at a Cyberthon convention in San Francisco in 1991: 'We live in this very weird time in history where we're passive recipients of a very immature, noninteractive broadcast medium. Mission number one is to kill TV.'[16]

Furthermore, by the mid-1990s, television's technological 'second chance' was often represented in popular discourses as a reprieve for the United States in its bid for international supremacy in the high-tech industry. Such reassuring national metanarratives resonated in the USA at a time when even the wide-eyed technophilic 1992 *Newsweek* article confessed:

> You remember the future, right? When we were kids, comic books and 'Star Trek' readied us for some kind of gleaming techno-paradise. So far, the future hasn't delivered. Technology hasn't yet solved any of the really Big Problems—you know, poverty, war and injustice. High-tech industries we saw as our great hope have been mastered by determined foreign rivals. We can't even control the technology in our own homes, which is why our VCRs are still blinking 12:00 . . . 12:00 . . . 12:00 . . .[17]

But now, the *Newsweek* cover article insisted, the convergence of computers, telecommunications, and consumer electronics promises 'an explosion of supergadgets and services that could change all our lives. As toy-loving cover boys Wayne and Garth might say, really *excellent* tech.'[18] In a similarly optimistic vein, the opening paragraph of the May 1993 *Newsweek* cover story on interactive technologies invoked the heroic American West, another era of 'virgin territory and a future that was literally there for the taking'.[19] An advertisement promoting an issue of *Forbes* business magazine with a cover story on 'Smart TV' put it starkly: 'Silicon Valley, this is your wake-up call.'[20]

---

14 John Schwartz, 'The Next Revolution', *Newsweek* (6 Apr. 1992), 45.

15 'Are New Realities More or Less Real?', *US News and World Report* (28 Jan. 1991), 59.

16 Peggy Orenstein, 'Get a Cyberlife', *Mother Jones* (May–June 1991), 63. Typically contrarian, cyberpunk novelist William Gibson told the Cyberthon crowd when asked if VR would be an electronic utopia: 'I think it could be lethal, like free-basing American TV. . . . I don't think that anyone that read my book seems to have understood it. It was supposed to be ironic. The book was really a metaphor about how I felt about the media. I didn't expect anyone to actually go out and build one of those things.' 'Get a Cyberlife', 64.

17 Schwartz, 'The Next Revolution', 42.

18 Ibid.

19 'Interactive: The Future is Here', 35.

20 Advertisement appearing in *New Yorker* (6 Apr. 1992), 41.

The *Forbes* article, by conservative economist and media pundit George Gilder, described the loss of the US consumer electronics market to Japanese manufacturers as a telling symbol of industrial America in decline. Nevertheless, Gilder offered US readers some hope for America's eventual triumph:

> But a second chance looms. Over the next few years there will be sweeping technological changes that will create a window of opportunity for American companies and a window of vulnerability for the Japanese. . . . A worldwide electronics market worth hundreds of billions of dollars will be at stake. It will dwarf the present home entertainment market, which the Japanese control.[21]

Gilder promised readers in his 1990 book *Life after Television* that 'the death of television . . . would be the salvation of American competitiveness'.[22]

Making people feel powerful

Much of the 1990s discussion addressing the entire spectrum of electronic high tech was inflected with the rhetorical project of remasculinizing the television apparatus through fantasies of power and control, a fantasy of technological terror and mastery for a masculinity under siege. Jaron Lanier told an interviewer in 1990: 'The whole point of Virtual Reality is to make people feel powerful. . . . When you're a kid, you get the shocking realization that you're not all-powerful. You learn that you can't bend the world to your own wishes, and adulthood sets in. We never recover from that.' VR, according to Lanier, 'gives adults technological permission to return to childhood'.[23] Claudia Springer has examined the gender politics of the merging of body and machine in films like *Robocop*, *Terminator*, and *Eve of Destruction*, linking it both to Western culture's long-expressed ambivalent desire and aversion toward the human body and to what she sees as a specifically contemporary crisis in masculinity and its representation.[24] Much of the discourse around VR in the 1990s shared these thematic and formal features with contemporary science fiction in films, novels, and comics.

A major strand of popular interest in VR in the mid-1990s was utopian; Lanier and other VR visionaries celebrated VR not only as the technological leveller of prejudices of gender, age, and physical appearance, but as the mechanism for extinguishing language, sexual difference, and even species differentiation. 'Virtual Reality is the ultimate lack of race or class distinctions or any other form of pretense, since all form is variable,' Lanier told the San Francisco Cyberthon audience.[25] Lanier told one journalist he imagined 'a world of "postsymbolic communication," a world without words', evoking perhaps less the post-symbolic than the Lacanian pre-symbolic in a denial of sexual difference.[26] Elsewhere Lanier spoke of using VR as an

---

21 George Gilder, 'Smart TV', *Forbes* (14 Oct. 1991), 188.

22 Ibid. 75.

23 A. J. S. Rayl, 'Making Fun', *Omni* (Nov. 1990), 47–8.

24 Springer, 'The Pleasures of the Interface', 303–18.

25 Orenstein, 'Get a Cyberlife', 63.

26 Sallie Tisdale, 'It's Been Real', *Esquire* (Apr. 1991), 147.

instrument of self-transformation, allowing its user to 'trade eyes' with another person, even to swap nervous and motor systems with another species such as a lobster:

> The interesting thing about being a lobster is that you have extra limbs. We found that by using bits of movement in the elbow and knee and factoring them together through a complex computer function, people easily learned to control those extra limbs. When we challenge our physical self-image, the nervous system responds very quickly.[27]

As Vivian Sobchack argued in a 1991 *Artforum* article, 'New Age Mutant Ninja Hackers', the VR motto 'reality isn't enough anymore' might be psychoanalytically recast as 'reality is too much right now', and she called some of the prevailing fascination with virtual reality 'a potentially danger-ous and disturbingly miscalculated attempt to escape the material space and specific politics (dare I say the "real" reality?) of the body's mortality and the planet's fragility'.[28] Citing cyberpunk fanzine *Mondo 2000*'s description of cyberspace as 'like having your everything amputated', Sobchack sees in the anxious rejection of the human body a reaction to contemporary fears of mortality in the face of AIDS, nuclear annihilation, and ecological suicide.[29] Journalist's Sallic Tisdale's account of the 1991 San Francisco Cyberthon concludes with the rueful observation about the computer-generated envir-onments she sampled: 'There is something terribly familiar about the flying pillars and smashed television sets, something smacking of comic books and Saturday-morning cartoons. . . . Here is a technology with massive power, stuck in the tiny paradigm of the white American male.'[30]

Many commentators noted the connections between the cyberpunk and hacker communities, sources of much of the popular press interest in VR, and a wider New Age-inflected interest in psychotropic 'smart' drugs, recalling the era of 1960s psychedelia. Ex-Grateful Dead lyricist John Barlow, writing in *Mondo 2000*, argued: 'The closest analogue to virtual reality that I know is the psychedelic experience, and, in fact, cyberspace is already crawling with delighted acid heads.'[31] The connection was underscored by widespread 1990s popular press reports of the efforts of LSD-pioneer-turned-VR enthu-siast Timothy Leary on behalf of VR, activities 'distress[ing to] . . . serious pioneers in the new technology', according to *Fortune* magazine.[32] Leary told one interviewer:

> Virtual reality means we won't have to lug our bodies around anymore! The only function of the human body of the future will be for acts of grace! Barriers of class and geography will fall! Kids in the inner city will be moving their brain anywhere they like! . . . The only reason to use cars

27 Bennett Davis, 'Grand Illusions', *Discover* (June 1990), 41.

28 Sobchack, 'New Age Mutant Ninja Hackers', 24–5.

29 Ibid. 25; for a collection of *Mondo 2000* writing on VR, see Rudy Rucker, R. U. Sirius, and Queen Mu, *Mondo 2000: A User's Guide to the New Edge* (New York: Harper Collins, 1992), 262–75.

30 Tisdale, 'It's Been Real', 147.

31 John Barlow, quoted in Rucker et al., *Mondo 2000*, 262.

32 Leary's role was described 'as a virtual reality barker' in Judith Stone, 'Turn on, Tune in, Boot up', *Discover* (June 1991), 35; Gene Bylinsky, 'The Marvels of "Virtual Reality" ', *Fortune* (3 June 1991), 142.

and planes will be for sports and pleasure. You're saying no, no, no. But what if I had said to you a hundred years ago, 'In the future we'll only use horses for sports and to show off our elegance?'[33]

'Our aim is to get the system as inexpensive as a pair of Nikes,' Leary has said; 'If kids in the inner city can have Nikes, we'll see to it they have this technology!'[34]

War and the living room

While Leary's born-again VR proselytizing may provide a nostalgic buzz of 1960s mind expansion and social activism, VR's discursive link with 1960s psychedelics also evokes some less savoury associations. While the history of psychedelic drugs reveals early ties to US military and covert intelligence research, the links between Pentagon spending and the computer imaging technologies behind VR is one of near-paternity.[35] Like some time-warped 1960s acid pioneer, contemporary VR partisans sometimes speak with a near-religious fervour, such as Thomas Furness, who, after spending twenty years working for the US Air Force on artificial environments, told an interviewer in 1991: 'With the technology of virtual reality we can change the world. . . . I'm like an evangelist. . . . It requires a kind of religious fervor at this point to get the word out.'[36] Furness's work with the Air Force included a 1981 F-16 flight simulator, including a $5-million-dollar helmet, along with eight computers to run it.[37] Each technological strand of advanced television and computer imaging—flat-panel displays, computer hardware and software, fibre optics—was similarly the product of substantial and sustained US military research and development expenditures.[38]

The association of the US military and the technologies of VR was also evoked, in a quite distinct discursive context, by the VR-inspired TV advertising campaign for the US Marine Corps in the early 1990s (Fig. 5.1). The tropes associated with the then-ubiquitous promotional discourse of virtual reality—the cybernetic mutation of the body, fantasies of unrestrained male power, and the masculinist subculture of computer games—were remarkably condensed in the Marine Corps's recruitment campaign, presumably aimed at Timothy Leary's young Nike purchasers. Shot in the same desert location as the original *Star Trek* television series with a $2 million budget and a 100-person crew, the commercial presents a dizzying pastiche of pop culture and techno-subculture imagery of the contemporary American adolescent male. The advertisement, produced before, but aired after, the

33 Stone, 'Turn on, Tune in, Boot up', 33; Andrew Ross places Leary's interest in VR in a typology of radical critiques of technology in 'The New Smartness', in Gretchen Bender and Timothy Druckrey (eds.), *Culture on the Brink: Ideologies of Technology* (Seattle: Bay Press, 1994), 334.

34 Stone, 'Turn on, Tune in, Boot up', 33.

35 See Martin A. Lee and Bruce Shlain, *Acid Dreams: The CIA, LSD, and the Sixties Rebellion* (New York: Grove Press, 1985), especially ch. 1.

36 Davis, 'Grand Illusions', 36.

37 Ibid. 41.

38 Herbert I. Schiller, 'Media, Technology and the Market: The Interacting Dynamic', in Bender and Druckrey (eds.), *Culture on the Brink*, 34–5.

US–Iraq War of 1991, underscored the Marine Corps's efforts to address hard-to-reach teenage males; the effort included related theatrical advertisements screened in US cinemas and print ads in *Dirt*, a teenage-male magazine launched in 1991, described by its 23-year-old editor as devoted to 'sports, music, art, chicks, cars, celebrities, style, motorcycles, females, global issues, current events, women, junk food, video games and stone cold babes'.[39] Directed at a similar demographic target as *Dirt*, the US Marine Corps TV advertisements provoked a sceptical reaction from some in the advertising trade press; columnist Barbara Lippert wrote in *Adweek:*

> This commercial is in a Twilight Zone of its own. . . . A bizarre mixture of teenage male fantasies, it suggests Darth Vader, heavy metal laser shows, Nintendo, Dungeons and Dragons, all stirred up by the possibility of mind-altering drugs. There's also some medieval weekend-festival garb thrown in, oddly enough. Parents have sued rock groups for less; Tipper Gore would not be amused.[40]

Despite the producer's intention to create a news-free, 'symbolic, metaphoric approach', Lippert, for one, was struck by the similarity of the commercial's imagery to that of the US–Iraq War, the news coverage of which dominated US airtime around the commercial's launch: 'Unlike those military news conferences that showed carefully edited videotapes of smart bombings (no shots of eviscerated Iraqis allowed), this brings the idea of "collateral damage" to new techno-surreal heights,' she wrote.[41]

At the same time, though far from the military-funded technological cutting edge of VR, the more prosaic world of consumer electronics advertising was reinvesting the ubiquitous domestic TV set with similar masculine scenarios of interaction and mastery. In part, this marketing strategy reflects precisely the dearth of genuine technological innovation in the largely stagnant consumer electronics industry of the early 1990s. *The Economist* magazine's 1992 survey of the international consumer electronics market identified several major decade-long product innovation cycles in home electronics since 1920 (including the gramophone in the 1920s, radio in the 1930s, black and white TV in the 1950s, colour TV in the 1960s, audio equipment in the 1970s, and the VCR in the 1980s), and wondered: 'What next? Before the VR machine can become the breadwinner for the industry (probably in the early 2000s), history suggests there will be a blockbuster product in between.' The promise of product innovation, according to the magazine, has led to a frantic search by hardware manufacturers for the 'next big thing', including pocket camcorders, DAT, satellite TV, and HDTV. In spite of these industry efforts, *The Economist* predicted tough times for the consumer electronics industry in the 1990s; in a weak global economy and without major new products on the near horizon, manufacturers faced jaded and saturated consumers, it argued.[42]

---

39 Cyndee Miller, 'Will *Dirt* fly? Only Time Will Tell', *Marketing News* (14 Oct. 1991), 2.

40 Barbara Lippert, 'The Marines' Chessboard in the Sand', *Adweek* (25 Mar. 1991), n.p.

41 Ibid.; the production information comes from a telephone conversation with a staff member of the commercial's production company, GMS, 4 Dec. 1991.

42 Nicholas Valery, 'Consumer Electronics: Purveyors of Dreams', *The Economist* (13 Apr. 1991), 50.

Fig. 5.1 Using VR-imagery to market military service to adolescent males: US Marine Corps recruitment television advertisement, 1991

Fig. 5.2 Rehabilitating the domestic TV receiver; artist and model and TV set: television advertisement for Sony XBR television, 1992

Fig. 5.3 Terrors of domestic technology and the embattled armchair: television advertisement for Toshiba Home Theatre, 1992

Reflecting the subdued state of the consumer electronics industry in the post-VCR age, in a 1984 interview entitled 'Design vs. Technology', Michael Schulhof, head of Sony-USA, argued that cutting-edge consumer electronics technology 'is an indispensable entry fee for the competitive marketplace. But since all players pay it, technology doesn't separate winners from also-rans. That is the function of design.' Citing the successful innovations of the Sony Walkman and Watchman, which originated from designers, not engineers, and used largely off-the-shelf technologies, Schulhof called consumer electronics a 'technologically mature' industry, arguing that technological leadership was now measured in days or months, not years, and in any event does not guarantee market strength: 'It is a fleeting thing at best, and not something on which to build a company's design or market strategy,' Schulhof said of such technological leadership.[43] Even in the widely disparate marketing contexts of consumer electronics and military recruitment, however, the figuration of masculinity and technology in 1990s television advertisements spoke to similar concerns, whether offering scenarios of a new science fiction battlefield or the familiar domestic TV set.

Partly as the result of the paucity of genuinely new consumer electronics products for the home, many TV commercials from electronics manufacturers in the 1990s strove to reinvest existing prosaic products like remote-control televisions with new scenarios of masculine power, as in Sony's 1992 'Portrait' commercial for their XBR television set (Fig. 5.2). The commercial's classical music, its affluent but bohemian *mise en scène*, but especially the condensation of quotidian manipulation of a TV's remote control with the active, creative, and masculinist high-art scenario of male artist and female model (the TV's remote control becomes both the artist's brush and conductor's baton synchronized with the music) all seek to reassure the male consumer that he remains uncontaminated by the traditional emasculating associations of TV viewing.

In a related marketing strategy in the first half of the 1990s, the solitary male viewer depicted in a commercial for the Pioneer Home Theatre is first sketchily located in the domestic iconography of a cosy TV armchair only to be magically transported out of the domestic space through his interaction with the 'new' home-theatre technology (Fig. 5.3). Enacting a fanciful literalization of the VR experience, the commercial dramatizes the recurrent ambivalence of terror and comfort provoked by new digital-media technologies and experiences, doubly ironic since here the couch-potato-turned-combatant is a near-casualty of the exterminating machines of the dystopic *Terminator 2* he has conjured into his living room. The terrors of too-complete interaction with the cinematic vision of the anything-but-benign technological future are briefly evoked, then dispelled by the protagonist's comforting return to the domestic space, albeit with lingering collateral damage to his TV armchair, icon of television's stubborn and problematic domesticity.

43 Michael Schulhof, 'Design vs. Technology', *Design News* (3 Dec. 1984), 11; for a discussion of the history of the Sony Walkman, see Paul du Guy, Stuart Hall, Linda James, Hugh Mackay, and Keith Negus, *Doing Cultural Studies: The Story of the Sony Walkman* (London: Open University/Sage Publications, 1997).

Conclusion   These examples of the early 1990s efforts of consumer electronics manufacturers to associate the domestic TV set with new scenarios of multi-sensory
interaction and masculine control served to revive the 1950s advertising
trope promoting television as a 'home theatre'. Historian Lynn Spigel argued
in 1992 that 'virtual reality is not only being extolled as an escape from the
mundane social world, it is also being implemented as an improved form of
"new age" domesticity where people can literally enter another world while
remaining in the safety of their private homes'. According to Spigel, the
promotional discourses surrounding technologically enhanced television
once again offer 'consumers an electronic cornucopia that promises to solve
social problems and replace the doldrums of everyday life with thrilling,
all-encompassing entertainment spectacles'.[44]

More than a decade after the explosion of popular speculation about the
future of virtual reality, it remains unclear in what form VR systems will meet
their eventual spectator-participant in the living room, dildonics-chamber,
workplace, amusement park, public auditorium, or battlefield. Despite the
conspicuous failure of the confident predictions from the early 1990s concerning virtual reality as an economic force and cultural form, it is important to consider the historical agency of the ephemeral, fantastic, and utopian
discursive responses to new communication technologies alongside their
less fanciful reception contexts. In any event, by the end of the 1990s, both
popular and policy debates had moved from the imaginative visions of
virtual reality to the very real changes brought about by the introduction
of digital technologies into the prosaic world of the domestic TV receiver.
In both cases, however, the predicted consequences of the technological
innovation in digital moving-image technologies, both fearful and euphoric,
were widely debated in the trade and popular press, provoking a striking
range of utopian and dystopian media worlds in both the USA and the UK.

44 Spigel, *Make Room for TV*, 186, 182.

6

Weather Porn and the Battle for Eyeballs: The Transition to Digital Broadcasting in the USA and UK

Introduction

AS POPULAR PRESS interest in the fanciful imaginative landscapes of virtual reality faded, the late 1990s marked the culmination of a long technological, policy-making, and marketing campaign waged by a diverse set of private interests to bring digital television into American and British homes. An examination of digital television's distinct fortunes in the United States and Great Britain offers revealing insights into some of the most persistent and difficult issues in media historiography, including the roles of national culture, market structures, and ideological valence in setting the course of technological innovation. The transition from analogue to digital standards for electronically stored and transmitted moving images marked a profoundly unsettling moment for the established policy rationales and commercial structures of broadcasting in both the USA and the UK. Digital television seemed to threaten not only to alter fundamentally traditional relationships among programme producers, station owners, broadcast networks, and satellite and cable operators, but also to attract powerful new economic actors to the business of providing programming and services to the domestic television audience. The tangle of rivalries and alliances between sectors of the television industry and multinational firms in consumer electronics, telecommunications, retailing, financial services, and computer hardware and software testifies to the contentious and uncertain nature of technological innovation in contemporary electronic media. In addition, the proliferation of channels and delivery systems associated with digital television promised to alter existing programming forms, as well as international programme flows and institutional alliances across an increasingly globalized media landscape. Finally, in the promise of enhanced visual quality, multiple programme channels, and the capacity for complex interactive exchange, digital television inspired many observers to proclaim the overturning of the prevailing and long-established models of television viewing with quite different, if still uncertain, scenarios. This chapter traces some of the concrete struggles within and outside the television industry which accompanied the introduction of digital television in the USA and UK at the end of the 1990s in order to trace the continuing power of ideas about home, gender, and nation in shaping both commercial rhetoric and policy outcomes.

The commercial and regulatory contexts for digital television

Preliminary to such a project is recognition that the term 'digital television' constitutes an over-determined and sometimes strategically ambiguous signifier, encompassing the distinct promises of enhanced picture quality (various formats of so-called 'high-definition television'), greater viewer–programme interactivity, and a significant expansion of programme channels delivered to the home. These distinct technological components of the term 'digital television' correspond to the competing commercial interests of different sectors of the television industry, leading to occasional public and policy disputes over the preferred applications of digital television. For the consumer electronics industry in the USA, for example, digital television represented the financial potential of a vast market for high-definition TV sets, as American TV households are forced to replace or adapt every existing receiver in order to receive higher-quality pictures (and, eventually, any pictures at all, as existing analogue television channels are shut down and auctioned off in 2006, according to the present timetable of the FCC). However, for TV broadcasters, cable operators, and direct broadcast satellite operators, digital television offered instead a means to multiply the channels of standard-definition television (SDTV) they might offer by a factor of five, ten, or even more; in their view, digital television primarily represents the chance to increase so-called programme 'tonnage', or the number of standard-definition television channels available for sale to viewers and/or advertisers. Finally, for cable operators and for some major interests outside the traditional broadcasting industry, including computer software and hardware manufacturers, telephone companies, and firms in retailing, publishing, and banking, digital television offered the fulfilment of the long-promised era of interactivity, where viewers become Web surfers and electronic point-of-sale consumers in their own living rooms.

If such clear strategic differences can be identified among competing sectors of the putative post-television market, there was also a striking, if somewhat unexpected, defensive tone in much of the trade discussion of digital television at the end of the 1990s. In spite of the general economic expansion in the USA and Western Europe through much of the 1990s, many of these diverse economic interests approached the prospect of digital television with a measure of uncertainty about their own commercial fortunes. For example, commercial television networks in the UK and USA were facing long-term declines in their shares of prime-time audiences and national advertising revenues; the long-stagnant consumer electronics industry had been desperate for new breakthrough products since the VCR and audio CD of a decade or more earlier, and the UK direct broadcast satellite (DBS) market, while more significant than that of the USA, nevertheless faced the rising challenges of static viewership, subscriber churn, and the limitations of a largely sports-driven, male-targeted, and somewhat down-market

audience.[1] At the same time, the US cable industry was worried about growing competition from DBS, phone companies, and the Internet. Furthermore, the growth of the US computer industry had slowed by the end of
the decade (and what growth remained was largely in the under-$1,000 PC
market), with household penetration rates still hovering around 40 per cent;
Intel's chairman, Andrew Grove, declared that future prosperity of the chip
industry depended on markets beyond the PC.[2] John Malone, head of US
cable giant TCI, described the mood among broadcast and cable executives
in the summer of 1998: 'Look, a lot of this is fear of the computers, fear of
Microsoft, fear that . . . somehow or other Bill [Gates] got some trick up his
sleeve and he's going to own the world—which really is only a timing difference, because he is going to own the world anyway. It's a question of whether
this is his route or some other route.'[3]

High-definition
politics

Given the defensive mood across the US and UK television industries at the
end of the 1990s, the tensions between the competing definitions and interests occasionally surfaced in acrimonious public debate and recrimination.
One example can be found in the aftermath of the prolonged and successful
campaign by US broadcasters and network operators for the free award
of valuable spectrum allocations for digital television service by the Federal
Communications Commission. The spectrum awards were achieved in the
face of formidable commercial and political opposition, which argued that
the channels should instead be allocated to non-television applications
via multi-billion-dollar spectrum auctions. With the support of a consumer
electronics industry eager for high-definition television services to revive a
sluggish domestic market, the US broadcasters successfully lobbied Congress
and federal regulators with stirring talk of the appeal of higher-resolution
images for American TV viewers and of the technology's strategic importance for the American economy. The FCC's spring 1997 granting of free
duplicate UHF channels to each US broadcaster, valued at $10 billion by
some observers, followed a decade-long political and policy campaign by
broadcasters and consumer electronics firms which traded heavily upon
discourses of economic nationalism and fears of Japanese ascendancy.

1 On declining ITV audience shares and advertising revenues, see Market Tracking International, 'The
Interactive Media Handbook 1998', *M2 Presswire* (24 Feb. 1998); on UK DBS prospects, see Maggie
Brown, 'Sky's Nightmare Vision of the Future', *Evening Standard* (4 Feb. 1998), 53; Jane Robins,
'Coming Soon to a Screen near you—Weather-Porn: Digital Television is Poised to Offer Hundreds of
New Channels. But What will they Show?', *Independent* (18 Aug. 1998), 14.

2 On the mood of the US cable industry, see Peter H. Lewis, 'Internet Ties Help to Revive the Cable
Industry as Satellite Sales Lag Behind', *New York Times* (15 Dec. 1997), D6; on growth prospects in the
computer industry, see Louise Kehoe, 'Battle for the Eyeballs: The US is Setting the Standard and Pace
of the Digital Television Revolution', *Financial Times* (28 Nov. 1996), 3, and Andrew S. Grove, *Only the
Paranoid Survive: How to Exploit the Crisis Points that Challenge Every Company and Career* (New York:
Doubleday, 1996), ch. 9, 'The Internet: Signal or Noise? Threat or Promise?' For contextual material on
HDTV, see Joel Brinkley, *Defining Vision: The Battle for the Future of Television* (New York: Harcourt
Brace, 1997) and Michel Dupagne and Peter B. Seel, *High-Definition Television: A Global Perspective*
(Ames: Iowa State University Press, 1998).

3 'TCI's Malone Discusses HDTV and Must-Carry at NCTA Convention', *Multichannel News* (11 May
1998), n.p.

Leading the chorus was conservative pundit George Gilder, who in 1989 saw in Japanese-developed analogue HDTV 'a kind of Pearl Harbor in the offing' for the US consumer electronics industry.[4] In 1992 Gilder warned that 'if the US fails to keep pace technologically or goes into a siege of bashing the rich and competent, the Japanese will become the world's dominant power'.[5] Such appeals to nationalist sentiment and geopolitical self-interest were crucial in the public and political campaigns for high-definition television in the early 1990s in the United States and continue to have a powerful force within public and policy debates over digital television, despite, or perhaps because of, the continuing internationalization of media ownership and programme flows.

Within months of their 1997 high-definition allocation victory, however, network and broadcast executives appeared to back away from their commitment to high-definition television, expressing new reservations about TV-set costs, viewer interest, and station conversion expenses involved in high-definition television service. ABC network president Preston Padden and other broadcasters complained that they saw no way to make money from high-definition television and announced that they would use their new channels for multiplexing pay per view and additional SDTV programming.[6] Padden told a group of security analysts in August 1997: 'Our share of the viewing audience will continue to erode as long as we remain a single channel in an expanding multi-channel universe.' David Smith, president of Sinclair Broadcasting Group, owner of twenty-nine stations in the USA, complained around the same time: 'We have yet to see how anyone makes money as an HDTV broadcaster.'[7] The broadcasters' new public scepticism about HDTV may have reflected their recalculation of the economic appeal of the distinct technical possibilities provided by digital broadcasting, in favour of using the new high-definition channels to multiplex additional proprietary SDTV channels and abandoning high-definition television entirely. Others in the industry suspected that the broadcasters' new scepticism merely reflected their earlier bad faith in the political debates over the HDTV allocations. TCI head John Malone told a journalist in July 1998 that broadcasters were holding back on announcing non-HDTV strategies only 'because the broadcasters are building up their intestinal fortitude to decide how much risk they take on these licenses and just how greedy they can afford to look'.[8] At a congressional hearing in the summer of 1998, Republican Senator John McCain, an opponent of the earlier HDTV spectrum giveaway, responded to the pleas of broadcasters to extend the transition period for high-definition television: 'You got tens of billions in free spectrum . . . over my vociferous objections . . . and now you're complaining that we expect

4 George Gilder, 'IBM-TV?', *Forbes* (20 Feb. 1989), 72.

5 George Gilder, 'Is America on the Way Down?', *Commentary* (May 1992), 22.

6 Joel Brinkley, 'Warning to Broadcasters that Renege on Running HDTV', *New York Times* (15 Sept. 1997), D1; also see Kyle Pope and Mark Robichaux, 'Promise of Digital Television is Fading as Broadcasters Complain about Costs', *Wall Street Journal* (12 Sept. 1997), 1.

7 Joel Brinkley, 'A Gulf Develops among Broadcasters on Programming Pledge', *New York Times* (18 Aug. 1997), D1.

8 'TCI's Malone Discusses HDTV', n.p.

you to put that to good use in a timely fashion. All along I knew, you knew and the broadcasters knew there wasn't a snowball's chance in Gila Bend, Ariz., that you were going to meet the 2006 deadline.'[9] Disappointed leaders of the consumer electronics industry, as well as mobile communication companies competing for the spectrum resources given away to the putative high-definition broadcasters, viewed the on-again, off-again campaign by the broadcast industry for high-definition television as a cynical, if successful, public relations and political lobbying effort in pursuit of free spectrum allocations. Former FCC chair Reed Hundt told the *Wall Street Journal* in 1997 that 'HDTV turned out to be more a lobbying idea than a business strategy'.[10]

While broadcasters, constrained by the public relations, political, and regulatory hazards of being seen as reneging on their promises of high-definition service, have more recently offered at least half-hearted expressions of support for high-definition television, other sectors of the US television industry have been more frank about their lack of interest in the increased visual resolution offered by digital television in favour of its potential for multicasting and interactivity.[11] One powerful set of declared antagonists to high-definition television includes most US cable operators, led by TCI's John Malone, and computer hardware and software firms eager to sell set-top boxes and software for interactive standard-definition television. In the summer of 1998 Malone's TCI attempted to lure broadcasters into eschewing high definition in favour of multiplexing standard-definition television channels and interactive services by offering to share transaction fees for electronic commerce conducted via digital television. In response to the public resistance to high-definition television from cable operators, Gary Shapiro, head of the Consumer Electronics Manufacturers Association, complained during a broadcasters' convention in January 1988: 'TCI's 14 million customers may never have a chance to see HDTV. This is a huge tragedy for the American consumer.'[12] At the same time, other powerful firms at the periphery of the traditional television business were eager to organize the new economy of digital television to their advantage. The *New York Times* reported in February 1998 that 'for more than a year, the Microsoft Corporation has been cajoling the nation's television broadcasters into abandoning high-definition television and using only the computer industry's favored, lower-resolution transmission formats when digital broadcasts begin in the fall'.[13] Indeed, by the end of 1998, with the exception of HBO and other premium movie channels, it appeared that the only unequivocal American champion of high-definition television, once hailed as the saviour of US broadcasting, the domestic electronics industry, and

---

9 Alicia Mundy, 'Digital's Ball of Confusion', *Mediaweek* (13 July 1998), 6.

10 Kyle Pope, 'Executives Play Down Prior Indications They Might Scrap High-Definition TV', *Wall Street Journal* (18 Sept. 1997), B7.

11 On the broadcasters' renewed assurances on HDTV, see Joel Brinkley, 'Under Pressure, 2 Broadcasters Decide They Will Now Run HDTV', *New York Times* (18 Sept. 1997), D1; Pope, 'Executives Play Down Prior Indications They Might Scrap High-Definition TV', B7.

12 Joel Brinkley, 'TV Cable Box Software May Blur Digital Signals', *New York Times* (23 Feb. 1998), D6.

13 Ibid.

national competitiveness, was the consumer electronics firms, themselves struggling to produce a high-definition set for less than the $7,000–10,000 demanded for initial models. The confusion and delay led the *Wall Street Journal* in September 1997 to complain: 'Rarely in the history of American business has there been a new technology that promised so much—and delivered so little.'[14] A year later, the *New York Times* described the regulatory handling of HDTV's introduction in the USA as 'a slow-motion train wreck'.[15]

Digital television and national identity

The tangled alliances and uncertain fortunes of high-definition television in the United States in the late 1990s underscore the very different terms upon which digital television was introduced in the UK during the same period. These distinct fortunes highlight the concrete roles of political and regulatory institutions involved in broadcasting and the more general ways in which popular and public policy debates around broadcasting inevitably serve to both invoke and construct myths of national identity. On one level, in both the USA and UK, the transition to digital television has been overseen by a relatively *laissez-faire* regulatory philosophy and spurred by the desire of both governments to capture revenues through the eventual auction of existing analogue TV channels (indeed, the US Congress has already incorporated these anticipated revenues in current budgets). In a suggestion of the prevailing anti-regulatory mood in the USA concerning high-definition television, FCC chair William E. Kennard in 1998 expressed his belief that federal regulators should be involved in industry policy disputes only 'when arguments are distorted by the prism of self-interest', without attempting to specify when this might not be the case.[16]

Despite the anti-regulatory political moods of both nations in the 1990s, however, one can argue that the USA and UK have more generally stood as the defining other in broadcast policy-making and popular imagination since the origins of radio broadcasting in the 1920s. The imagined community of the national broadcast audience and the political rationale for national regulation remain powerful, despite the increasing globalization of programme markets and corporate ownership. The transition to digital television in the late 1990s underscored the differing competitive and policy forces acting upon the television industries in the USA and UK. In each nation, traditional broadcasters, direct satellite broadcasters, and cable operators attempted to direct the development of digital television via their control of an existing delivery system. However, the respective market power of each of the three sectors was quite different in the two nations; while cable enjoyed relatively low penetration levels in the UK (2.5 million of Britain's 23.5 million households in 1998), and terrestrial broadcasting was limited to five

---

14 Pope and Robichaux, 'Promise of Digital Television is Fading', 1.

15 Denise Caruso, 'Digital Commerce: A Slow-Motion Train Wreck in Setting Technology Standards for a Forthcoming Era of Television', *New York Times* (28 Sept. 1998), C3.

16 Joel Brinkley, 'FCC Responds to its Digital-TV Critics', *New York Times* (16 Sept. 1998), C2.

channels, Rupert Murdoch's ten-year-old direct broadcast satellite service, BSkyB, offered forty analogue channels to 3.6 million British homes.[17] Thus, unlike the case in the USA, where there are many more conventional broadcasters, higher cable penetration rates, and a smaller percentage of homes using satellite television, Murdoch's new 140-channel (including forty-eight pay-per-view channels) digital satellite service became the first delivery platform for digital television into UK households, even though the digital service requires replacement of existing receiving dishes and decoder boxes. Murdoch's chief rival was OnDigital, a consortium of ITV broadcasters, who launched a thirty-channel, non-interactive digital service in mid-November 1998.

Thus, the competitive context and delivery paths of digital television in the USA and UK were quite distinct. OnDigital offered no interactive features, and Murdoch's digital BSkyB offered only limited interactive features for some months after its October 1998 launch, unlike the promise of more technologically and economically efficient interactivity via cable service, more common in the USA. More strikingly, digital television in the UK, unlike the USA, was never promoted to policy makers and consumers as a high-definition service requiring new TV receivers, but instead largely as a way to increase the number of standard-definition channels available to existing sets. As we shall see, these differing promotional strategies depended upon quite distinct models of the place of digital television in the home.

In offering a means of greatly increasing the number of television channels, digital television in both the USA and UK promised to destabilize traditional programme-making and scheduling practices. One immediate effect was the frantic efforts by traditional programme producers to 'repurpose' existing programming and personnel to feed the new digital channels; for example, the BBC announced plans to supplement its two existing channels on digital BSkyB with BBC Choice, BBC News 24, BBC Learning, and a digital text service. Programme budgets for BBC Choice, a channel offering wall-to-wall 'repurposed' reruns of previous BBC programmes, were estimated at $16,000 to $32,000 an hour, compared to about $728,000 an hour for BBC drama on its most popular channel. The BBC Choice budget, in turn, was much higher than many other satellite channels offered by Murdoch's digital satellite service.[18] The sometimes-desperate efforts to fill expanded programme hours with inexpensive repackaged reruns of existing programming led the *Guardian* to suggest that 'soon there'll be UK Weather Gold—a channel devoted to classic weather reports'.[19]

Other critics in the UK have worried that digital television will bring a proliferation of so-called 'weather porn', US-produced weather and natural disaster documentaries which can be cheaply acquired and quickly re-edited to feature a British narrator and nominal UK content; such generic

17 Rachel Unsworth, 'Dawn of Television's Digital Age', *Mail on Sunday* (13 Sept. 1998), n.p.

18 Sally Kinnes, 'Consumer: Box of Tricks: Digital TV will be with us from Next Month', *Guardian* (21 May 1998), n.p.

19 'Isn't it Choice?', *Guardian* (7 Oct. 1998), 21.

documentaries, they fear, will crowd out traditional nationally produced documentaries addressing specific social and political topics.[20] Such 'repurposed' programmes increasingly travel in both directions across the Atlantic, and the proliferation of digital channels and inexpensive digital post-production in both the USA and UK will make the economic logic of such exchanges more compelling in the future.

Some of the changes foreseen with the global take-up of digital television at the end of the 1990s represent a radical recasting of the function of broadcasting as both product and producer of national identity. Such technologically inspired predictions of the waning power of the live national television broadcast as instrument and expression of national identity dominated journalistic responses to the launch of UK digital television in the autumn of 1998. A few days before the launch of Sky Digital, a British journalist wrote of Murdoch executives: 'Together they are in the business of persuading us that the age of television as a force of national cohesion is over: that we no longer wish to sit down all together on a Monday night to watch *EastEnders*, and that, instead, we are ready to embrace a world of hundreds of channels.'[21] Another journalist reported BBC chairman John Birt's statement that 'the end may be in sight for broadcasting as a communal experience', and a third journalist lamented: 'Television has up to now been a unifying feature, for people in any one country tend to watch the same programmes—if only because they have had little choice. Now we will have that choice. That is wonderful. But we will lose a nationally unifying force.'[22]

Meanwhile, Microsoft CEO Bill Gates and others happily predicted the replacement of such technologically antiquated artefacts of electronic media with a single global popular culture, what *Fortune* magazine in 1990 called 'a one-world pop-tech civilization', whose products happen to be overwhelmingly American in content and origin.[23] As Gates argued in his 1995 bestseller *The Road Ahead*: 'American popular culture is so potent that outside the United States some countries now attempt to ration it. They hope to guarantee the viability of domestic-content producers by permitting only a certain number of hours of foreign television to be aired each week. . . . The information highway is going to break down boundaries and may promote a world culture.'[24] Other US observers saw the global economic power of American cultural products in the new digitally linked media landscape of the second half of the 1990s as an important weapon in a wider and long-running ideological and nationalistic battle. In stark contrast to his

20 Robins, 'Coming Soon to a Screen near you', 14.

21 Jane Robins, 'Liz and Mark's Satellite Love-in', *Independent* (29 Sept. 1998), 14.

22 Ibid.; Chris Barrie, 'Pity the New Digital Underclass', *Guardian* (6 Nov. 1998), 21; Hamish McRae, 'Unleashing the Digital Divide', *Independent* (17 Nov. 1998), 5. The position of at least some in the popular press in the United States about the effects of audience fragmentation on national identity was quite different from that in the UK; in January 1999 the *New York Times* editorial board complained: 'to the lament that we are losing a sense of national community as television grapples with its recombinant future, there is only one thing to say: Get a life.' 'Whither Television?', *New York Times* (4 Jan. 1999), A18.

23 John Huey, 'America's Hottest Export: Pop Culture', *Fortune* (31 Dec. 1990), 50.

24 Bill Gates, *The Road Ahead* (New York: Penguin, 1995), 263.

early-1990s vision of America as 'a graying and gullible nation, slipping into churlish senility', by 1996 conservative pundit George Gilder was celebrating the 'technological and entrepreneurial culture of bourgeois America that is now sweeping the globe'. For Gilder, digital television represented a formidable instrument in a global ideological battle between the values of capitalism and what he termed 'the bohemian intelligencia'. According to Gilder, digital television 'threaten[s] the key remaining bastions of the power of bohemian intellectuals: the universities, Hollywood, the broadcast networks, and the government/social-work complex. Intellectuals like to describe these mostly depraved institutions as the core of the nation's identity and common purpose, but in fact they serve chiefly as the pork barrels, subsidy mills, and agitprop centers of the bohemian intelligencia.'[25]

For Gilder, the predicted decline of such politically suspect institutions of national identity reflects a kind of technological and, ultimately, theological manifest destiny of US-style capitalism. In 1994, Gilder argued that the growth of computer networks, infiltrating and finally taking over the traditional uses of television, would eventually destroy the national institutions of broadcasting, to the benefit of conservative forces in an undeclared cultural war: 'The downfall of the liberal media, the rout of the rodent kings of the networks, the . . . "three blind mice" gnawing at the pillars of civilized life in America—what, one might wonder, could be sweeter news for conservatives?' Gilder concluded that 'the information superhighway promises to revitalize capitalism and culture in the US and around the globe and to retrieve the hopes of a conservative era in politics'.[26] Expounding a determinism both technological and theological, a feverish Gilder told readers of *The Economist* in 1993: 'Television will die because it affronts human nature; the drive to self-improvement and autonomy that lifted the race out from the muck and offers the only hope for triumph in our current adversities . . . commercial television is necessarily the enemy of civilization.'[27] Ultimately, Gilder's faith in technological progress was a theological one, as he explained in 1991: 'I think secular culture is an irredeemable fiasco; estranged from God as the source of all truth and beauty, art rots to triviality and evil. Nonetheless, I believe that this culture has produced one incomparable achievement, scaled a summit as beautiful and true as any Gothic cathedral. That pinnacle is its technology.'[28] The messianic tone and sweeping scale of Gilder's late 1990s writings echo late nineteenth-century claims for the linked teleologies of technology and Christianity which accompanied the introduction of the telegraph and wireless in the USA. While Gilder's extravagant political and theological rhetoric celebrating technological change remains exceptional (and his specific technological predictions largely refuted), similar claims for digital television in service of wider national and ideological goals were common during the US dot-com investment bubble of the 1990s.

25 George Gilder, 'The National Prospect', *Commentary* (Nov. 1995), 62.

26 George Gilder, 'Breaking the Box', *National Review* (15 Aug. 1994), 37–8.

27 George Gilder, 'The Death of Telephony', *The Economist* (11 Sept. 1993), 76.

28 George Gilder, 'The Shape of Things to Come', *National Review* (8 July 1991), 27.

The Tom Cruise in Microsoft's windows

Despite the grandiloquent moral certainties of conservative techno-pundits like Gilder, the actual effects of digital television on traditional institutions and representations of national identity remained uncertain at the end of the 1990s. At the same time, the introduction of digital television provoked speculation about mutating programme forms among promoters of the new technology. In *The Road Ahead*, Bill Gates wrote enthusiastically about digital television's promise of new merchandizing opportunities for television programme makers and broadcasters in the form of enhanced product placement: 'In the future, companies may pay not only to have their products on-screen, but also to make them available for you to buy. You will have the option of inquiring about any image you see . . . you'll be able to pause the movie and learn about the glasses or even buy them on the spot.' Using the hypothetical example of actor Tom Cruise's on-screen accessories, Gates explained: 'If the movie's star carries a handsome leather briefcase or handbag, the [Internet] highway will let you browse the manufacturer's entire line of leather goods and either order one or be directed to a convenient retailer.'[29] In late 1998, Microsoft's digital television website suggested that digital television broadcasters adopt a merchandizing device from the World Wide Web, the un-deletable interactive banner advertisement: 'Use banner ads or other clickable graphics. While commercials appear for short intervals, banner ads can be constantly displayed, even as the video continues to play.'[30] Elsewhere on its website, Microsoft advised would-be digital broadcasters:

> Develop associated revenue streams. An obvious business model makes use of formerly unrealized, complementary revenue . . . associated revenue streams might pair CDs with a dance or music review, weather experiment kits for kids who watch the evening weather report, books suggested by talk show hosts, airline tickets or holiday packages suggested by travelogues, among many others. The key is in the partnership and how you share your audience with the merchandiser.[31]

As Microsoft dreamed of digital television's possibilities for enhanced product placement and inescapable on-screen marketing logos, others in the industry posited the development of gendered segmentation of television services according to day part, with interactive standard-definition programming offered in the daytime to a presumed predominantly female audience, and high-definition, non-interactive programming offered to the more masculine audience presumed in prime time.[32] This linking of programme form, implied audience, and advertising strategy in contemporary digital television echoes the practices of early commercial radio broadcasting

---

29 Gates, *The Road Ahead*, 165–6.

30 Microsoft digital television website, updated 13 Nov. 1998.

31 Ibid.

32 'TCI's Malone Discusses HDTV', n.p.

concerning so-called direct and indirect advertising and of early television regarding the design of programmes according to anticipated viewer attention and day part. A CBS publication on television in 1945 suggested that 'programs requiring full attention of eye and ear should be scheduled in the evening hours when viewers feel entitled to entertainment and relaxation'.[33] In this regard, the prevailing marketing assumptions of the putative post-television era at the end of the 1990s seem remarkably consistent with long-established beliefs and practices concerning the domestic audience of American broadcasters and advertisers.

'Sad unhappy people who live in lofts': new paradigms of the television viewer

In addition to throwing into question at least some of the traditional assumptions about the television industry's competitive structure, programme forms, and national role, the long-term enforced transition from analogue to digital television initiated in late 1998 in the USA and UK also provoked a reconsideration of some traditional conceptions of the television audience and the activity of TV viewing. The three competing applications and business models for digital television—improved image quality, multiple standard-definition channels, or enhanced interactivity—activate distinct and incompatible scenarios of television viewing, scenarios which nevertheless resonate with a repertory of popular images of media audiences going back to the beginning of the twentieth century. The introduction of digital television at the end of the 1990s threw such established figurations into confusion and crisis in both the USA and UK. For example, the provision of 140 channels on digital television systems like Rupert Murdoch's digital BSkyB required an electronic programme guide (EPG) resembling an Internet search engine more than the traditional printed *TV Times*. The introduction of the new EPG activated disjunct and competing images of the domestic TV audience in Great Britain; defending his company's thirty-channel, non-interactive terrestrial digital system against Murdoch's more technologically complex system, OnDigital's CEO Stephen Grabiner told a British journalist in 1998: 'There will be people who want 200 channels and there will be people who spend their lives playing with the EPG. But these are sad unhappy people who live in lofts.'[34] Grabiner's social and spatial marginalization of the electronics enthusiast as distinct from middle England's non-technophilic media consumer tapped into long-running popular culture figurations of the lonely male hobbyist in the basement, attic, shed, or garage. These alternately heroic and pathetic masculine figures recur in the popular literature on electronic media, from the 1910s amateur radio enthusiast,

33 On the radio split, see William Boddy, 'The Rhetoric and the Economic Roots of the American Broadcasting Industry', *Cinetracts*, 6 (Spring 1979), 37–54; on the split in early television, see William Boddy, *Fifties Television: The Industry and its Critics* (Champaign: University of Illinois Press, 1990), 21; the CBS publication is CBS, *Television Audience Research* (1945), 6.

34 Peter Thal Larsen, 'Can Digital TV Convert the Dish-Hating Viewer?', *Independent* (29 July 1998), n.p.; Grabiner told another British journalist in 1998: 'There is a market for people who want 200 television channels. They live in dark attics and don't come out very often. OnDigital's market is middle England, people who want more choice in their viewing.'

through the post-war audiophile or ham radio operator, to the contemporary computer hacker.[35]

Given these persistent discursive traditions, it is suggestive to consider at least briefly the ostensible convergence of the computer and TV set from the point of view of some prominent writers and executives in the computer industry at the end of the 1990s. As the previous chapter outlined, many technological and political pundits voiced deep pessimism in the early 1990s concerning the future competitiveness of American high tech in the face of Japanese economic expansionism. Such observers constructed a broad opposition between conventional broadcast television and the then much-hyped phenomenon of virtual reality, and the deep-seated gender and cultural positioning of domestic television as object and activity served as a remarkably consistent foil for enthusiasts of a range of advanced electronic imaging systems, what a chorus of diverse commentators at the time identified as 'television's second chance'. However, by the late 1990s, as attention to virtual reality in the popular press dwindled into such prosaic headlines as 'Virtual Reality at the Dentist: Better than Novocain', the Internet moved into VR's discursive space as antipode to the culturally degraded domestic television receiver.[36] Thus, from the point of view of many Web partisans in the 1990s, the putative merging of the computer and TV set was seen as more a threat than a promise. One can observe this anxiety in a number of sites, including the flurry of interest and controversy in 1995 around so-called push technologies as a business model for the Internet (VR pioneer Jaron Lanier in *Wired* magazine denounced push technologies as 'TV all over again'[37]), the marketing of TV-like computer interfaces, and studies of the phenomenology of computer and television use. While interactive digital television has reactivated some of the oldest tropes celebrating masculinist mobility and adventure from the earliest days of wireless (George Gilder wrote in 1991 that via digital video, 'a tourist could visit a Third World country and view any chosen set of scenes or events without having to drink the water'),[38] its discomforting proximity to the conventionally scorned object of the domestic TV receiver has also provoked anxiety and resistance. Apple Computer CEO Steve Jobs told a group of educators in December 1998 that while viewers use television to 'turn their brains off, people go to the PC to turn their brain on'. Of the supposed convergence of personal computer and television set, Jobs said: 'These things don't go together, and I think it's crazy to expect this is going to happen.'[39]

35 For a discussion of the gendering of the 1950s male audio enthusiast in opposition to the feminized TV viewer, see Keir Keightley, '"Turn it Down"!', She Shrieked: Gender, Domestic Space, and High Fidelity, 1948–59', *Popular Music*, 15 (1996), 149–77; for a discussion of the development of the early personal computer subculture, see Sherry Turkle, *The Second Self: Computers and the Human Spirit* (New York: Simon and Schuster, 1984), especially ch. 5.

36 'Virtual Reality at the Dentist: Better than Novocain', *Computer Review*, advertising supplement to the *New York Times* (5 June 1994), n.p.

37 Jaron Lanier, 'Mass Transit!', *Wired* (May 1995), 156.

38 George Gilder, *Microcosm: The Quantum Revolution in Economics and Technology* (New York: Simon and Schuster, 1989), 314.

39 Wendy J. Mattson and Matthew Rothenberg, 'Apple's Jobs Candid about Technology's Role in Education', *MacWeek Online* (10 Dec. 1998), n.p.

In a similar vein, in his 1997 book *Interface Culture*, Steven Johnson protested the use of the verb 'surf' to describe what Internet users do, since, according to Johnson, the term derives from the existing television practice of channel surfing via cable television and the remote control. 'What makes the idea of cybersurf so infuriating is the implicit connection drawn to television,' Johnson complained.[40] In place of the culturally contaminated figure of the Web 'surfer', Johnson proposed the masculinist figures of Baudelaire's nineteenth-century urban *flâneur* or the solitary frontiersman 'trailblazer', 'a term', he argues, 'that would have fitted well with the "new frontier" rhetoric of recent cyber-boosterism. It certainly would have been an improvement on the couch-potato passivity of the "surfing" argot.'[41] Johnson is likewise scornful of Microsoft Bob, a software shell unsuccessfully launched in 1995 which offered users a simplified graphical interface based on domestic iconography and talking cartoon-character guides.[42] For Johnson, 'Bob represents the domestication of the personal computer, in the pejorative sense of the word . . . the mother's-little-helper of interface design.'[43]

Notwithstanding such protests from Internet enthusiasts, Microsoft's late 1990s moves into the interactive digital television market gave the company a strong strategic interest in blurring the phenomenological and normative differences between television viewing and computer use, refuting the conventional opposition between Web user and domestic TV viewer. Microsoft's digital television website argued that 'watching TV is already interactive. Many viewers seldom watch complete programs, but channel surf and graze through a variety of channels. . . . An increasing number of viewers simultaneously watch a TV set and use a computer to surf the Internet. With over 2,000 broadcast stations in the United States, hundreds of cable channels, and millions of websites, the war for eyeballs has grown even fiercer.'[44]

Indeed, what Intel chief Andrew Grove calls the 'battle for eyeballs' between computers and TV sets in the home has provoked his own microprocessor company to look beyond the traditional computer industry for new markets. While digital television tuner cards for personal computers, including those capable of receiving high-definition programming, would be a relatively inexpensive path for digital television into the home, the problems of integrating the device within the domestic space, configuring screen–user distance, and managing social aspects of their use remain daunting to many observers. At the same time, as Bill Gates admitted in *The Road Ahead*: 'A big-screen TV across the room doesn't lend itself to the use of a keyboard, nor does it afford privacy.'[45] As one industry sceptic noted about the prospects for interactive television as a means for Web access: 'People

40 Steven Johnson, *Interface Culture: How New Technology Transforms the Way We Create and Communicate* (New York: HarperCollins, 1997), 107.

41 Ibid. 67, 118.

42 For the ideas of two Stanford professors who consulted with Microsoft on the design of Bob, see Byron Reeves and Clifford Nass, *The Media Equation: How People Treat Computers, Television, and New Media Like Real People and Places* (Stanford, Calif.: CSLI Publications/Cambridge University Press, 1996).

43 Johnson, *Interface Culture*, 62–3.

44 Microsoft digital television website, updated 13 Nov. 1998.

45 Gates, *The Road Ahead*, 71.

have computers. People are continuing to buy them. I expect that computers will continue to be the primary way people get online.' Another industry analyst concluded: 'Maybe in 25 years PC/DTV may be the mode of operation for watching programs, but right now generations of consumers like to go home, sit down on the couch, turn it on and flip their clicker. No one wants to boot up their TV or have it crash on them during their favorite program.'[46]

Selling new media to the home

Notwithstanding the sometimes bitter tactical debates and long-term commercial uncertainties concerning the place of new digital media in the home, US consumer electronics manufacturers in the late 1990s faced the immediate challenge of selling their new digital hardware by appealingly enacting their domestic use in print advertisements and TV commercials. These brief, self-serving, and ephemeral television commercials can illuminate some of the wider issues involved in the take-up of new domestic electronic media, since they typically enact dense and affective scenarios of socially embedded technologies; in indirect and unacknowledged ways these 30-second dramas often point to the wider culture's fears and ambivalences about new technologies. One 1998 television commercial for a Toshiba DVD player depicts a traditional family group (parents and two young children) in front of their living-room TV set as dad inserts a DVD of the 1997 action-adventure film *Eraser* (Fig. 6.1). The images which follow, unaccompanied by any narration or dialogue, offer a disjunctive series of reverse angles alternating between the thrilled and immobilized family audience, close-ups of the DVD player, and assorted on-screen explosions from the feature film they are viewing. The commercial's analogy between domestic television viewing and theme-park thrill-ride, insistently evoked by acrobatic camera movements, arbitrary lighting changes, blurred rapid zooms, and extreme close-ups of hands clutching sofa armrests, is literalized by the sign above the living-room door glimpsed in the commercial's opening frames: 'Warning: This Ride is Intense. Please Remain Seated at all Times.' While Toshiba's commercial employs the familiar advertising trope conflating domestic viewing space with hyper-real TV screen action, what is conjured here is less the traditional advertising scenario of television as home theatre than television as public amusement park attraction. The assertive animated titles leaping out to viewers after the domestic scene fades to black—'You've Got Senses. Use Them.'—underscore the commercial's attempts to evoke a visceral, body-centred scenario of television viewing via a flurry of interpolated extreme close-ups of the eyes, ears, and open mouths of the family audience. The assaultive, transgressive nature of the depicted DVD television experience is reinforced by the commercial's extreme close-ups of shaking teaspoons and pearl earrings, icons of traditional domesticity. The overall effect of the commercial, however, is suggestive less of a new and novel media technology than of conventional TV on steroids; the ad is able to eschew narration and dialogue only because the electronic technology and viewing experience it depicts are presented as merely a hyperbolization of existing television

---

46 Peter Brown, 'Chipmakers Reject the PC/DTV', *Electronic News* (16 Nov. 1998), 27.

Fig. 6.1 Selling home theatre as living-room thrill ride: television advertisement for Toshiba DVD player, 1998

Fig. 6.2 Selling the convergence of TV set and computer monitor: television advertisement for Panasonic SVGA-TV monitor, 1998

viewing scenarios, albeit one which pushes the traditional marketing distinctions between domestic and public spaces to their limit. Only implicit in the Toshiba commercial is DVD's noteworthy threshold status as a contemporary consumer electronics product, serving at once as a software platform for both personal computers and television sets. On one level simply an enhanced delivery vehicle for Hollywood films already available on videotape and laser disc, the DVD also represents the first moving-image format launched simultaneously for both PCs and TVs. In January 1997 the *New York Times* quoted one industry analyst who noted that 'this is the first consumer product that will come into the home through two doors, both the living room and the den', and DVD's dual status sidesteps some of the social and phenomenological shortcomings of the computer as a moving-image display device.[47]

In contrast to the Toshiba commercial's hyperbolic fluency in evoking a new TV viewing paradigm, a 1998 Panasonic commercial for the firm's large-screen SVGA-TV, a combination TV set and computer monitor, suggests the marketing challenges involved in launching a genuinely new and unfamiliar electronic device in the home (Fig. 6.2). Unlike the terse

47 Lee Isgur, Jefferies & Company consumer electronics analyst, quoted in John Markoff, 'Companies Roll the Dice on Digital Videodisks', *New York Times* (9 Jan. 1997), D2.

and evocative Toshiba DVD commercial, the cluttered and loquacious Panasonic ad relies on non-stop narration, a generic action-adventure musical score, a number of superimposed titles, and even several arbitrary strings of binary 0s and 1s superimposed over the diegetic action. The commercial depicts a pre-adolescent male, first seen seated close to the TV screen with a computer keyboard on his lap, apparently calling up Internet Web pages containing images of spaceships; after the boy's chair magically slides several feet away from the monitor, he is shown watching sci-fi TV programming on the same large-screen monitor. While the commercial offers a comforting social scenario suggesting the domestication of the pre-adolescent male's potentially unruly relationship to electronic technology (echoing a trope established in the popular representations of the early twentieth-century radio hobbyist), it nevertheless suggests some of the difficulties in representing hybrid digital media in the home. The commercial's opening narration, 'It's one world. Why view it through two windows?', is heard over an image of two animated globes which merge in the centre of the screen, below a browser-like animated graphic in the top corner of the screen. However, the implied equivalence between Internet browsing and TV viewing begs the question of the adequacy of the single-window metaphor for both devices and activities; unlike Web browsing, the activity of TV viewing is less commonly understood in such an instrumental fashion. Moreover, the unlived-in look of the commercial's domestic *mise en scène*, with its minimalist decor and wall of built-in electronic apparatus, suggests that domestic spaces need to be purpose built around these new digital-media devices, rather than providing a scenario of their seamless integration into existing domestic routines and spaces. Most strikingly, the commercial's magical solution to the central problem of the disparate screen distances appropriate for computer and television set use—the boy's chair which slides autonomously across the room as he shifts from Internet browsing to TV viewing—suggests the difficulties of representing the shifting modes of attention and physical space embedded in the hybrid computer–TV-set device. The solitary figure in the abstracted domestic space also evades the challenge of integrating interactive digital technologies into the social activities of the household; would the family gather around the living-room television to watch the son's Web surfing on their TV set? As we have seen, similar misgivings were expressed about the introduction of television into the domestic living room in the mid-1940s, when one industry official wondered if 'the father of the house would be willing to have the lights turned out in the living room when he wants to read because his children want to watch a television broadcast of no interest to him'.[48] However, current domestic battles over channel surfing and control of the remote control would very likely pale in comparison to the anticipated domestic friction generated by collective living-room Internet browsing. Given all these challenges, viewers of the Panasonic SVGA-TV commercial were likely to remain sceptical or merely puzzled about the possible domestic scenarios for interactive digital television on offer.

---

48 Quoted in Lyndon O. Brown, 'What the Public Expects of Television', in John Gray Peatman (ed.), *Radio and Business 1945: Proceedings of the First Annual Conference on Radio and Business* (New York: City College of New York, 1945), 137.

Conclusion Discourses around the launch of digital television have already supplanted traditional figurations of the television audience with competing dystopian images of pathetic loft dwellers and utopian scenarios of new armchair Columbuses. Clearly, the cultural valuation of a range of domestic electronic devices, from computer and television set to satellite dish, has been put into question by the introduction of digital television. There are significant competitive advantages and policy outcomes at stake in the discursive battles among competing figurations of the television audience in the popular imagination and commercial market place, and an analysis of these battles can offer insights into the wider social process of technological innovation. As we have seen, the celebration of the speculative birth of yet another 'revolutionary' communication technology at the end of the 1990s suggests the cultural and ideological battles evoked in the prosaic and everyday activity of television viewing.

From the perspective of five years beyond the 1998 launch of digital television in the USA and UK, the full impact of digital television on the competitive conditions, regulatory regimes, and popular assumptions regarding television remains quite uncertain in both countries, However, the subsequent fortunes of Britain's OnDigital, the terrestrial broadcasting-based rival to Rupert Murdoch's BSkyB, are instructive. While by August 2003 the UK had the highest penetration rate of digital television of any nation in the world (44 per cent of TV homes), OnDigital was no longer around to share the audience.[49] Despite a £10 million effort by joint owners Granada and Carlton Communications to rebrand OnDigital as ITV Digital in mid-2001, a year later the company laid off 1,700 workers and went into receivership, following losses of £1.2 million. Its digital broadcast licences were acquired by a new free-to-air digital service, Freeview.[50]

Technical, marketing, and management problems beset the terrestrial digital television service immediately upon its lavish, £90 million launch in October 1998, beginning with the company's failure to bring set-top boxes to the market for the 1998 holiday season. In mid-1999 OnDigital chief executive Stephen Grabiner resigned and launched an extended public lawsuit against ITV over his compensation. More seriously, OnDigital's broadcast signal was inaccessible to over 30 per cent of the UK population, and where available, its image was prone to freezing and fuzziness, offering viewers an image quality later described by Carlton chairman Michael Green as 'softer than an electric razor'.[51] The technical problems led to a persistent churn rate among OnDigital subscribers of 25–30 per cent, more than twice the turnover of BSkyB customers.[52] Despite pleas from OnDigital executives,

---

49 George Trefgarne, 'Ball Skills that Made Sky Mentionable at a Dinner Party', *Daily Telegraph* (13 Aug. 2003), 27.

50 Mark Ritson, 'Inside-out Conception of Brand Triggered ITV Digital's Downfall', *Marketing* (9 May 2002), 18.

51 Quoted in Nic Paton, 'Monkey Business: It's a Jungle Out There, and the ITV Digital Monkey Suffered Due to Mismanagement and Intense Competition', *Personnel Today* (20 Aug. 2002), 2; Raymond Snoddy, 'A Bad Omen that Haunted Channel to the Bitter End', *The Times* (28 Mar. 2002), n.p.

52 The churn rate was identified by ITV Digital marketing executive Phillip Manzi, quoted in Maggie Brown, 'Vision Impossible: A Pioneering Media Venture, Maybe, an Unrealistic Plan with Severe Technical Problems, Definitely', *Guardian* (29 Apr. 2002), 2.

the government refused to sanction an increase in transmitter power, a position Stuart Pebble, Grabiner's successor as OnDigital's CEO, later attributed to the Labour government's unwillingness to displease BSkyB's Rupert Murdoch.[53] In addition to signal problems, the service was also plagued by a high number of pirated users, estimated between 100,000 and 300,000 households, alongside the service's 1.2 million paying customers.[54] Technical and regulatory obstacles were accompanied by management mistakes, including over-bidding for second-tier football matches and devoting limited channel capacity to low-performing in-house speciality channels like Granada's Men and Motors and the Carlton Food Channel.[55] Beyond accusations against BSkyB of predatory pricing of Sky programming for the terrestrial service, BSkyB also forced Granada and Carlton into a costly bidding war in June 1999 when Murdoch began giving away its set-top boxes to subscribers.[56] While BSkyB went into £1.44 million debt over the following eighteen months, the set-top box giveaway boosted the number of subscribers from 800,000 to just under 5 million during the same period, and the share price of BSkyB corporate parent Newscorp remained largely unaffected. Meanwhile, Granada and Carlton executives, who had earlier estimated it would take an investment of £300–400 million before the digital service became profitable, were faced with unrecovered costs two or three times that amount, and the share prices of both ITV Digital's corporate owners were punished by investors.[57] Also contributing to investor pressure upon Granada and Carlton was an unprecedented 13 per cent drop in UK TV advertising revenues in 2001, damaging the core business of the commercial television operators.[58]

The failure of OnDigital/ITV Digital reverberated in British corporate boardrooms and government ministries through 2002 and 2003. On the one hand, Freeview, a twenty-three-channel terrestrial digital TV service launched by the BBC and Crown Castle in late 2002, received quick government approval to increase transmitter power 300 per cent, and the new service inherited ITV Digital's one million-plus households with set-top boxes (although ITV Digital's bankruptcy administrator contacted subscribers to demand the purchase or return of the 'free' set-top boxes).[59] On the level of consumer uptake, the new free digital television service, which carries BSkyB's Sky News, Sky Sports News, and Sky Travel, alongside a number of BBC channels, was an unexpected success, attracting a million subscribers within a year. Indeed, by late 2003 Freeview was responsible for reviving the general economic prospects for digital terrestrial television and

53 Maggie Brown, 'Prebble Fears TV's Future is in Sky', *Guardian* (6 June 2003), 21.

54 'Digital Disaster: Rule 1: Never Try to out-Sky BSkyB', *Observer* (31 Mar. 2002), 5.

55 Ibid.; Brown, 'Vision Impossible', 2.

56 Saeed Shah, 'Trying to Use ITV Digital to Break BSkyB's Monopoly has Only Strengthened Murdoch', *Independent* (1 May 2002), 2.

57 Ibid. Raymond Snoddy puts the original break-even point for OnDigital at £700 million; see Snoddy, 'A Bad Omen', n.p.

58 Snoddy, 'A Bad Omen', n.p.

59 Shah, 'Trying to Use ITV Digital', 2.

providing a model for other European nations.[60] At the same time, however, the service's limited number of channels made provision of pay-TV channels unfeasible, vitiating Freeview's competitive threat to BSkyB's core business. BSkyB, having eliminated a rival digital pay-television platform in ITV Digital, viewed Freeview chiefly as a potentially lucrative promotional vehicle; as one commentator noted in 2002: 'For the first time in its 13-year history, BSkyB will be able to market its wider pay offering via give-away channels on a free-to-view basis.'[61] By mid-2002, pay TV on the new digital platform in the UK was a lopsided duopoly split between BSkyB, with nearly 6 million subscribers, and two major cable firms with a total of 2 million subscribers.[62] As reporter Tim Webb concluded in 2003: 'Murdoch will have to accept that Sky cannot have the whole multi-channel market—just the bit that makes all the money.'[63]

The spectacular failure of ITV Digital also had implications for corporate governance and national identity across the British media industries. Coincident with the implosion of ITV Digital were efforts by its corporate parents, Granada and Carlton, to merge into a single commercial broadcasting company. However, immediately upon the heels of the UK's Competition Commission's approval of the merger in October 2003, the two companies' institutional investors, led by the American firm Fidelity Investments (the largest shareholder of each company), insisted upon the removal of Carlton CEO Michael Green, labelled by one journalist as 'the architect of the OnDigital/ITV Digital disaster'.[64] Green found himself, according to the *Daily Mail*, 'on the wrong end of the most brutal boardroom coup in City history', and the *Independent* reported that Green had confided to a friend about OnDigital/ITV Digital that 'he wishes he'd never heard of it'.[65] The incoming CEO of the new ITV, former Granada head Charles Allen, immediated promised to cut costs across the company by £100 million, and many industry observers predicted widespread layoffs and cuts in programme budgets.[66] At the same time, the removal from the new ITV of Green and other Carlton and Granada executives associated with the OnDigital/ITV Digital debacle was seen by many trade observers as increasing the chances that the new company would become 'prey to one of the American groups routinely mentioned as predators', in the words of the *Independent*.[67] The US trade paper *Variety* speculated that 'The prospects of a U.S. media combine

60 Chris Wynn and Alexandra Wales, 'Europe Looks to UK's Freeview Model for DTT', *New Media Markets* (14 Nov. 2003), n.p.

61 Graham Lovelace, 'Britain Began a New Chapter This Past Week in its Bold Attempt to Become the World's First Completely Digital Television Nation', *Business* (7 July 2002), n.p.

62 Ibid.

63 Tim Webb, 'Three Years Ago, Reporters at Sky News Complained that Reporting the Results of Parent Company British Sky Broadcasting Company (BSkyB) Was a "Poisoned Chalice"', *Business* (17 Aug. 2003), n.p.

64 Maggie Brown, 'Cost-Cutting the Key Consequence of ITV Merger', *Stage* (30 Oct. 2003), n.p.

65 Sean O'Grady, 'Michael Green: Behind the Screen: The Private Man Who Now Runs TV', *Independent* (11 Oct. 2003), 19.

66 Brown, 'Cost-Cutting the Key Consequence', n.p.; Dan Milmo, 'Allen Admits defeat in ITV Plc Contract Fight', *Guardian* (9 Dec. 2003), 21.

67 O'Grady, 'Michael Green: Behind the Screen', 19.

swooping in on ITV have improved' with Green's ouster.[68] As the *Financial Times* concluded in October 2003:

> The confrontation with shareholders during the Carlton–Granada merger may have reflected peculiarly British circumstances, but the affair should be viewed in the context of a global crisis of corporate governance. Have fidelity and its supporters simply opened the door to a US takeover of ITV?[69]

Former ITN editor-in-chief Richard Tait linked the earlier business success of Michael Green and Charles Allen to regulatory decisions by Conservative governments of the 1980s and 1990s, but attributed Green's recent 'defenestration' to the determination of major shareholders' groups, still smarting after the OnDigital disaster, to insist upon an independent management executive for the new ITV firm:

> The independent chairman, once appointed, will be explicitly there to look after shareholders' interests—and that means, in the last resort, changing the chief executive. And while the way we got here is as much about regulation and political decision as it is about entrepreneurship, from now on, the market will likely have the last word. This is the final opportunity for British-owned commercial television to build a really significant media business—if it fails, the next shareholders' putsch could be to call in the Americans.[70]

At the same time, according to Nils Pratley writing in the *Sunday Times* in October 2002, 'the government has become so embarrassed by the disgraceful state of ITV that it is beyond caring whether it ends up in the hands of an American company such as Viacom, or AOL Time Warner'.[71]

The tangled fallout of the collapse of OnDigital/ITV Digital provides an ironic coda to OnDigital's earlier nationalistic marketing profile as a digital service for non-technophilic 'middle England' viewers, versus Sky's image 'as a service for football fanatics', 'selling ugly great satellite dishes door-to-door on housing estates, and delivering television that was cheap and largely poor quality', according to Jane Robbins, writing in the *Independent* in 1998 as the digital rivalry began.[72] She pointed to 'a strong class division over satellite, with the middle classes still sniffy about dishes', and noted the American origins of the BSkyB leaders:

> Mark Booth and Elizabeth Murdoch are on a mission to change the television habits of Britain. The task would be daunting enough for anyone, but these two are American—and if they are to succeed they

68 Steve Clarke, 'ITV Defenses Down: Clash over Toppers Spurs U.S. Takeover Talk', *Daily Variety* (21 Oct. 2003), 6.

69 Barry Riley, 'Crossing the Thin Green Line: There is a Danger that the Listed Market will Start to Shrink', *Financial Times* (27 Oct. 2003), 28.

70 Richard Tait, 'Dramatic Twist in ITV Soap Opera: Michael Green was Doomed by Decisions made by People Elsewhere', *Financial Times* (28 Oct. 2003), 4.

71 Nils Pratley, 'I'm an ITV Shareholder . . . Get me Out of Here', *Sunday Times* (13 Oct. 2002), 4.

72 Robins, 'Liz and Mark's Satellite Love-in', 14.

not only need to understand British culture very quickly; they need also to change it.[73]

By the end of 2003, however, it was Britain's conventional commercial broadcasters' misadventures with digital broadcasting which seemed to bring ITV itself closer to an American takeover. Meanwhile, by August 2003 BSkyB CEO Tony Ball could boast that 'saying you've got Sky is no longer embarrassing at a dinner party. Those who haven't got it are odder than those who have.'[74] In late 2003 Granada and Carlton announced generous severance packages to executives associated with its failed digital broadcasting service, including £1.4 million to Michael Green, a gesture described by the *Daily Mail* as 'cocking a snook at shareholders who removed him from office'.[75] The same day, the British press reported that Standard and Poor's had raised the credit rating of BSkyB from junk bond to investment status.[76] The potent, if elusive, role of class and national identity in the discourses of digital television at the end of the twentieth century suggests the way in which technological innovation remains enmeshed in the social.

---

73 Ibid.

74 Trefgarne, 'Ball Skills that Made Sky Mentionable at a Dinner Party', 27.

75 '[By the] standards of BSkyB where former chief executive Tony Ball has marched off into the sunset with a GBP 10.7m "non-compete" payment, the severance package for Michael Green of Carlton is relatively modest', *Daily Mail* (9 Dec. 2003), n.p.

76 S&P's credit analyst drily explained: 'BSkyB's solid operating performance, profitability, and cash generation have led to consistent reductions in its debt burden. We consider these improvements to be sustainable, taking into account the near-term prospect for a possible reinstatement of the group's equity dividend.' Quoted in 'Allen Accepts [£] 1m One-Year Contract as ITV Plc Chief Executive', *Herald* (Glasgow) (9 Dec. 2003), 24.

7

Redefining the Home Screen: The Case of the Digital Video Recorder

Introduction

ONE WAY TO ASSESS the significance of recent technological innovations associated with the shift from analogue to digital television platforms in the United States is to chart their impact upon traditional assumptions about television and its audience, assumptions themselves informed by specific historical forces within and beyond the television industry. The turmoil which accompanied the medium's transition to digital standards at the end of the 1990s threw into stark relief how far the industry had moved from the instrumental fantasies of reception, ontology, and national identity associated with the era of network television in the USA from the 1940s into the 1980s, with its apotheosis in the period of the early 1960s described in Chapter 3. The first four decades of post-war American television, dominated by the formidable economic and cultural power of three network firms, is noteworthy beyond the phenomenal economic prosperity and relative structural stability that the TV industry enjoyed. Equally telling is the way in which a remarkably consistent and enduring set of ideas about the general nature and function of the television medium was also elaborated as commercial television was consolidated within American economic and cultural life. Responding in complex ways to the self-promoting discourses of powerful industry interests, especially the three dominant TV networks, a web of 'commonsensical', if largely implicit, propositions about the medium permeated public and trade discussions of television. These assumptions found a place within both popular and elite criticism of television, were invoked by both defenders and critics of the industry, and guided policy makers and legislators concerned with the medium, sustaining an common image of television, as we have seen, as quotidian, advertising dominated, audio driven, visually impoverished, female centred, and passively consumed. In American media scholarship, it was not until the belated impact of cultural studies-inflected audience studies in the 1980s that such constructions underwent systematic revision. Unlike the cultural positioning of cinema in the USA since the 1940s, increasingly associated with the possibilities for artistic status, personal expression, cosmopolitanism, and high cultural prestige, American television was generally construed in terms of its domesticity, liveness, and its role as an indispensable agent of national identity. The significance of contemporary technological innovation within moving-image culture is suggested by the ongoing erosion of many of these traditional propositions about the nature and uses of the television medium.

TV nation   Leaders of the three dominant US networks at the height of their enormous post-war prosperity and power had their own reasons for ratifying these imagined essentialized features of the medium. Countless network statements in the mid-1950s linked commercial television's role as nation builder with the medium's purportedly all-powerful relationship with its domestic audience. In 1954, the year that CBS became the world's largest single advertising medium, CBS network president Frank Stanton told a gathering of journalists: 'The most remarkable thing is what the *Public* does. Putting aside all other considerations, the public glues its eyes and ears to newspapers, loudspeakers and television tubes; seeing everything, hearing everything and—heaven help us all—*believing* everything.' Stanton outlined the importance of the commercial media in constituting American national identity for such a credulous population: '*We give America its daily consciousness of being a Nation.* If it weren't for us, private individuals all, and private businesses all, America would not know where it stood or what it felt.' Stanton concluded by defending television's role as nation builder: 'I am far from saying we are a perfect mirror, or even always a well-polished one . . . but if this mirror were shattered, the National Countenance would disappear.'[1]

The US television networks had specific motives in the mid-1950s for claiming the role of national looking-glass and consciousness maker. Two network firms, CBS and NBC, which controlled only 11 per cent of total television industry assets, took in an estimated 43 per cent of industry-wide profits in 1955.[2] The previous year, CBS alone captured 28 per cent of the profits of the entire television industry, boosted by an annual return of 1,800 per cent from the operation of its New York City station.[3] Given their vulnerability to public and regulatory complaints of monopoly power, the networks defended their monopoly provision of live nationwide programming with appeals to national identity and necessity. For example, CBS's Frank Stanton told a congressional committee in 1956 that 'to curtail or destroy the networks' unique quality of instantaneous national interconnection would be a colossal backward step. It would make the United States much more like Europe than America. In fact, it would be a step in the direction of the *Balkanization*, the fragmentation, of the United States.'[4] Stanton's appeal to received notions of America as privileged site of unified national identity against a tribalized Europe resonated with Cold War era claims of American distinctiveness and global hegemony. If network leaders in the 1950s claimed that US national identity depended upon their unfettered market power, they also argued for their own legitimization via a quasi-electoral mechanism of viewer channel choice; as Stanton told the congressional committee, 'a

---

1 Frank Stanton, talk to Sigma Delta Chi convention, Columbus, Oh. (13 Nov. 1954), 14–15. Collection of CBS Reference Library, New York. Emphasis in original.

2 US Congress, House, Committee on Interstate and Foreign Commerce, *Network Broadcasting*, House Report no. 1297, 85th Cong., 2nd sess. (Washington, DC: Government Printing Office, 1958), 194.

3 US Congress, Senate, Committee on Interstate and Foreign Commerce, *The Network Monopoly*, *Report* by Senator John W. Bricker (Washington, DC: Government Printing Office, 1956), 3, 5, 15.

4 Frank Stanton, 'Statement of Frank Stanton, President, Columbia Broadcasting System, Inc. before the Senate Committee on Interstate and Foreign Commerce, June 12, 1956', 6. Collection of CBS Reference Library, New York. Emphasis in original.

network draws its validity in precisely the same fashion as an elected official of government—from election by and of the people'.[5] Thus the long-running image of US commercial television as a quasi-statist oligopoly serving a domesticated and credulous audience was reinforced by network leaders who sought to defend their monopoly powers from the threats of regulation and competition.

For similar purposes, network TV leaders defended their oligopolistic commercial practices before a series of congressional committees in the mid-1950s by associating their operations with contemporaneous ontological and aesthetic claims for the privileged status of live television, what CBS's Frank Stanton called 'the very lifeblood and magic of television'.[6] During the 1950s, the networks posited this strategic ontology of liveness against competition from potential pay-television services built upon the feature-film libraries of the Hollywood studios. In CBS's *Annual Report* for 1955, Stanton argued that such film-based networks would 'highjack the American public into paying for the privilege of looking at its own television sets'.[7] In a 1955 CBS pamphlet, Stanton denounced pay television as 'a booby trap, a scheme to render the television owner blind, and then rent him a seeing eye dog at so much per mile—to restore to him, only very partially, what he had previously enjoyed as a natural right'.[8] CBS's mid-1950s evocation of pay television as a violation both of television's ontological destiny of liveness and of the 'natural rights' of television viewers resonated with the pervasive nationalistic political discourse of the time and implicitly aligned advertising-supported television with the legitimizing operations of the state. In any event, television's association in both elite and public opinion with viewer credulity, liveness, consumer sovereignty, and national identity was sustained by industry leaders and critics alike over the three or four decades of network domination of the US television industry after the Second World War.

The end of simultaneity?

If many of the truisms about American commercial television can be traced back to the era of network ascendancy of the mid-1950s, such associations endured long after network power began to fade in the mid-1970s. The traditional opposition in reception sites between the domestic television receiver and the public cinema screen, with its persistent gender implications, has recently been challenged both by the growing popularity of domestic home-theatre installations and by the prospect of the electronic distribution and projection of feature films in public cinemas.[9] While decried by some

---

5 Frank Stanton, 'Statement of Frank Stanton, President, Columbia Broadcasting System, Inc. before the Senate Committee on Interstate and Foreign Commerce, June 12, 1956', 36. Emphasis in original.

6 Frank Stanton, speech to Second General Conference of CBS Television Affiliates, Chicago (13 Apr. 1956), 10. Collection of CBS Reference Library, New York.

7 Frank Stanton, 'Free vs. Pay-Television', pamphlet (New York: Columbia Broadcasting System, 19 May 1955), n.p.

8 Ibid.

9 For a discussion of digital cinema's disappointing commercial roll-out, see Carl DiOrio, 'Digital Gurus Can't Send in the Clones', *Daily Variety* (14 Feb. 2002), 1.

critics as the lamentable 'domestication' of the theatrical film experience, the 1990s home-theatre boom has provided new masculinist pleasures of technological fetishism and feature-film collecting and connoisseurship and has arguably changed the modes of attention and sociality around which at least some television is consumed in the home. More significantly, prospective changes associated with digital delivery and recording media in the home promise further to destabilize traditional notions of the nature of television, its audience, and its links to national identity, as we shall see in the debates around the introduction of the digital video recorder (DVR), also known as the personal video recorder (PVR), at the end of the 1990s.

It is symptomatic of the generally unsettled state of the US television industry that the mid-1999 commercial launch of the seemingly prosaic digital video recorder, a VCR-like appliance which records programmes on a computer hard drive and downloads programme schedules overnight via an internal modem, provoked apocalyptic warnings of the death of commercial television from a number of TV executives. While some major studios and television networks responded to what they saw as the commercial prospects of the digital video recorder by making direct investments in the two start-up manufacturers of the new devices, Replay Networks Inc. and TiVo Inc., other media firms threatened to sue the same manufacturers for copyright infringement of recorded programming. Four large media companies—Walt Disney, CBS, the News Corporation, and Discovery Communications— have, in fact, both made direct investments in, *and* threatened to sue, the DVR manufacturers.[10]

One of the novel features of the digital video recorder is its ability to record and replay material at the same time, allowing viewers to record an on-air programme as they watch it, leave the room for an interval, and resume viewing the recording at the point at which they left, jumping past commercials on playback as desired. Replay's vice-president of marketing reported that tests of the device among consumers indicated that 'after they've had the unit a while they stop watching live TV'.[11] This new form of time shifting is merely one sign of the ways in which digital technologies, at least in the eyes of many current industry leaders and pundits, are eroding the experience of simultaneity and liveness that has been traditionally seen as both part of television's essential nature and central to its relation to the nation. MIT's Nicholas Negroponte predicted in 1995 that 'digital life will include very little real-time broadcast. . . . With the possible exception of sports and elections, technology suggests that TV and radio of the future will be delivered asynchronously.'[12] In the same year, Microsoft CEO Bill Gates nostalgically described the communal aspects of the traditional live national television broadcast as

10 Bill Carter, 'Aiming a Little Persuasion at Makers of TV Recorders', *New York Times* (16 Aug. 1999), C5. The diverse corporate investors in Replay and TiVo also include Sony, Philips, DirecTV, America Online, and NBC; individual investors include Paul Allen (co-founder of Microsoft and America's third wealthiest individual), and Netscape founder Marc Andreesen. Emphasizing the ambiguous status of the new device within the television industry was Replay's September 1999 selection of Kim LeMasters, a former chief programmer for CBS, as the company's chairman and chief executive officer. See Bill Carter, 'Replay Network to Appoint Ex-CBS Programmer as Chief', *New York Times* (16 Sept. 1999), C8.

11 Replay executive Steve Shannon, quoted in 'Here at Last: A Brainy VCR', *Toronto Star* (29 Aug. 1999), n.p.

12 Nicholas Negroponte, *Being Digital* (New York: Alfred A. Knopf, 1995), 168–9.

instrument of national unity: 'When we Americans share national experiences, it is usually because we're witnessing events all at the same time on television—whether it is the *Challenger* blowing up after liftoff, the Super Bowl, an inauguration, coverage of the Gulf War, or the O. J. Simpson car chase. We are "together" at those moments.' However, Gates argued, 'it is human nature to find ways to create synchronous communications into asynchronous forms'.[13] Leaving aside such dubious appeals to human nature or technological will in forecasting the decline of the live nationwide broadcast, it is clear that many observers in the late 1990s expressed growing scepticism about television's role as agent of national identity, a central tenet of the network broadcasting era. Just as the three powerful networks had economic interests in proposing the nationwide live broadcast as television's unique aesthetic and nation-building mission in the 1950s, other sectors of the contemporary media industry have their own commercial motives in proclaiming the end of simultaneity in the late 1990s.

New threats to television advertising

If, as the previous chapter suggested, the prospect of digital delivery and storage of television programming put into crisis the long-standing privileging of the live nationwide broadcast as guarantor of national cohesion, the launch of the digital video recorder also reignited 1950s debates over advertising-supported versus subscription-supported television. The ease with which viewers might skip commercials recorded via the new device led some industry observers to offer doomsday scenarios for commercial television, as declining advertising revenues force networks to bail out of bidding wars with pay-television platforms for the most desirable programming. One Young & Rubicam executive told the *New York Times*: 'I think conventional television, while not quite dead, is going to do a slow death here', and the chairman of Viacom's MTV Networks told the paper: 'I hate to think about Replay and TiVo. We kind of like the world the way it is now.'[14] At the same time, the television networks at the end of 1990s seemed uncertain about how to frame the perceived threat to commercially supported television in the stark ideological terms of their 1950s opposition to pay-television proposals. For Garth Ancier, head of NBC Entertainment, the prospect of the migration of the most popular television programmes from advertiser-supported to pay television brought about by the ad-busting digital video recorder 'is either anti-American or totally American, depending on how you look at it'.[15]

The prospect of large numbers of TV viewers using their digital video recorders to evade television commercials quickly led to predictions that advertisers and broadcasters would respond by creating advertising formats impossible for viewers to escape, including intensive product placement within programmes, on-screen banner advertisements, and programme-length

---

13 Bill Gates, *The Road Ahead* (New York: Penguin, 1995), 66. Microsoft, through its WebTV subsidiary, was developing its own version of the personal video recorder at the time.

14 Bill Carter, 'Will this Machine Change Television?', *New York Times* (5 July 1999), C1.

15 Ibid.

commercials.[16] A spokesperson for Replay Networks told journalists in August 1999: 'We know there will be people who want to skip commercials. The goal for us is to find other ways for companies to deliver their messages.'[17] Robert Tercek, senior vice-president of digital media for the Columbia-TriStar Television Group at Sony Pictures, described the programming logic of Sony's partnership with WebTV and TiVo by invoking mail-order catalogues as programme models:

> There's no reason why TV programs in this new media have to be 30 minutes or an hour long. In fact, there are a lot of reasons why you want to make them shorter. It costs you a lot to keep an audience there. ... J. Crew could be a show—it already is a show, look at the catalog. Or Abercrombie & Fitch. Catalogs already attempt to create a narrative drama to give their products more mystique.[18]

Through such programming 'innovations', at least some commercial broadcasters and advertisers hoped to adapt to even the most alarmist scenarios regarding the effects of the DVR upon television advertisers.

Helping to assuage sponsor and broadcaster fears about audience defection during traditional TV commercials is the ability of the digital video recorder to continuously track users' viewing preferences, offering sponsors and broadcasters the long-sought prospect of delivering specific commercials to individually targeted consumers. General Motors, for example, has partnered with TiVo to allow the replacement of GM's conventional broadcast ad with another commercial already downloaded on the household's DVR, this one more suited to the consumer's specific viewing habits and demographic profile.[19] Such flexibility for advertisers would be achieved at some cost to the digital video recorder user, however. As one industry official told *Electronic Engineering Times*: 'We are beginning to see some system operators setting aside a portion of the HDD [hard disk drive] real estate for revenue-producing applications.' As the trade journal explained, this application was pursued 'rather than leaving the entire storage space under the consumer's control'.[20] In addition to recording actual viewing patterns, the TiVo device prompts viewers to make simple 'thumbs up' or 'thumbs down' responses to programme titles on the weekly programme guide and aggregates and uplinks these preferences for use by advertisers. Despite the rudimentary nature of such viewer data, Jim Barton, TiVo's chief technical officer, argued that 'there's actually not that many different types of people ... They tend to [fall into] socioeconomic buckets.'[21] Barton's remarks suggest that, notwithstanding the current industry upheaval in the face of new digital technologies, many contemporary characterizations of the television

---

16 'Taking the Ads out of Television', *The Economist* (8 May 1999), n.p.

17 'Networks Buy into New Personalized TV Technology', *Calgary Herald* (19 Aug. 1999), F5.

18 Robin Berger, 'The Name of Tercek's Game is Interactive', *Electronic Media* (13 Sept. 1999), 22.

19 'Companies Consider Ways to Target TV Advertising', *Marketing News* (15 Mar. 1999), 11.

20 Junko Yoshida, 'Digital VCRs Packing HDDs Seen as First Front in War to Establish Non-PC Home Networks', *Electronic Engineering Times* (2 Aug. 1999), n.p.

21 Jon Healey, 'New Technology Customizes Television Program Selection to Viewer's Tastes', *San Jose Mercury News* (18 Aug. 1999), n.p.

audience conform with the reductive and instrumental models generated by decades of post-war US marketing and mass communication research.

Competing models of the new TV viewer

More broadly, the opposing reception scenarios conjured up by the digital video recorder—technologically empowered TV viewers rebelliously zapping commercials versus passive and unwitting consumers being sold to advertisers in ever more perfectly commodified form—suggest the extent to which contemporary digital technologies can evoke wildly differing fantasies of domestic television viewing. In this regard, the digital video recorder is merely one case study activated by the long-predicted merging of television set and personal computer, a convergence which activates quite distinct connotations of media use. As John Markoff of the *New York Times* wrote of the digital video recorder, 'the idea is to permit people to use television the way Web surfers now use the Internet', including the construction of customized viewer 'channels' of favourite programmes.[22] *Business Week* saw in the launch of the two competing digital video recorders a 'race to convert television from a one-way affair into an Internet-age interactive medium', and this discursive opposition of interactive Web user and passive TV viewer pervades trade and public discussions of digital television, as we have seen in previous chapters.[23]

In addition to its effects upon traditional television advertising, another source of industry interest in the digital video recorder concerns its potential as an Internet portal, chiefly as a tool for what *Business Week* called 'couch commerce'.[24] As one journalist explained: 'If you like the shirt being worn by Bill Cosby on his sitcom . . . all you'll have to do to purchase it is press a button on your remote and be linked to the site of a major retailer or manufacturer, which already have [*sic*] all your measurements and credit card information.'[25] In August 1999, America Online (AOL), the largest Internet service provider in the USA with 20 million subscribers, announced it had acquired a minority stake in TiVo; AOL president Robert Pittman told the press that 'AOL has always focused on making the online experience a key part of our members' lives. As consumers want to extend that interactive experience to devices beyond the PC, we see TiVo as a great way to help us deliver our hallmark, ease-of-use and convenience, to the television.'[26] At the same time, Internet-access rivals to AOL see Internet-enabled digital video recorders as a way to challenge AOL's dominance of the Internet-access market for the PC by expanding Internet provision beyond the computer desktop.

Such a shift involves the speculative redefinition of the traditional television screen, its location, and the nature of social interaction around it. An executive at the AT&T-owned Excite@Home told the trade journal *Telephony*:

---

22 John Markoff, 'Two Makers Plan Introductions of Digital VCR', *New York Times* (29 Mar. 1999), C13.

23 Janet Rae-Dupree and Richard Siklos, 'Here's the Next "Big Thing" ', *Business Week* (9 Aug. 1999), 38.

24 Ibid.

25 'Here at Last: A Brainy VCR', n.p.

26 'TiVo and America Online Announce Alliance for AOL TV', *Business Wire* (17 Aug. 1999), n.p.

'We expect that a high percentage of consumers will want both TV and PC Internet. . . . The PC experience in the den is typically very task-oriented, whereas the television experience is more driven by convenience.'[27] One industry official noted that the central question about the success of the DVR remained 'how couch potatoes might respond to potentially interactive features'.[28] As the *New York Times* put it: 'some question whether ReplayTV and TiVo, in predicting revolution, are misreading how viewers watch television: as either passive lumps not sure what they want until they notice that it is on, or as reflexive hunters for new, unanticipated viewing alternatives.'[29] This already well-rehearsed rhetoric of empowerment, freedom, and interactivity has marked much of the press coverage of the DVR, frequently explicitly contrasting the active, in-command viewer of new interactive TV with that fabled and disreputable figure of the previous era of network broadcasting, the barely sentient, lump like couch potato. However, at least some journalistic observers have expressed scepticism about the likelihood of the digital video recorder overturning that long-established figuration of the television audience. The new device, according to one journalist, 'allows the couch potato to settle even deeper into the cushions', and an enthusiastic DVR reviewer at *Newsweek* concluded that 'you may never get up off that couch again'.[30]

While it remains to be seen how much appetite US consumers will demonstrate for the time-shifting and interactive capabilities of the digital video recorder, it is clear that the launch of the DVR in 1999 has already challenged some of the long-standing conventional notions of television's purported essence, reception, and social function. Moreover, the ongoing marketing battles over the definition of the television medium and audience have more than merely commercial consequences; such scenarios of media reception become powerful, if largely unexamined, tools with which the public and policy makers alike make sense of a changing media environment. The real historical agency wielded by these representations suggests that media historians have much to learn from a consideration of the ephemera of corporate press release and TV commercial.

---

27 Kelly Carroll and Brian Quinton, 'Gaining Ground on a Giant', *Telephony* (23 Aug. 1999), n.p.

28 Jim Porter, president of Disk/Trend Inc., quoted in Yoshida, 'Digital VCRs Packing HDDs', n.p.

29 Carter, 'Will this Machine Change Television?', C1.

30 Ernest Holsendolph, 'Play it Again; or, Maybe, for the First Time', *Atlanta Journal and Constitution* (22 Aug. 1999), 1; N'Gai Croal, '(Re)play that Funky Television Show', *Newsweek* (3 May 1999), 67.

8

Marketers Strike Back: Virtual Advertising

BY THE END of the 1990s, the possible effects upon traditional television practices and programme forms brought about by the move to digital broadcasting and the introduction of the digital video recorder were hotly contested within the industry. The distinct capabilities of digital processing of the television signal—high definition, channel proliferation, and interactive services—together with the time-shifting and ad-zapping abilities of the digital video recorder, caused many to question whether advertisers would be able to reach increasingly fragmented and recalcitrant viewers armed with new devices to avoid conventional TV commercials. At the end of 1999, the nascent practice of virtual advertising—the ability to map imported video material seamlessly into the illusionistic space of live action—was seen by many within the TV industry as a timely technological counter-weapon to the domestic television viewer newly armed with anti-commercial digital defences.

Both the digital video recorder and the technologies of virtual advertising operate by intercepting the digital flow of television images, allowing real-time image processing at any stage, from a camera feed to the consumer's set-top box. One advertising executive argued that virtual advertising 'begins to highlight that a lot of people in the future will be able to touch content—and change it'.[1] Another industry figure called virtual advertising 'one of the first little gremlins to come out of the box of digitalization'.[2] A New York advertising executive told the *New York Times* in October 1999: 'If the digital future in some cases precludes commercials', as wealthier viewers—'the most valuable consumers'—buy digital video recorders to delete them from programmes, 'virtual advertising might work just fine in order to reach them'.[3] London's *Daily Telegraph* sternly warned the industry in December 1999: 'One thing's for sure, advertisers need to get it right—and quickly. The advent of digital television may soon allow viewers to skip the traditional commercial break altogether. And there's a certain irony in the fact that it's also digital technology which could enable advertisers to put their messages across in new and ever more invidious ways.'[4] In January 2000, the British magazine *The Economist* likewise argued that diffusion of the digital video

---

1 Stuart Elliott, 'Real or Virtual? You Call It: Digital Sleight of Hand Can Put Ads Almost Anywhere', *New York Times* (1 Oct. 1999), n.p.

2 Alec Gerster, chairman at Mediacom in New York, the media buying unit of Grey Advertising, quoted ibid.

3 Steve Saldano, partner and media services director at the Deutsch Inc., quoted ibid.

4 Jim Davies, 'Connected: Advertising Conjuring Ads out of Thin Air', *Daily Telegraph* (11 Dec. 1999), 6.

recorder would encourage broadcasters to take up virtual advertising.[5] As one US advertising executive told the *New York Times*: 'Heaven knows, in an era of fractionalization and remote controls, television can use all the help it can get.'[6]

Given industry concern at the end of the 1990s over the digital video recorder's threat to traditional advertising practices, the prospect of virtual advertising 'rendering the remote control useless' was clearly appealing.[7] The website of one of the major virtual advertising providers, SciDel USA, argued that 'commercials lose much of their effectiveness due to viewers' ability to do other things during the commercial breaks, whether they are switching to other stations or engaging in other short-term activities such as bathroom breaks'.[8] A June 1999 SciDel press release boasted that 'because messages appear during action, on the "field of play" when viewers are focused on programs of choice the SciDel system is zap-proof'.[9] Princeton Video Images (PVI), the most prominent firm in the US virtual advertising industry, laid out the technology's rationale on its investor relations website:

> Smart marketers love television because it generates such intensity with viewers. With conventional commercial breaks, advertisers are close to such magic moments as a home run blast or a stunning goal. With PVI technology, however, the message becomes part of the excitement itself. That's the core of our business. And that's also PVI's growth strategy: Be a part of the excitement—and a part of the new revenue that virtual advertising will generate by providing a complete range of virtual advertising services to the smart marketers who want to get right into those events.[10]

As well as placing the virtual ad directly in the frame of action, the technique is typically used at precise moments of peak audience attention, as the baseball crosses the plate or the football spins toward the goal posts.

The virtual advertising industry

Princeton Video Images, the dominant player in the early virtual advertising industry in the USA, supplies the proprietary L-VIS (Live Video Insertion System) hardware and software it acquired in 1995 for use in sporting venues, television newsrooms, and Hollywood syndication companies in exchange for 20–50 per cent of the resulting virtual advertising revenues.[11] The company provides three distinct services: so-called 'sports enhancements' in

5 'Virtual Advertising', *The Economist* (15 Jan. 2000), n.p.

6 Stuart Elliott, 'A Video Process Allows the Insertion of Brand-Name Products in TV Shows Already on Film', *New York Times* (29 Mar. 1999), C11.

7 Josh Rolnick, 'Virtual Billboards are Becoming a Reality at Sporting Events', Associated Press State & Local Wire (2 Aug. 1998), n.p.

8 www.scidel.com/who.htm.

9 'SciDel Presents a Whole New Ballgame in Sports Advertising and Sponsorship', *PR Newswire* (21 June 1999), n.p.

10 www.pvi-inc.com/investor/index.html; for Princeton Video Images' announcement of its acquisition of SciDel, see www.pvi-inc.com/news/currentb.html.

11 Terry Conway, 'Computer-Generated Ads are Marching into the Wide World of Sport', *Philadelphia Business Journal* (30 Apr.–6 May 1999), 26.

the form of virtual finish lines at horse races and first-down markers in football games, virtual billboards at live sporting and news events, and 'virtual product placements' inserted into entertainment programming. The image-recognition and adaptive occlusion processing technologies enabling virtual advertising have their roots in 'military technology designed to pick out missiles from their surroundings and track and destroy them', according to London's *Financial Times*.[12] Two of the four global firms providing virtual advertising services are partly owned by Israeli defence contractors, and Princeton Video Images' proprietary technology is licensed from the Sarnoff Center, formerly owned by RCA.[13] According to its website, 'PVI employed Sarnoff to develop the first L-VIS prototype and has licenses to all the appropriate Sarnoff intellectual property'.[14] Press accounts place PVI's origins in CEO Brown Williams's experiments 'in his New Jersey garage in 1990'; originally known as Princeton Electrical Billboard, PVI was initially underwritten by private investors in 1993, later joined by institutional investors before a public stock offering in December 1997; by April 1999 Williams claimed an accumulated $60 million expenditure in technology and business development.[15] According to PVI's management, 1998 was a pivotal year, marking a strategic shift from a technology company to a marketing company, the introduction of a new generation of the L-VIS which enabled the insertion of moving as well as static images, and expansion into domestic and international markets with licensing agreements with partners in Latin America and South Africa.[16]

PVI began its sports-related virtual advertising activities in June 1995, with an agreement with Comcast Cablevision of New Jersey to use the technology during a Trenton Thunder minor league baseball game.[17] The company signed deals with major league baseball's San Francisco Giants in 1995 (the team was first to use the L-VIS system in part because it did not control the signage revenues in Candlestick Park) and with the San Diego Padres and Philadelphia Phillies in 1996. In baseball, the virtual ads are typically sold in half-inning units and placed behind the plate, within the centre-field camera shot which constitutes one and a quarter hours of the average nine-inning broadcast.[18] Via a partly owned Mexican licensee, Publicidad Virtual, formed in 1993, Princeton Video Images created virtual ads for toothpaste and potato chips in the centre circle of a Mexican soccer field and was 'paid $130,000 for a package of two soccer games and a bullfight'.[19] Publicidad Virtual has also been active in creating virtual product placements in several *telenovelas* produced by the Mexican TV network Televisa, involving several

12 Norma Cohen, 'Giants Score on TV Ads', *Financial Times* (18 June 1996), T11.

13 Davies, 'Conjuring Ads out of Thin Air', n.p.

14 www.pvi-inc.com/investor/index.html.

15 Conway, 'Computer-Generated Ads are Marching into the Wide World of Sport', 26.

16 'Princeton Video Image, Inc. Announces Fiscal 1998 Third Quarter Results', *Business Wire*, 14 May 1998; 'Princeton Video Image, Inc. Announces Fiscal 1998 Fourth Quarter and Year-End Results', *Business Wire*, 2 Sept. 1998.

17 Chad Rubel, 'What you See on TV is not What you Get at Stadium', *Marketing News* (6 May 1996), 2.

18 Ibid.

19 Ibid.

Colgate-Palmolive products, and for Carter Wallace's Nair depilatory cream.[20] Princeton Video Images began its US colleqe football activity in winter 1996 with ABC's telecast of the Sugar Bowl and ESPN's coverage of the Holiday and Peach Bowls.[21] PVI signed deals with ESPN in 1997 for arena-league football and in 1998 with CBS for virtual first-down markers for regular-season NFL games, after two years of experiments during pre-season games.[22] In January 1999, PVI acquired virtual advertising rights for the Super Bowl for viewers in Mexico, Japan, Germany, and the United Kingdom, including an agreement with Canadian broadcaster Can West to insert virtual moving spectator cards advertising Coke seen by 3 million Canadian viewers.[23] The 1999 Super Bowl also marked the first time that PVI's L-VIS system was used by a broadcast network to create original pro-gramming—the introduction of the Super Bowl team line-ups—for a US audience as well as providing virtual advertising insertions for Canadian and Mexican broadcasters.[24] In November 1999, PVI signed a multi-year deal with CBS to employ the E-VIS system on a regular basis for the relaunch of CBS's morning news programme, *The Morning Show*. The technology was also used in the New Year's Eve-related broadcasts of *CBS Evening News* and *48 Hours*. By the beginning of 2000, PVI could point to its involvement in over 1,200 sporting, entertainment, and news broadcasts around the world.

The emerging business model of virtual advertising has a characteristically postmodern relation to traditional broadcast construction of the nation, allowing multinational capital to operate more efficiently and flexibly on both global and local levels. Indeed, the worldwide practice of virtual advert-ising began with European sport broadcasts, especially involving soccer, where the lack of commercial breaks during matches had long encouraged advertisers to place billboards on stadium walls and logos on players' uniforms. One industry executive predicted as early as January 1997 that 'different markets will have different levels of receptivity. In Europe, where corporate sponsors have been on jerseys for years, it will be much more read-ily accepted.'[25] In December 2000, *Sports Marketing* recalled that 'virtual's relationship with football began as a cloak-and-dagger affair. In the UK there were reports of behind-the-scenes tests by rights owners, generally followed by silence, fueling rumors of problems with the technology.'[26] Also making European football especially well suited to virtual advertising was its audience and advertising appeal across borders, allowing multinational advertisers to tailor messages to specific national markets viewing the same live event; as *Sports Marketing* explained: 'The big, big pay-off was that

20 Sinclair Stewart, 'Virtual Ads Hold Big Promise', *Strategy* (1 Feb. 1999), 1; Robin Berger, 'Digital Technology Virtually Blurs Reality', *Electronic Media* (5 Apr. 1999), 14.

21 Jack Craig, 'A Virtual Slew of Advertising Opportunities', *Boston Globe* (10 May 1996), 98.

22 'CBS and Princeton Video Image Sign Deal for NFL Telecasts', *Business Wire* (10 Nov. 1998), n.p.

23 'Global Hopes to Score with Virtual Ads', *Globe and Mail* (23 Jan. 1999), B1. The virtual ads inserted by PVI in the 28 Jan. 2001 Super Bowl were seen by an estimated 700 million viewers in 200 nations; see 'SuperBowl Viewers to Get a Taste of Virtual Advertising', *Sports Marketing* (16 Jan. 2001), 1.

24 'Fox TV Uses Princeton Video Image System for Super Bowl to Create Spectacular Player Introductory Sequence', *Business Wire* (2 Feb. 1999), n.p.

25 Terry Lefton, 'The New Sign Age', *Brandweek* (27 Jan. 1997), 35.

26 'Grim Reality for Virtual Advertising', *Sports Marketing* (Mar. 2000), 12.

virtual technology allowed rights owners, for the first time, to carve up their international TV footprints and sell multiple narrowcasted ad packages worldwide.'[27] Reacting to the decision of a subcommittee of the international soccer federation to lift its outright ban on virtual advertising in April 1999, PVI CEO Dennis Wilkinson wrote: 'Worldwide soccer is an especially good market for virtual advertising, as so many games are shown in countries other than the country in which the game is actually played. Now advertising can be placed in the game for each country into which the game is transmitted. This is especially important in Europe and Latin America.'[28]

Concomitant with the global reach of virtual advertising in European football broadcasts, however, is its potential for running afoul of the unsettled and competing national, league, team, and stadium policies regarding broadcast advertising. In fact, British audiences had their first glimpse of virtual advertising in 1998 only inadvertently, when the BBC unwittingly took a feed from French TV featuring an indelible virtual ad in the centre circle.[29] In January 2000, FIFA, the international football federation, after two years of study, adopted formal restrictions on the use of virtual advertising, including prohibiting its use on the figures of players or spectators themselves and on the surface of the field when players are present.[30] The FIFA regulations also prohibit the use of virtual advertising 'without the express permission of all parties involved, notably the match organisers, rights-holders, host broadcasters and advertisers', according to *Sports Marketing*.[31]

The formation in 1999 of the Virtual Imaging Alliance (VIA), headquartered in Brussels, reflected the consolidation of efforts by the five major international virtual advertising firms to lobby for minimal and consistent regulation of virtual advertising across Europe and beyond.[32] The European debates over virtual advertising moved beyond the specific case of football to take up the fundamental distinctions between programme and commercial. The European Commission's regulatory principles, initiated in its 1989 Television Without Frontiers Directive, set strict limits on the number of advertising minutes per hour and per broadcast day. Furthermore, a spring 2000 European Commission document, 'Principles for Regulation of the Audiovisual Sector in the Digital Age', reaffirmed the Commission's determination 'to ensure that basic principles such as the prohibition of surreptitious advertising and the need for a clear separation between advertising and other material continue to apply'.[33] After quoting the European Commission

---

27 'Grim Reality for Virtual Advertising', *Sports Marketing* (Mar. 2000), 12; the then-CEO of PVI explained to a journalist in 1996 that 'the system is geared primarily for large global advertisers. Instead of buying 30-second spots throughout the world, the advertiser can buy the signage at one source and reach as many countries as needed.' Quoted in Rubel, 'What you See on TV is not What you Get at Stadium', 2.

28 'Princeton Video Image Endorses FIFA Subcommittee Recommendation to Allow Virtual Advertising during Televised Soccer Games', *Business Wire* (7 Apr. 1999), n.p.

29 'Grim Reality for Virtual Advertising', 12.

30 The English version of the FIFA regulations can be found at: **www.fifa2.com/fifa/handbook/Va/downloads/VirtualRegs_e.pdf**.

31 'Grim Reality for Virtual Advertising', 12.

32 The Virtual Imaging Alliance website can be found at **www.virtualimaging.org**.

33 Quoted in Paul Schuchhard, 'Brussels Update', June 2000, found at **www.virtualimaging.org** and reprinted in *Sports Marketing* (July 2000), n.p.

document, VIA spokesperson and lobbyist Paul Schuchhard wrote that 'this last sentence worries me very much because it shows old media thinking in a new media world. . . . I believe that it will be extremely difficult in the future to keep commercial communications in general separate from the programming.'[34] The clear conflict between the regulation of traditional television commercials which interrupt a programme and of virtual advertising messages within programmes themselves could hardly be more stark, and the result has been a patchwork of national regulations and unresolved European-wide policy.

The prospect of the widescale adoption of virtual advertising has particular implications for debates within the UK about broadcasting's role in constructing national identity within an ethos of public service broadcasting. For some observers, virtual advertising would be especially appealing to the BBC, which is prohibited from selling conventional advertising, in maintaining its ability to bid successfully for major sporting events. Noting the BBC's loss of major cricket test matches and football highlight programming to commercial broadcasters, the *Financial Times* argued in August 2000 that virtual advertisements 'embedded in the sports event would be the only advertising on the BBC and more attractive to potential advertisers'. Moreover, the author noted, 'The advertiser would pay the rights holder who would discount the fee charged to the BBC, neatly side-stepping' the prohibitions against direct advertising revenues. 'It may not be the pure, uncommercialised sports coverage the BBC or its viewers would be used to, but represents a possible solution to the flow of sports events away from the BBC to pay-TV channels,' the writer concluded.[35] While the BBC's use of virtual imaging has so far been limited to unbranded sports enhancements, the special appeal of virtual advertising for public service broadcasters otherwise proscribed from the broadcast advertising market raises questions about the political rationale and economic model of public service broadcasting. In the meantime, foreign audiences for UK Premiership football matches have already been treated to electronically inserted virtual stadium billboards announcing the British Tourist Authority's VisitBritain.com website.

Other observers of virtual advertising in the UK have imagined the day when the technology of virtual imaging joins those of video streaming and interactive television to tailor broadcast commercials to individual households: 'In five years time two *Coronation Street* fans sitting next to one another watching the same episode but on different PC's could quite literally see a totally different set of advertisements—geared totally towards their own individual tastes and preferences. With the consumer targeted, the virtual adverts then allow the user to click onto the brand logo to obtain more information about the product or make a purchase.'[36] This vision of television as a PC-based, individually tailored, point-of-sale device is far from the traditional construction of the television set as the binding point of an imagined national community.

---

34 Ibid.

35 Matthew Garrahan, 'Broadcasting Watchdogs and Sports Rights' Holders Keep a Wary Eye on Virtual On-screen Advertising', *Financial Times* (2 Aug. 2000), 4.

36 'If Audience Fragmentation is the Problem are Virtual Ads the Answer?', *New TV Strategies* (21 Dec. 2000), 8.

Virtual product placement

Like World Cup football, the *telenovelas* produced by the Mexican TV network Televisa represent programming with a diverse international audience and the use of PVI's E-VIS system for product placement within these popular soap operas follows the same global/local marketing logic of European sports broadcasting. The head of PVI's Mexican partner, Publicidad Virtual, told *Electronic Media*: 'Televisa sells to 136 countries. They don't want to give that message to any potential advertiser for free.'[37] The firm's chief technical officer boasted that 'with our system, we can do a 30-second insertion in about 10 minutes', and in 1999 Televisa charged advertisers $4,500 to $6,000 for three product insertions in a single episode, each lasting about 10 seconds.[38]

Beyond its use in *telenovelas*, the use of virtual advertising and product placement to tailor multinational advertising campaigns within a single television event or programme seems as compelling for the huge and ever-growing inventory of US prime-time entertainment shows available for international syndication as for the Super Bowl or the World Cup. Just as US sports broadcasters looked to the additional revenues that virtual advertising offered to redress flat viewership levels and rapidly escalating programme fees, in the late 1990s Hollywood production companies explored virtual product placement to alleviate a similar squeeze between rising production costs and static network licensing fees as audiences and advertising revenues were dispersed across an increasingly multi-channel universe.[39] *The Economist* in January 2000 argued that 'the big challenge for the nascent virtual advertising industry is to persuade television networks to allow the inclusion of virtual advertising in such programmes as soap operas and comedy shows', and PVI's Wilkinson was reportedly making the rounds to the major networks and production houses to sign up virtual product placement deals for both current network shows and off-network syndicated programming.[40] In February 1999, PVI's chief financial officer outlined the familiar global/local marketing logic of virtual product placement in exporting US telefilm:

> It creates a new revenue stream for syndicators. We now have the ability to insert a cereal box or a drink on a kitchen counter after a show has already been taped. And because it's being done for syndication, it could be a Coke in the US, a Labatt's in Canada, and a British beer in the UK—it can all be targeted by market.[41]

Just as baseball's virtual ads change each half-inning and the Super Bowl's live digital field might contain different corporate logos for each nation

---

37 'Digital Technology Virtually Blurs Reality', 14. In September 2001 PVI announced the acquisition of Publicidad Virtual; see PVI's press release of 20 Sept. 2000 at www.pvi-inc.com/news/currentb.html.

38 Ibid.

39 Stephen Battaglio, ' "Virtual" Product Placing Gets Real in UPN Debut', *Hollywood Reporter* (25 Mar. 1999), 26.

40 'Virtual Advertising', *The Economist*, n.p.; Battaglio, '"Virtual" Product Placing Gets Real in UPN Debut', 26.

41 Stewart, 'Virtual Ads Hold Big Promise', 1.

receiving the broadcast, the virtual products placed inside a syndicated TV episode could be adapted to each TV market or air date. PVI's Wilkinson argued that while 'it's clearly fair to say the sports applications have caught on faster than the entertainment applications, the opportunity to place advertisements where without a doubt they have to be noticed' would eventually lead to the adoption of virtual advertising in network and syndicated entertainment programming as well. 'As long as it's done in good taste, as if it's part of the program and doesn't stick out like a sore thumb people will accept it, embrace it, because it will pay for the shows,' he told the *New York Times*.[42]

The immediate reaction from the advertising industry to the possibilities of virtual advertising has been ambivalent. While some within the TV industry expressed concern about the implications of virtual advertising for advertising clutter, creative integrity, contractual rights, and viewer backlash, the economic logic of virtual product placement in the face of shrinking audience shares and ever more elusive viewers of conventional TV commercials struck many as inescapable. 'You are seeing the first glimpse of the future of advertising', one advertising executive told the *New York Times* in October 1999, 'where the product and the program are integrated in a fashion that's more seamless than we ever could have imagined.'[43] However, in January 1997 *Brandweek* noted that 'adding more messages to an already-cluttered environment has raised the eyebrows of some of the industry's most influential marketers', and many industry leaders expressed reservations about the widespread adoption of virtual advertising in sports and entertainment programming.[44] The previous president and CEO of PVI admitted to a journalist in 1997 that 'this technology can be intrusive if not used properly', and a New York ad exec told the *New York Times* in 1999: 'I'm big on exploitation, but not to the point where it's self-defeating. [Virtual product placement is] just another way to clutter up the screen and distract people from the programming. . . . The quality of the viewing experience is something we glom onto. It's not good for us if the people who want to watch the programs are alienated.'[45] An executive at a Chicago advertising firm told the paper, 'I would just hope the networks will be very careful with this and don't allow it to become a runaway train.'[46] Meanwhile, National Basketball Association Commissioner David Stern told a journalist, 'I don't see it necessarily as something that will kill the goose that laid the golden egg, but it has the capacity to,' and a vice-president of Anheuser-Busch beer company, a major television sports sponsor, warned that virtual signage 'will be the downfall of TV sports if not managed well'.[47]

42 Ibid.

43 Elliott, 'Real or Virtual? You Call It', n.p. Specific problems of verisimilitude may attend the placing of virtual advertising for contemporary products within older syndicated shows; PVI's L-VIS was used to insert virtual product placement in the 1960s *Bewitched* TV series for syndication in Mexico.

44 Lefton, 'The New Sign Age', n.p.

45 Michael Burgi, 'TV Exec Sees Virtual Signs', *Media Week* (10 Feb. 1997), 13; Elliott, 'A Video Process Allows the Insertion of Brand-Name Products', n.p.; Lefton, 'The New Sign Age', n.p.

46 Elliott, 'A Video Process Allows the Insertion of Brand-Name Products', n.p.

47 Lefton, 'The New Sign Age', n.p.

The ambivalence with which some in the advertising industry have greeted the prospect of virtual advertising involves a normative quasi-aesthetic debate about the tactics of virtual imaging: should the practice be self-effacing, used only to mimic the appearance and spatial logic of actual signage and products, or should advertisers use the technology to arrange and animate virtual images in a patently non-naturalistic manner? One ad executive quoted in the *New York Times* described his misgivings about virtual advertising: 'I'm not in love with the idea', he said, because on the one hand 'it runs the risk of being obtrusive', and, on the other hand, if the virtual image is 'there for only a couple of seconds so it doesn't smack viewers in the face, the question is whether the advertiser has gotten any real value'.[48] Another industry executive warned that 'if it becomes distracting . . . it could result in the twin banes of every advertiser—clutter and viewer annoyance'.[49]

This tension between self-effacement and foregrounding is also reflected in press statements by leaders of virtual advertising technology firms. For example, while Princeton Video Images CEO Dennis Wilkinson told the *Hollywood Reporter* in March 1999 that 'everyone we talk to wants it done discreetly. They want it to blend into the overall fabric of the show, and we can do that', a few months earlier another PVI executive told the *Los Angeles Times*: 'The ads need to be noticed. . . . We want to use it in a place where you would never put a sign—that's the way to use it. . . . We want people to know the images were put there virtually.'[50] Similarly, while an executive at PVI's Israeli-based competitor Orad Hi-Tech Systems told the press that if a virtual ad is designed correctly, 'the viewer shouldn't even know it's virtual',[51] the actual practices by PVI and others in the industry have frequently contradicted this self-effacing aesthetic. Examples include virtually inserted exploding virtual fireworks behind the plate in Philadelphia Phillies baseball games, US Army jets zooming out of goalposts during Fox's Super Bowl team line-up announcements, and winking Gerber babies and exploding food tins in the centre circle of European and Latin American football games. The most notorious example of the anti-self-effacing aesthetic was cited by London's *Daily Telegraph*, describing a Greek football broadcast which 'showed the players running around, and occasionally through, giant deodorant cans, which appeared to be magically squirting their contents into the enthusiastic—but unaccountably dry—crowd'.[52] One advertising executive saw a generational split among viewers regarding the self-effacing versus foregrounding debate: 'People who have grown up with digital editing

48 Elliott, 'A Video Process Allows the Insertion of Brand-Name Products', n.p.

49 Stewart, 'Virtual Ads Hold Big Promise', 1.

50 Battaglio, ' "Virtual" Product Placing Gets Real in UPN Debut'; Mo Krochmal, 'Company Cashes in on Computer-Generated Ads', *TechWeb News* (25 Jan. 1999). Later the same year, PVI CEO Wilkinson told a reporter: 'It has to be done in a seamless way that doesn't impact on the integrity of the show. But I think the consumer will accept it,' quoted in Richard Natale, 'The Surreal Thing', *Los Angeles Times* (Sept. 1999), n.p.

51 Josh Rolnick, 'Here's One Pitch the Stadium Crowd Never Sees', *Seattle Times* (6 Mar. 1998), n.p.

52 The baseball example is discussed in William Power, 'The Virtual Ad: On TV You See It, at Games You Don't', *Wall Street Journal* (30 July 1998), n.p.; Davies, 'Conjuring Ads out of Thin Air', 6. For more information on the virtual imaging firm responsible for the Greek football broadcast, see www.symah-vision.fr/vhtml/epsis.html.

in movies are less bothered than a generation who might complain, "Hey, they're messing with my reality." ' The sanguine executive told the *New York Times*: 'If you say to the viewer, "This detracts from the integrity of advertising," . . . the viewer is going to say "Excuse me, there's integrity in advertising?" ' [53]

If the prospect of unrestrained virtual advertising has provoked measured reservations within the television industry, the reaction of some observers outside the industry was one of undisguised horror. The leader of one US public interest group described virtual advertising as 'yet another incursion into the public life by marketers who are dreaming up every possible way to sneak into our consciousness'.[54] The *Washington Post* quoted a University of California communication professor who denounced virtual advertising as 'another way for advertisers to make the programs subservient to their needs . . . part of a trend in which the advertiser, more and more, shapes the entertainment and information content of this society'.[55] *New York Times* advertising columnist Stuart Elliott, describing virtual advertising as 'a sign of the never-ending efforts of marketers to blanket consumers in a continuous fog of sponsored pitches', quoted Gary Ruskin, director of Commercial Alert, an organization founded by consumer advocate Ralph Nader, who argued that 'people are being bombarded with ever-craftier ways of getting them to desire products. It's another good reason they ought to be giving up their TV sets.'[56]

Meanwhile, the ambivalence within the television production community toward virtual product placement was succinctly expressed by CBS president and CEO Leslie Moonves in the *Hollywood Reporter*: 'As a creative person I hate it. As a business person, it's interesting.'[57] Although the major networks have not employed virtual product placement in entertainment programming, Viacom's UPN made a 1999 demonstration deal with PVI to insert five virtual products (a Wells Fargo Bank sign, Kenneth Cole shopping bags, a Blockbuster videotape, and bottles of Coca-Cola and Evian) into an episode of its science fiction series *Seven Days*. Described by Viacom as a 'trial balloon', the experiment moved the *New York Times*' Stuart Elliott to suggest that the broadcast 'may give American consumers a preview of a future where their efforts to avoid advertising by switching channels or muting the sound when commercials come on are thwarted by marketers using sophisticated technological tactics'.[58] In May 1999 Warner Bros.' syndication division, which controlled 20 per cent of the domestic syndication market, announced a demonstration deal with PVI to create virtual product placements in several of its most popular situation comedies, including

53 Ellen Oppenheim, media director at the New York office of FCB Worldwide, quoted in Elliott, 'Real or Virtual? You Call It', n.p.

54 Michael Jacobson, executive director of the Center for Science in the Public Interest, quoted in Elliott, 'A Video Process Allows the Insertion of Brand-Name Products', n.p.

55 Dale Kunkel, communications professor at the University of California—Santa Barbara, quoted in Paul Farhi, 'Finding Versatility in the "Virtual" Ad; Sports Broadcasters, Advertisers Warm up to Billboards That Aren't Really There', *Washington Post* (18 Aug. 1998), C1.

56 Elliott, 'Real or Virtual? You Call It', n.p.

57 Battaglio, ' "Virtual" Product Placing Gets Real in UPN Debut', 26.

58 Elliott, 'A Video Process Allows the Insertion of Brand-Name Products', C11.

Friends and *The Drew Carey Show.*[59] London's *Dally Telegraph* quoted PVI's Wilkinson in December 1999: 'Digital product placement is a real sleeper, potentially it's huge business.'[60] A spokesman for Fox Television told the *New York Times* in October 1999: 'at the moment it's not allowed, because we're purists. But we do not rule out all future applications. We're not Luddites.'[61] The *New York Times* quoted *TV Guide* editor Steven Reddicliffe about the prospects for virtual product placement: 'There's a good chance it will come, and faster than we imagine.'[62]

While of clear appeal to multinational advertisers and programme syndicators in the global market, virtual advertising also appealed to advertisers too small or too local for the traditional television advertising market. The general manager of the cable company that debuted PVI's E-VIS system in a 1995 minor-league baseball game told a journalist that a local cable operator 'could sell the real estate to smaller advertisers, which may not have well-produced commercials, but which may possess snappy logos'.[63] Virtual signage in sporting events allows the same screen space to be sold simultaneously to multiple regional sponsors, a practice that PVI's former CEO analogized with the placing of local print ads in national magazines and local spots on cable TV networks.[64]

The possible scope of virtual advertising localization, however, goes beyond such traditional advertising practices of whatever scale. In 2000, the Princeton Video Images website claimed that its US and European patent umbrella 'covers any image insertion into video that uses pattern recognition as part of the process. This includes its use on all video distribution mechanisms, including the Internet.'[65] PVI CEO Dennis Wilkinson told investors in November 1999: 'The initial reaction to our product development for the Internet and interactive television has also been enthusiastic. We believe that although these emerging markets will take time to develop, they represent significant new potential revenue streams.'[66] Announcing the award of a new US patent in October 1999, a PVI press release pointed to the appeal of the technology in targeting audiences in more discriminating ways:

> On conventional broadcast TV narrow-casting allows advertisers to target different geographic areas with tailored messages embedded as part of the program in each market. Used on broadband Internet video transmission, PVI's adaptive occlusion technology will allow demographic targeting by URL.[67]

59 Chuck Ross, 'Warner Bros. to Test "Virtual" Ad Concept', *Advertising Age* (17 May 1999), 1, 64.

60 Davies, 'Conjuring Ads out of Thin Air', n.p.

61 Elliott, 'Real or Virtual? You Call It', n.p.

62 Ibid.

63 Linda Haugsted, 'Advertisers Eye, Try Virtual Billboards', *Multichannel News* (14 Apr. 1997), 36A.

64 Rubel, 'What you See on TV is not What you Get at Stadium', 2.

65 www.pvi-inc.com/investor/index.html.

66 'Princeton Video Image, Inc. Announces Increased Fiscal 2000 First Quarter Revenues', *Business Wire* (5 Nov. 1999), n.p.

67 'Princeton Video Image Inc. Granted New US Patent; New Patent Protects PVI's Adaptive Occlusion Processing Technology', *Business Wire* (14 Oct. 1999), n.p.

Its technology, according to the company, 'allows PVI to insert advertisements or program enhancements from remote locations. Using this technique, individually tailored inserts can be done in a set top box in the home.'[68] The goal is to integrate PVI's virtual advertising technology into interactive television applications, whether PC based or delivered to a conventional television set via a set-top box. In announcing their fourth-quarter 1999 earnings, PVI boasted that the company was 'developing what could be one of its most exciting new products—virtual images that are interactive. This product, designed for the Internet and ultimately, interactive television, is based on PVI's patented, proprietary technology and will offer advertisers revolutionary new ways to reach viewers, whether they are watching television broadcasts or streaming video.'[69] Given the diverse possible applications of virtual imaging, it is easy to envision a combination of virtual advertising and the digital video recorder which would allow the remote insertion of a virtual ad tailored to the demographics and viewing habits of a specific household. Thus, the digital video recorder, initially both feared and praised for offering viewers the technological means of evading conventional television advertisements, may become the technological enabler of a more pervasive and individuated delivery system for commercial messages to the home.

Virtual advertising in the news

Despite the extensive discussions of the present and prospective applications of virtual advertising in the late 1990s trade press, many Americans were unlikely to have heard of the technology until it landed on the front page of the *New York Times* in January 2000 under the headline 'On CBS News, Some of What You See Isn't There'.[70] The article reported on some of the on-air results of a November 1999 deal between Princeton Video Images and the CBS network to expand the use of virtual imaging beyond the virtual first-down marker in NFL football games. In November 1999 CBS News began using PVI's L-VIS system on a nearly daily basis on *The Early Show*, placing a virtual CBS logo on the pavement of New York's Fifth Avenue, the back of Central Park horse-drawn carriages, a window of the adjacent Bergdorf Goodman department store, and the fountain in front of the Plaza Hotel. The network's deal with PVI was part of its efforts to raise the ratings of the $30 million CBS morning news programme, which was number three in the ratings, and Princeton Video Images' press release announcing the CBS deal quoted the news programme's executive producer: 'PVI's virtual imaging technology allows us to extend our brand beyond traditional borders. Our new neighborhood in mid-town Manhattan gives us countless opportunities to do so.'[71] 'We were looking for some way to brand the neighborhood with

68 'Princeton Video Image is Granted New European Patent for Remote Insertion of Virtual Images', *Business Wire* (27 Oct. 1999), n.p.

69 'Princeton Video Image, Inc. Announces Record Fiscal 1999 Fourth Quarter and Year-End Revenues', *Business Wire* (10 Sept. 1999), n.p.

70 Alex Kuczynski, 'On CBS News, Some of What You See Isn't There', *New York Times* (12 Jan. 2000), A1.

71 'CBS News and Princeton Video Image Announce a Multi Year Deal for Insertion of Virtual Images in CBS' the Early Show', *Business Wire* (3 Nov. 1999), n.p.

the CBS logo', the show's executive producer told the *New York Times* in January 2000, 'It's a great way to do things without ruining the neighborhood. Every day we have a different way of using it, whether it's logos or outlines. And we haven't even scratched the surface of its uses yet.'[72]

Notwithstanding CBS's routine use of the Princeton Video Images equipment to digitally insert its advertising logo unannounced upon the New York City landscape during its morning news programme, what caught the attention of the press was CBS's use of the L-VIS in news broadcasts around the New Year's Eve celebrations in New York's Times Square at the end of 1999. During the *CBS Evening News* with Dan Rather on 30 and 31 December, as well as the New Year's-themed *48 Hours* episode of 30 December also hosted by Rather, CBS used the PVI technology to obliterate two existing Times Square billboards—for Budweiser beer and for the NBC television network—with its own advertising logo, without alerting viewers to the practice.

Journalistic and public reaction to CBS's use of virtual imaging in its Times Square New Year's Eve news broadcasts was emphatic. As the London *Times* reported a few weeks later: 'The fact that the once revered news division of the so-called "Tiffany Network" would resort to such illusionism provoked a rumpus in New York media circles.'[73] Britain's *Guardian* newspaper quoted veteran CBS anchorman Walter Cronkite: 'It's flat-out dishonest. CBS and the rest of the broadcasters must pledge to refrain from the use of the technique in any manner.'[74] Dan Rather himself, after originally declining to comment on the affair, told the *New York Times* the following day that the virtual Times Square billboard was 'a mistake'; 'there is no excuse for it. I did not grasp the possible ethical implications of this and that was wrong on my part. At the very least we should have pointed out to viewers that we were doing it.'[75]

Other CBS personnel, however, were less apologetic about the network's use of virtual imaging in its newscasts. CBS news president Andrew Heyward defended *The Early Show*'s use of virtual branding as 'a whimsical and creative way to display our logo in various and unlikely places'. Defending the use of virtual advertising in the morning news programme, Heyward argued: 'If somebody comes to New York and is surprised that it doesn't say *The Early Show* in the middle of Fifth Avenue, I don't think we've committed a journalism sin. I don't want to apologize for being aggressive in exploiting this.'[76] Heyward allowed that its use in CBS's Times Square New Year's Eve coverage was 'a closer call', but argued that 'on New Year's Eve with confetti in Dan's hair, I saw this as an extension of our graphics, a change in this very festive, in effect, set'.[77] CBS network head Leslie Moonves went further in defence of the virtual billboard which obscured the actual signage of CBS's network competitor, describing a new corporate news policy: 'Anytime there's an NBC

---

72 Kuczynski, 'On CBS News, Some of What You See Isn't There', A1.

73 James Bone, 'Illusion Blacks out CBS Rival', *The Times* (13 Jan. 2000), n.p.

74 Jane Martinson, 'US Row as Network Alters News Pictures', *Guardian* (14 Jan. 2000), 13.

75 Bill Carter, 'CBS is Divided over the Use of False Images in Broadcasts', *New York Times* (13 Jan. 2000), C1.

76 Ibid.

77 Ibid.

logo up on our network we'll block it again.'[78] Indeed, Eric Shapiro, director of the *CBS Evening News*, told *Broadcasting and Cable* a few days before the New Year's Eve telecast that L-VIS 'has other applications [besides branding] that I think are very valid and lend themselves perfectly to news, such as obscuring things you don't want in the frame', including, he told the magazine, blocking a competitor's logo or signage.[79]

If some CBS executives seemed nonplussed in their initial reactions to the Times Square virtual billboard controversy, expressions of disapproval from outside the industry were emphatic. Commercial Alert's Gary Ruskin accused the network of 'a violation of public trust' and called the episode 'a really good example of how low television has sunk. Journalism is based on public trust. I think it's going to be pretty hard for CBS to recover that in the minds of many.'[80] However, as public criticism of its New Year's newscasts grew, CBS executives began to express new ethical reservations about the use of virtual imaging in journalism, with Andrew Heyward telling the *New York Times*: 'We are not in the deception business, We're in the reality business; we're in the accuracy business. To the extent that this technology interferes with that core belief we're not going to do it. We will absolutely take seriously the use of this tool.'[81] Meanwhile, Princeton Video Image executives welcomed the company's increased visibility growing out of the CBS News controversy; as CEO Dennis Wilkinson told *Broadcasting & Cable*: 'It gets us out of the closet. People now know this technology works. In all of the coverage, no one's complained that it doesn't work. If anything, it works too well.'[82] Not coincidentally, during the controversy PVI's stock price rose to a high of $11.87 a share.[83]

Conclusion   It should be noted that most of the commercial practices associated with virtual advertising were not new. Conventionally televised billboards and logos on stadium walls, scoreboards, and player uniforms are well established, and product placement in feature films and television entertainment programmes has been familiar for decades. In addition, the use of digital image manipulation has been familiar to viewers of Hollywood films for some time, from science fiction special effects to inserting fictional characters into historical footage, as in *Zelig* and *Forest Gump*; even its use as virtual fig leaves to cover nude figures in the US release of *Eyes Wide Shut*. Finally, the

78 Ibid.

79 Glen Dickson, 'CBS Goes Virtual for the Millennium', *Broadcasting and Cable* (3 Jan. 2000), n.p.

80 Don Aucoin, 'CBS Faulted for Digital Inserts', *Boston Globe* (13 Jan. 2000), D12.

81 Carter, 'CBS is Divided over the Use of False Images in Broadcasts', C1.

82 Glen Dickson, 'CBS' Virtual Logos a Real Pain', *Broadcasting & Cable* (17 Jan. 2000), 20.

83 Indeed, the fortunes of PVI have declined drastically since its association with CBS's millennium New Year's Eve broadcast. Despite management changes and an infusion of additional capital in 2002, in March 2003 the company was delisted by Nasdaq and in May 2003 it filed for bankruptcy. A 20 Aug. 2003 company press release drily noted: 'It is expected that there will be no distributions to Princeton Video Image's shareholders under the plan and that Princeton Video Image will subsequently be dissolved.' For a copy of the press release, see **www.pvi-inc.com/pvi/news-archive/Aug202003_PVI_ CompletesSaleOfAssets.html?ticker=PVII.ob&script=410&layout=6&item_id=442483.**

ontological implications of the crisis of indexicality provoked by digital image making has received a good deal of scholarly and trade attention over the past several years. Nevertheless, the prospect of the widespread application of virtual imaging in television raised the stakes of such academic and professional disputes, suggesting that the transition to digital television has the capacity to alter radically the programme forms, advertising formats, and ontological expectations of traditional television. In any event, the changes in lived experience attending our cultural entrance into an era of digital moving images will have more to do with the commercial, political, and social choices involved than with any essential qualities of the digital image. As such, scholars of contemporary media might play some small role in shaping those debates and choices through the analysis of the specific struggles over the fate of the image in digital culture.

9

How God Watches Television: Early Responses to Digital Television

Introduction

UNDER THE HEADLINE 'TiVo Revolutionizes TV', a technology review in *Chicago Sun-Times* on 8 May 2001 opened with this enthusiastic flourish: 'At the end of your first day with TiVo, you will finally blink and shout, "Holy cats, this must be how God watches television!" ' In the brief column which follows, columnist Andy Ihnatko first described TiVo as 'a powerful video bouncer, making sure that the VIPs get through and the losers stay behind the velvet rope', and argued that 'TiVo will definitely terminate your rut of scavenging for entertainment. No longer do you gobble up anything even marginally palatable just because it's in front of you. You will become a gourmet, selecting just the stuff you really want.'[1] The propensity for metaphor and hyperbole, in this case alternately theological, class based, or culinary, suggests both the long tradition of overheated pronouncements about technological change in media industries and the specific challenges that the current wave of digital technologies has brought to traditional figurations of the television set and television viewer. As we have seen repeatedly, popular figurations of technological innovation in electronic communication have insistently conjured up a reformed and empowered spectator to supplant the disparaged couch potato. Ihnatko ends his column with an equally sweeping vision of industry instability as the television spectator merges into the computer user:

> Before long, TV watching becomes like e-mail. TV shows start accumulating on the hard drive, and instead of sitting down to watch shows as they air, you sit down when you damned well please, punch the 'list' button on the remote and choose from shows that have been delivered. You're totally divorced from networks, air times or the commercials you fast-forward through. No wonder the broadcasters and advertisers are all terrified.[2]

This chapter examines the first few years of life with the digital video recorder in the United States, in order to revisit some of the widespread predictions of imminent upheaval in the businesses of broadcasting and advertising at the hands of the new device and to analyse some of the changes it has brought to long-running accounts of the television audience.

1 Andy Ihnatko, 'TiVo revolutionizes TV', *Chicago Sun-Times* (8 May 2001), 50.
2 Ibid.

The transition from analogue to digital television in the United States and elsewhere since 1998 has provoked widespread predictions of fundamental change in moving-image culture, including forecasts of the slow death not only of commercially supported network television but of the entire economic and cultural logic of mass marketing that has supported commercial broadcasting for half a century.[3] The technological promise of digital television, in the form of higher-definition images, greater bandwidth, and interactive services, has thrown into crisis, or at least historiographic relief, long-established industry practices, business relationships, and textual forms. The uneven adoption of digital technologies across the fields of consumer electronics, programme production, and delivery systems has exposed new fissures among sectors of the television industry and brought new economic players into the business, in the form of both start-ups and well-established firms, with significant amounts of venture capital being raised even in the wake of the collapse of dot-com share prices on Wall Street.[4] The ongoing uncertainty has also put into question traditional industry and popular accounts of the medium's role as signifier of national identity (and public service broadcasting's political rationale in the UK and elsewhere), its ontology of liveness and photographic realism, and its place as a consumer product within the gendered household. One place where these shifting scenarios of identity and utility are enacted is the ephemeral 30- and 60-second commercials for a range of emerging digital television products and services, including high-definition television receivers, digital video recorders, and interactive television services. While some of the recent digital television consumer products and technologies, like the hugely successful DVD player, fit comfortably within already-established business models and viewing practices, others, notably the digital video recorder and virtual advertising, are seen by many within the industry as potentially disruptive of the medium's established textual and economic practices. In the eyes of at least some observers, who evoke the full convergence of the TV set and home computer, digital technology will thoroughly transform the TV industry, its programming and advertising practices, and the position and function of the apparatus in the home.

The US network television industry has reacted with deep ambivalence to the transition to digital television and to the wider reconfiguration of the medium's role in American society. While the at-best modest fortunes of high-definition television since its public launch at the end of 1998 have underscored the distinct interests of consumer electronics manufacturers, broadcasters, and cable operators, it has been the prospect of the wide diffusion of hard drive-based digital video recorders that has provoked the greatest anxiety among broadcasters and advertisers and the most extravagant visions of a moving-image landscape altered almost beyond recognition by smart TV sets and empowered viewers. In this chapter, I will address some of the early and often highly speculative responses to digital television and suggest the ways in which the move to digital technologies has already altered some widely shared cultural and economic assumptions about the medium.

---

3 See, for example, Michael Lewis, 'Boom Box', *New York Times Magazine* (20 Aug. 2000), 36–41.

4 May Wong, 'Digital Television Gold Rush is Starting', *Toronto Star* (1 May 2001), n.p.

The context for the transition to digital television

It is important first to note the unusual historical circumstances in which the US television industry has confronted the transition to digital television. The long-term decline in network audience share as the result of an increasingly fragmented television audience (its effects mitigated in the 1990s by a strong advertising economy and the spectacular success of a few low-cost prime-time network programmes, including *Who Wants to Be a Millionaire* and *Survivor*) has thrown into crisis the perennially disputatious economic relations between networks and their affiliates, advertisers, and programme producers. The continuing consolidation of TV station ownership into ever-larger chains fuelled by permissive federal regulators has alarmed network leaders who have long envied the more stable and substantial profit levels of station owners. On the other hand, affiliates, facing networks which are increasingly merely parts of larger media conglomerates with interests in cable, satellite, and Internet platforms, worry that their status as the dominant delivery vehicle for network programming is in jeopardy. The economic foundation of the network–affiliate relationship, the networks' payment of compensation to stations in return for affiliate airtime, is under concerted network attack; these efforts have spurred a number of group owners to launch a regulatory challenge to network business practices, provoking in turn two networks to withdraw from the National Association of Broadcasters in retaliation. Thus, the uncertainty about the long-term viability of the fundamental economic premises of a half-century of American commercial television have made the networks and others extremely sensitive to the perceived threat of the emerging digital television technologies, especially the digital video recorder.

Other, more short-term, developments within the TV industry have also affected the way in which new digital technologies have been perceived. At the end of the 1990s, the US networks, faced with escalating programme licence fees for star- and writer-producer-driven prime-time dramatic programming, embraced a range of inexpensive reality-TV formats, with often extremely lucrative short-term results. In addition, the threat of Hollywood talent strikes in the middle of 2001 encouraged networks to stockpile such scriptless and actor-free programming before the 2001–2 season. Coincidentally, these non-traditional entertainment formats were seen as best suited for the design of integrated interactive features and intensive product placement, further encouraging networks to pursue these applications of digital technology. Meanwhile, the bursting of the dot-com speculative bubble and the precipitous cooling of the national advertising market at the beginning of 2001 brought the first decline since 1974 in the so-called upfront network TV market, where networks solicit spring commitments from advertisers for the upcoming autumn television season. The downturn in network advertising made the networks fearful of any erosion of their audience at the hands of the TV-commercial-evading digital video recorder and eager to work with advertisers on forms of advertising which would be impervious to such technological agents, including enhanced sponsorship, product placement, and other forms of 'embedded commerce'.

Finally, events in the US computer and consumer electronics industries have also shaped the short-term economic prospects for enhanced digital television products and services. The *New York Times* in May 2001 reported the first ever *decline* in the number of residential Internet customers, following the extinction of several free ISPs; the same newspaper reported that US personal computer sales had actually shrunk in the previous two quarters.[5] Meanwhile, prospects for continued high levels of spending in the consumer electronics and computer technology sectors appeared dim in early 2001; as one observer put it: 'It's a truly disquieting moment for the sellers of technology. They're in the difficult position of trying to unload a trunk full of cheesecakes in the parking lot of an all-you-can-eat restaurant.'[6] Previous growth forecasts of the entire range of interactive and digital television products and services were suddenly put in a new context of shrinking consumer confidence, falling technology share prices, restricted access to venture capital for start-ups, and a retrenched advertising market.

The business fortunes of the digital video recorder

Notwithstanding both the early optimistic predictions of digital video recorder sales and the alarmist claims for the destabilizing effect of the device's commercial-evading capabilities, sales of the devices were modest through most of 2001. As the *Washington Post* noted in April 2001: 'In 1999, Boston-based Forrester Research predicted that 50 million homes would have DVRs by 2005. Fewer than 300,000 have sold so far.'[7] By October 2000, weak sales forced ReplayTV, whose earlier plans for a $119 million initial public offering were aborted by the sell-off in technology stocks, to withdraw from manufacturing stand-alone digital video recorders altogether, in favour of attempting to license its technology for integration into other consumer devices, from cable boxes to DVD players and TV sets.[8] In February 2001, after failing to attract additional private capital, ReplayTV was acquired by Sonicblue, the maker of the Rio MP3 player, in a stock swap valued at $120 million; as ReplayTV's vice-president for marketing confessed to the *Washington Post*: 'It certainly is not the billions of dollars we were calculating a year ago.'[9] In April 2001, ReplayTV's rival TiVo announced that it intended to lay off 25 per cent of its staff and cut overall expenses 35 per cent; at the same time, TiVo also raised its lifetime subscription fee 25 per cent.[10]

---

5 Bob Tedeschi, 'The Rush to the Web Appears to be Slowing, but has the Audience Peaked or will it Keep Growing?', *New York Times* (21 May 2001), C9.

6 Scott Kirsner, 'Diminished Appetites', *Boston Globe* (30 Apr. 2001), C1.

7 Christopher Stern, 'DVR, Stuck on Pause; Digital Video Has Lowered Makers' Stock, Staff, Hopes', *Washington Post* (6 Apr. 2001), E1; for similarly optimistic predictions from Forrester, see Tobi Elkin and Hillary Chura, 'PVRs Revolutionizing TV Ad Buys', *Advertising Age* (18 Sept. 2000), 16, and Josh Bernoff, *TV Viewers Take Charge* (Cambridge: Forrester Research Inc., 1999).

8 Steve Gelsi, 'ReplayTV Clicks IPO off for Now', CBS.MarketWatch.com, 22 Aug. 2000; Tobi Elkin and Richard Linnett, 'Replay Strategic Shift Marks Victory for TiVo', *Advertising Age* (4 Dec. 2000), 6. In May 2001, Replay announced a deal to supply its personal video recorder software to Motorola, the US's largest manufacturer of cable set-top boxes; see Jon Healey, 'ReplayTV to Supply Video-Recording Software for Motorola Converter Boxes', *Los Angeles Times* (1 May 2001), C7.

9 Jon Healey, 'Sonicblue to Buy ReplayTV for $120 Million', *Los Angeles Times* (2 Feb. 2001), C1; Stern, 'DVR, Stuck on Pause', E1.

10 See the TiVo press release, **www.tivo.com/news/pr_detail.asp?article=10968&frames=no**.

Meanwhile, by the spring of 2001, TiVo stock was trading as low as $4, down from its previous high of $78 in June 2000; as TiVo's chief technology officer admitted in April 2001: 'As we ramped up our distribution and marketing, we all came to the realization that it is going to be harder than we thought.'[11] The *Washington Post* quoted one stock analyst of the digital video recorder business: 'We've switched from this euphoria surrounding the potential to a lot of doubt,' and one April 2001 survey of six financial analysts following TiVo noted that only one of them 'is rating the company higher than a "hold"'.[12] A senior vice-president at Thomson electronics told a journalist in December 2000 that 'we still have a lot of questions about that [stand-alone DVR] category because the business model is very, very difficult . . . All of those [stand-alone] products are subsidized to some extent, and it is still pretty open as to whether the revenue streams would really be out there long term to maintain that business model.'[13]

With digital video recorder sales much slower than earlier optimistic predictions, the device's anticipated effect in depressing the viewing of TV advertisements was small to non-existent up to the middle of 2001. While Forrester Research in January 1999 predicted that within ten years digital video recorders would be in 82 million homes and that the number of TV commercial messages actually watched by viewers would be cut in half, many in the industry remained sceptical of the device's impact on advertising practices.[14] One media executive told *Broadcasting and Cable* in February 2001: 'The impact right now is negligible. There are hardly enough boxes out there now to start a trend. It's really not even enough to experiment with.'[15] In January 2001, the *Financial Times* noted that TiVo executives, faced with slow digital video recorder sales, were now 'keen to pull back from the dire predictions that were being made about TiVo's impact on commercial broadcasting. Now the stress is very much on what the machines can offer broadcasters,' including fuller use of late-night time slots.[16] In fact, TiVo's accommodation to broadcasters and advertisers began with the original design of the device's remote control; according to TiVo Entertainment Group's publicity material aimed at potential advertising partners, unlike its rival ReplayTV, 'TiVo chose not to offer a skip button, which would eliminate the informative value of advertising. We will work with you to create advertising content that is most effective in a fast-forward environment.'[17]

This ambivalence on the part of TiVo is also expressed in the company's own television advertising. As one journalist noted, 'the problem facing the industry goes to the core of the clever, yet ambiguous, TiVo television ads that seem to encourage viewers to zap ads that they don't want to see. TiVo

11 Stern, 'DVR, Stuck on Pause', E1.

12 Rick Aristotle Munarriz, 'Fool Plate Special: Theory of TiVo-lution', MotleyFool.com, 6 Apr. 2001. http://biz.yahoo.com/mf/010406/plate_010406.html.

13 'Thomson Puts TiVo on Hold', *Consumer Electronics* (30 Oct. 2000), n.p.

14 Bernoff, *TV Viewers Take Charge*, 11.

15 Lee Hall, 'Coming Soon to a PVR near you; TiVo to Provide Uploadable Advertisements, While Giving Customers the Means to Skip Them', *Broadcasting and Cable* (26 Feb. 2001), 40.

16 'Creative Business: TiVo', *Financial Times* (23 Jan. 2001), 40.

17 TiVo Entertainment Group publicity material, n.p.

Fig. 9.1 Doing away with network programmers: television advertisement for TiVo digital video recorder, 2000

Fig. 9.4 'The revenge of the nerds': television advertisement for TiVo digital video recorder, 2001

touts its value to the advertising community, while pitching itself as a way for TV viewers to skip those same commercials.'[18] On the one hand, the eight 30-second national TV commercials made in 2000 and 2001 by TiVo's advertising agency, Goodby, Silverstein and Partners, offer a series of humorous, sometimes edgy vignettes illustrating life with TiVo, including a controversial commercial, 'Network Programmers', which the CBS network refused to run on its hit programme *Survivor* in July 2000 (Fig. 9.1). The commercial's single-take tracking shot follows two silent, well-muscled men sweeping past secretaries' desks and executive offices to calmly throw a 30-something male executive out of his high-rise corner office window, while a sardonic voice-over intones: 'Look at these guys. Network TV programmers. They decide what we watch and when we watch it. Who needs them. TiVo. TV your way.'[19] The other TiVo commercials in the campaign also evoke the viewer-liberating, anti-advertising ethos of the product, using everything from fake 'masculine itching' ads with ex-football heroes on a golf fairway to sober-sounding public service appeals for an end to an epidemic of 'people hurting TVs and TV's hurting people' staged in a hospital emergency room filled with human and TV-set casualties.

18 Hall, 'Coming Soon to a PVR near you', 40.

19 'Short Take: CBS Scraps TiVo Commercial', *Bloomberg News* (6 July 2000), n.p.

However, the anti-commercial inflection of TiVo's own commercials belies the company's more ambivalent business model. TiVo has a dizzying array of equity partners, including cable and satellite companies, consumer electronics manufacturers, and programme producers and networks, and the company strove to present the digital video recorder as a technology which will aid television advertisers, not put them out of business.[20] TiVo's efforts include four so-called 'branded areas' in where TiVo turns over screen space and hard disk storage capacity directly to advertisers, in the forms of TiVo Direct (thirty minutes of direct response video programming pre-installed on the device's hard drive), *TiVo Takes* (a TiVo Studios-produced weekly programme magazine, with interactive-encoded previews of upcoming programmes), Network Showcases (a on-screen menu of branded network partners), IPreview (interactive TV promos), and TiVolution Magazine (a weekly updated branded on-screen text preview of upcoming programmes).

Life with the digital video recorder

With only 154,000 TiVo units sold as of January 2001 (and less than half of US consumers reporting to have heard of the product), substantive research is scant on how the digital video recorder alters audience viewing habits.[21] Furthermore, it may be misleading to extrapolate from the experience of so-called 'early adopters', who are likely not to be representative of the eventual mass market, if any, for the device. However, in its promise of viewer sovereignty over the programme schedule, the digital video recorder has already provoked a revision of the cultural value of the entire television medium for some observers. Writing in opposition to 'TV Turnoff Week', an annual event organized by the TV-Turnoff Network (formerly TV-Free America, with media scholars George Gerbner, Todd Gitlin, Mark Crispin Miller, and Neil Postman on its board of directors) and endorsed by the American Medical Association, the National Education Association, and the American Academy of Pediatrics, one US journalist admonished readers instead to record 'absolutely everything for future viewing', and cited TiVo's suitability for this task. After all, she argued, 'we'd never walk into a library or bookstore, spin around blindfolded and decide to read whatever our hand fell on. We wouldn't tell our kids, "It's time for your bedtime story. Here's this month's *Playboy*." '[22] Thus, the promise of the digital video recorder to tailor the flood of programming to individual tastes and schedules has had the effect, at least among some trade observers, of reconceptualizing the medium as a valued domestic resource rather than an unwanted invasion.

20 The list includes AOL-Time-Warner (13%, with an option to buy 30%), Advance/Newhouse, CBS, Comcast Corporation, Cox Communications, DIRECTV, Discovery Communications, Encore Media Group, Liberty Media subsidiaries, Liberty Digital, NBC, Philips Electronics, Showtime Networks, SONY, TV Guide Interactive and The Walt Disney Company; see TiVo's website, **www.tivo.com/tivo_inc/partners.asp?frames=no**.

21 The percentage of Americans aware of the product was reported by Tim Spengler, Initiative Media, North America, at personal video recorder panel at the 2001 Association of National Advertisers Television Advertising Forum, 29 Mar. 2001, Plaza Hotel, New York City.

22 Gail Pennington, 'TV is Just Too Valuable to Turn off', *St Louis Post-Dispatch* (15 Apr. 2001), F9.

What TiVo's own market research has suggested is that early purchasers were 'decisively male', primarily between the ages of 25 and 44, with high levels of disposable income and leisure spending, likely to have computer skills and homes already replete with DVD players, personal computers with Internet access, and young children.[23] Proprietary ethnographic research data presented at the Association of National Advertisers annual Television Advertising Forum in March 2001 indicated that 75 per cent of TiVo users still begin their viewing sessions with live TV, turning to material recorded on their hard drives only if they find nothing on air that interests them.[24] The researcher also reported that while almost all TiVo users report using the device to avoid commercials, actual observation indicated that commercials were still being watched, although more selectively; the video recorder works as a commercial filter, not a commercial eliminator, according to the researcher.[25] In any event, it is likely that viewers highly averse to watching commercials before TiVo were already using other means to avoid watching them. The research also indicated that the recorded programming least likely to contain commercials skipped upon playback was children's shows, and men were more likely to avoid commercials than women.[26] A TiVo executive more recently estimated that 50–80 per cent of TiVo owners scanned through at least some commercials.[27]

The implied gender issues in the preliminary audience research found resonance in the trade discussions of the digital video recorder. One industry journalist in January 2001 wrote: 'I think pausing live TV is largely "a guy thing," another way that men can use the remote to prove we are the masters of our universe.'[28] While it is premature to describe the 'remasculinization' of the domestic television set with the introduction of the digital video recorder and other interactive television devices, the position of the TV set within the larger masculinist subculture of home-theatre technophilia and connoisseurship has already affected the medium's position within both the household and wider cultural life. One attempt literally to reposition the emerging 'Technographics segment' that Forrester Research calls the 'Mouse Potato' ('Technology-accepting, entertainment-focused, and with above-average incomes')[29] was a partnership announced in January 2001 between Microsoft and US furniture manufacturer La-Z-Boy Inc. to market a $1,500

---

23 Personal interview with Ken Ripley, National Director, Advertising Sales, TiVo, New York City, 27 Mar. 2001.

24 John Carey, Greystone Communications, 2001 Association of National Advertisers Television Advertising Forum.

25 Ibid.

26 Ibid. On the other hand, some TiVo users expressed the desire to be able to use TiVo to search for commercials as well as for programming for viewing. According to TiVo's behavioural research on TiVo users, Saturday is the most popular day for video playback; the most popular day part for viewing recorded material is early fringe time and late night; the heaviest taping target time is prime time, and the average interval between recording and playback is two days. According to TiVo, personal video recorder households watch an extra three hours of television per week; Ken Ripley, 2001 Association of National Advertisers Television Advertising Forum.

27 Michael McCarthy, 'Ads are Here, There, Everywhere: Agencies Seek Creative Ways to Expand Product Placement', *USA Today* (19 June 2001), 1B.

28 Craig Leddy, 'TiVo Hard Drives Raise Hard Questions', *Multichannel News* (15 Jan. 2001), 54.

29 Bernoff, *TV Viewers Take Charge*, 12.

Fig. 9.2 'Plug in, log
on and veg out':
'The Explorer' reclining
armchair from Microsoft
and La-Z-Boy, 2001

WebTV-equipped recliner, named 'The Explorer', complete with a WebTV
wireless keyboard, two months' free WebTV service, a fused, surge-
protected 110V power outlet and AC adapter for laptop use, a DSL port, and
a standard modem line; concealed within the other armrest is storage for
remote controls and a cupholder (Fig. 9.2). One Internet news site began
its announcement of the product launch with 'Internet junkies and couch
potatoes unite!', and the rhetorical and literal condensation of Web surfer
and television viewer, figures fixed in opposition in the trade and popular
press over the past decade, suggests the wider stakes of the putative merging
of computer and TV set via digital technologies.[30] Another commentator
on the new recliner evoked the incongruity of the imagined merger of Web
surfer and TV viewer in the characteristically comic and condescending

---

30 Jay Steinberg, 'For the Lazy Boy', 12 Jan. 2001, **www.edgereview.com/ataglance.cfm?category=**
edge&ID=162; for a discussion of the history of Microsoft's experiences in interactive television, see
the following chapter.

tone endemic to such discussions: 'Middle America, lie back and meet the Internet. . . . Plug in, log on and veg out.'[31]

In addition to Microsoft's attempts to revive early TV-set manufacturer DuMont's oxymoronic advertising appeals to the male viewer as an 'armchair Columbus' (Fig. 9.3), the current regendering of the television apparatus in the home can also be seen in the thriving subculture of TiVo hackers, sustained through a number of unofficial, if so-far TiVo-tolerated, websites. TiVo's Linux-based operating software has attracted a relatively large number of hackers who seem chiefly interested in installing higher-capacity hard drives, though hackers have also reportedly succeeded in changing the compression algorithms of the TiVo software.[32] In May 2001, the *New York Times* quoted an estimate from TiVo's customer relations director that about 1 per cent of the company's 150,000 customers had altered their devices, thereby invalidating their machines' guarantees; he told the paper that the company had rewarded some hackers with gifts of free service for telling the company about hacks they had accomplished.[33] A few months earlier, an article in the *Washington Post*, after quoting a number of male TiVo hackers, concluded: 'The "hackability" of a product can be appealing in its own right to some customers—the ones who are curious, technically minded or cheap. To a hacker, a modification doesn't even have to be particularly useful—just elegant.'[34] A full account of the meeting of the prosaic TV set with the gendered subculture of computer hackers would need to consider the ways in which the individual artefact of domestic technology may become powerful constructive and projective media, as suggested by Sherry Turkle, used by individuals to consolidate personal and social identities.[35] The diffusion of the digital video recorder promises to reconfigure the psychological and social meanings of these familiar domestic technologies.

While TiVo buyers are 'decisively male', the device's ambivalent position between the gendered technologies of domestic television, on the one hand, and the personal computer and home theatre, on the other, highlights tensions within the consumer electronics market going back to the development of high-fidelity audio as a male subculture in the late 1940s and 1950s, tensions enacted in countless quotidian battles over household spending, domestic space, and viewing and listening choices.[36] TiVo's website, for example, contains a number of testimonials from male customers related to such micro domestic battles across the United States, including 'my wife

31 Dan Richman, 'Microsoft, La-Z-Boy Team up for World's First "E-cliner" ', http://stacks.msnbc.com/local/pisea/M7203.asp?cp1=1.

32 Amy Vickers, 'Digital tv uk: TiVo Deal Fuels Questions over BSkyB Set-Top Choice', *New Media Markets*, 7 July 2000.

33 David J. Wallace, 'You Will Be Reprogrammed. Your Toaster, Too', *New York Times* (3 May 2001), G1.

34 Kevin Savetz, 'Breaking it Open, Making it Better', *Washington Post* (2 Mar. 2001), E1.

35 For an account of the role of domestic technologies as powerful evocative objects, see Sherry Turkle, *The Second Self: Computers and the Human Spirit* (New York: Simon and Schuster, 1984), 12; for a popular history of the social context of the growth of the personal computer market, see Phil Patton, *Made in USA: The Secret History of the Things that Made America* (New York: Penguin, 1992), ch. 17.

36 See Keir Keightley, ' "Turn it Down!" She Shrieked: Gender, Domestic Space, and High Fidelity, 1948–59', *Popular Music*, 15/2 (1996), 149–77.

Fig. 9.3 The male TV viewer as 'Armchair Columbus', DuMont magazine advertisement, 1944

normally cringes when I bring home a new gadget, but she LOVES TiVo, and calls it "hers"'; 'the only audio/electronic component that my girlfriend actually doesn't want to disconnect the moment it enters the system'; and 'even my wife, who is not quite the gadget nut I am, is thrilled with TiVo'.[37] Another TiVo promotional page, 'Celebrity Quotes', includes a quotation from retired football quarterback Steve Young which indicates how TiVo's entrance into the household may or may not disturb traditionally gendered household routines: 'I thought once I stopped playing football, things would be quieter. But with a new baby in the family, I'm more busy than ever. With TiVo, I can record all the games and watch them whenever I want. And with the ability to pause live TV for a diaper change, my wife may love TiVo even more than I do!'[38]

It is clear that the digital video recorder, itself a marriage of television and computer technologies, has evoked a range of consumer responses inflected by larger cultural figurations of the TV viewer and computer hobbyist. TiVo's website quotes one journalist:

> TiVo is like a drug. It enhances humdrum parts of your world, eats up your time, taps your wallet and is extremely difficult to explain to anyone who hasn't used it before. Fortunately, personal digital video recorders don't have the downsides of most drugs, and they're a lot cheaper than most illicit habits. But after using TiVo for a while, I'm finding it very hard to conceive of going back to plain old TV.[39]

While the rhetoric of addiction and time wasting here evokes the traditional figuration of the disreputable TV viewer, they also recall similar tongue-in-cheek portraits of the self-described 'radio maniac' of the early 1920s. Furthermore, the author's appeal to an exclusive subculture of initiated users also suggests the more elevated fraternity of the male hi-fi hobbyist and computer enthusiast, which since the 1950s has been rhetorically constructed as the antipode to the commercially debased, passive, and lowest-common-denominator activity of television viewing.

Significantly, in addition to retired football players and mid-tier show business celebrities, TiVo's 'Celebrity Quotes' Web page also features a prominent endorsement from legendary personal computer pioneer Steve Wozniak, co-founder of Apple Computer, and one of TiVo's customer testimonials includes the simple endorsement: 'best invention since the PC'.[40] Evoking the computer enthusiast in a different context, TiVo's national TV advertising attempts to link the digital video recorder to the heroic cultural narrative of the personal computer industry in a 30-second commercial, entitled 'Earl', which features a physically unprepossessing 20-something male driving his dilapidated automobile the wrong way up a freeway entrance, gleefully decapitating a parking meter, interrupting a graveside service with

37 www.tivo.com/entertain/talk/testimonial_category.asp?category=A&page=4&frames=no.

38 www.tivo.com/entertain/celeb_quotes_p2.asp.

39 Sascha Segan, 'A New View on TV: Digital Video Recorders Go Way beyond VCRs', abcnews.go.com, 11 Dec. 2000. The TiVo link is at www.tivo.com/news/product_reviews.asp?year=2000&frames=no.

40 www.tivo.com/entertain/talk/testimonial_category.asp?category=A&page=7&frames=no.

the 'Hallelujah' chorus, and demanding (successfully) of a bewildered zoo employee that he bring home a giant live tiger (Fig. 9.4; see p. 128). 'Now that I have TiVo, and I can watch whatever I want, I want to *do* whatever I want. . . . Not everyone understands. . . . Then again, not everyone's got TiVo,' he explains over the assorted incidents. The fantasy of technologically delivered interpersonal mastery of socially challenged male technophiles, the 'revenge of the nerds', has been a powerful mythic scenario of the personal computer industry in the United States.[41]

Conclusion

Beyond the ways in which the introduction of the digital video recorder may alter long-standing everyday understandings of the television medium, the mere threat of the DVR has already encouraged a range of new technological and advertising countermeasures to the digital recorder's ability to evade standard TV commercials.[42] The growing use of such 'embedded commerce' in the forms of intrusive product placement, star-talent product pitches, and sponsor-designed programmes represents an eerie echo of some of the earliest business practices in the US television industry, with important implications for a range of issues from creative freedom of TV writers and producers to the design of programme formats themselves. Despite, or perhaps because of, the networks' ever more desperate efforts to retain advertisers through increased product placement and branding opportunities, some observers predicted that, in the words of Forrester Research's Josh Bernoff, 'broadcast networks [will] lose their reputation for quality', in a downward spiral as viewers increasingly evade commercials, advertising revenues fall, and audiences rebel in turn against intrusive product placement.[43]

At the same time, it is important to keep in mind that the commercial prospects for interactive television generally and the success of any specific digital video recorder service like TiVo are by no means assured in the USA or elsewhere. Indeed, the question of which domestic device will serve as portal and recorder for digital television remains unsettled; contending platforms include satellite and cable decoder boxes, DVD players, video game consoles, and television sets themselves. Similarly unresolved are the contentious financial agreements among hardware makers, content providers, and delivery-system operators to share prospective interactive television revenues, leading one analyst quoted in *Advertising Age* in December 2000 to lament that 'there are too many pigs at the trough'.[44]

---

41 See, for example, Stephen Segaller, *Nerds 2.0.1: A Brief History of the Internet* (New York: TV Books Inc., 1999).

42 TiVo press release; for an account of increased interest among advertising-supported cable networks in advertiser-supplied programming, see Jim Forkan, 'On Some Cable Shows, the Sponsors Take Charge', *Multichannel News* (4 June 2001), 53; on the growth of product placement, see Wayne Friedman, 'Eagle-Eye Marketers Find Right Spot, Right Time: Product Placements Increase as Part of Syndication Deals', *Advertising Age* (22 Jan. 2001), S2.

43 Bernoff, *TV Viewers Take Charge*, 14.

44 David Card, senior analyst, interactive TV, Jupiter Research, quoted in Elkin and Linnett, 'Replay Strategic Shift Marks Victory for TiVo', 6.

10

High Tech in a Falling Market: Interactivity and Advertising Form in Contemporary US Television

Introduction

DESPITE a decade of both apocalyptic and utopian predictions about life in the 'post-television era', the effects of technological and industrial realignments upon actual viewing practices and the advertising and programme forms of American television are still quite uncertain. This chapter provides a context for understanding these contemporary disputes through two case studies: the long and unhappy commercial history of interactive television over the past thirty years, and the recent controversies over changing programme and advertising practices which are seen as one industry response to the challenge of a new, technologically empowered television viewer.

Dreams and nightmares of interactive television

Notwithstanding the manifest turmoil within the US television industry at the beginning of the twenty-first century, it is easy to be sceptical of the self-interested claims for technologically driven fundamental change in the medium, especially in light of decades of unsuccessful business ventures advanced under the banners of technological convergence and viewer interactivity. Such cautions were expressed as early as 1971 in a Rand Corporation report on interactive cable television, which noted that 'as is often the case with emerging technologies . . . the promise of two-way services on cable has at times been oversold'.[1] Likewise, a nearly unbroken string of failed commercial launches of interactive television, from Time-Warner's Qube system in Columbus, Ohio, in 1977 to the same company's costly trial of a state-of-the-art interactive television service in Orlando, Florida, in 1995, suggests the dangers of overestimating consumer appetite for interactive television services. Given the unhappy business history of interactive television in the

---

1 Walter S. Baer, *Interactive Television: Prospects for Two-Way Services on Cable* (Santa Monica, Calif.: Rand Corporation, November 1971), p. v.

USA to date, the scepticism underscored in the title of L. J. Davis's 1998 business history, *The Billionaire Shell Game: How Cable Baron John Malone and Assorted Corporate Titans Invented a Future Nobody Wanted*, does not seem unwarranted.[2] As one journalist concluded in March 2001: 'In general, the dream of combining PC technology with America's favorite entertainment medium has been a nightmare.'[3]

Similarly, the combined efforts of computer manufacturers, software designers, and Web entrepreneurs to introduce TV programme forms and business models into the PC market place have also fared poorly over the past decade. These efforts include the failure of integrated PC-TV devices from Compaq, Gateway, and others, slow sales of TV-tuner cards for use in PCs, a range of ill-fated mid-1990s TV-modelled computer interface designs and delivery systems (including Microsoft's Bob, Windows CE, and a flurry of so-called push technologies for the Internet), the slower than expected provision of broadband Internet service into the home, the quick court-ordered shutdown of TV-streaming Internet sites like iCraveTV, and the failure of many of the costly efforts by the traditional television networks to establish themselves as Web portals. (ABC-Disney alone spent an estimated $100 million on the Go.com portal before shutting it down.)[4] If the long-heralded convergence of personal computer and TV set indeed ever comes about, it will not be without leaving a formidable number of major corporate casualties and junked business plans in its wake.

Some of the lessons taken from the chequered history of interactive television can be seen in the shifting product and promotional strategies of a single firm, Microsoft, which has repeatedly and unsuccessfully attempted to create a viable business out of the intersection of the home computer and TV set. After the expensive failure of its early 1990s strategy built around cable television's set-top box as the platform for Microsoft's interactive television software (and the simultaneous failure of the original business model of MSN as an AOL clone providing limited and proprietary Internet access), by 1995 Microsoft responded to the spectacular growth of the Internet by shifting its attention to the Web as the path for interactive television.[5] The August 1995 initial public offering of Internet browser maker Netscape, the largest single IPO in history to that date, signalled, in part, the financial market's repudiation of Microsoft's plans for interactive television via cable's set-top box.[6] By the time of Bill Gates's second best-seller in 1999, *Business @ the*

2 L. J. Davis, *The Billionaire Shell Game: How Cable Baron John Malone and Assorted Corporate Titans Invented a Future Nobody Wanted* (New York: Doubleday, 1998).

3 Ian Fried, 'Microsoft Shifts WebTV Oversight to Redmond', CNET News.com, 2 Mar. 2001. http://news.cnet.com/news/0-1006-200-4997557.html.

4 Harry Berkowitz, 'Sparks Fly between Moguls at Conference', *Newsday* (4 May 2001), A62; on the brief history of iCrave, see Samantha Yaffe, 'Casters Fighting iCrave', *Playback* (17 Dec. 1999), 1 and Christopher Stern, 'Web's iCrave Caves: Settlement Shuts down Pirate Netcaster', *Daily Variety* (29 Feb. 2000), 7; for a discussion of the legal issues involved in streaming broadcast material on the Web, see Dick Wiley, 'Current Legal Issues no Audio (or Video) Hallucination for Webcasters', *Communications Today* (6 Apr. 2001), n.p.

5 Kathy Rebello, 'Inside Microsoft: The Inside Story of how the Internet Forced Bill Gates to Reverse his Corporate Strategy', *Business Week* (15 July 1996), 56–67.

6 Joshua Quittner and Michelle Slatella, *Speeding the Web* (New York: Atlantic Monthly Press, 1998), 249.

Speed of Thought, the author was willing to admit that Microsoft had taken too long to pull the plug on its mid-1990s interactive television efforts: 'as we proceeded, there was a slow realization that the costs were higher and the customer benefits lower than we had all assumed they would be. Interactive television wasn't coming together as soon as we expected or in the way we expected.'[7]

Microsoft's April 1997 $425 million acquisition of WebTV, a start-up founded in 1995 by three alumni from Apple Computer, reflected Microsoft's new interest in combining Internet access and television viewing in the same device, as well as an attempt to recoup some of Microsoft's substantial investment in interactive television software.[8] However, the number of WebTV subscriptions quickly stagnated at slightly over a million, despite price cuts, hardware give-aways, and enhanced features. The service was hurt by a history of network outages, an extremely high subscriber churn rate, a December 2000 FTC settlement over deceptive advertising claims, a March 2001 decision by Sony Pictures Digital Entertainment to withdraw its popular interactive TV game shows, and a general brand image of WebTV as a technologically enfeebled service for technophobes.[9] More fundamentally, as one journalist explained, 'selling the Internet on TV meant selling the Internet to consumers who understood the benefits of the Internet but didn't own a PC. And that's a market that is shrinking as PC prices have fallen.'[10] Finally, by most accounts, relations were strained between the Silicon Valley-based WebTV subsidiary and its corporate parent in Redmond, Washington; according to two CNET reporters in October 2000, the 'WebTV transition has been a sometimes-farcical exercise fraught with unclear direction, shameless politics and technological blunders that have already cost both companies untold sums in lost opportunity—if not their assured leadership of the entire interactive TV industry.'[11]

Microsoft's TV commercials marking the autumn 1999 US relaunch of WebTV, which introduced enhanced interactive television features and was part of a wider repositioning of the brand, tried to redress some of these weaknesses. The campaign, from the ad agency Foote Cone & Belding, consisting of six 30-second commercials and a single 60-second commercial, never depicts WebTV in use, but offers instead a procession of comic scenarios involving bewildered and sometimes humiliated users of the discredited 'Brand X'—in this case, traditional television. The 60-second commercial that launched the campaign, entitled 'Chaos Theory', draws on excerpts from the succeeding 30-second ads, depicting a series of TV viewers reacting with incomprehension to their television sets' display of a jumble of cut-and-

7 Bill Gates, *Business @ the Speed of Thought* (New York: Warner Books, 1999), 162.

8 Christine MacDonald, 'MS Tuned in to Convergence', CNET News.com, 7 Apr. 1997. http://news.cnet.com/news/0-1003-200-317912.html.

9 'Free WebTV Promotion', *Consumer Electronics*, 18 Sept. 2000; Lori Enos, 'WebTV Settles Deceptive Ad Charges', NewsFactor Network, 26 Oct. 2000; www.NewsFactor.com/perl/story/4653.html; Jon Healey, 'Sony Pulls Interactive Games from WebTV', *Los Angeles Times* (1 Mar. 2001), C4.

10 Richard Shim, 'Microsoft's Ultimate Challenge in Interactive TV', CNET News.com, 27 Mar. 2001. http://news.com.com/2100-1040-254788.html5255384.html?tag=pt.yahoofin.financefeed..ne.

11 Mike Yamamoto and Stephanie Miles, 'Picture Imperfect: WebTV: How Microsoft Lost its Vision with WebTV', CNET News.com, 12 Oct. 2000. http://news.cnet.com/news/0-1006-201-2950148-1.html.

Fig. 10.1 Traditional television's incompetent viewers: television advertisement for WebTV, 1999

pasted programme images and on-screen voices that form the repeated stuttered phrase 'I . . . could . . . do . . . so . . . much . . . more' (Fig. 10.1). Given the commercial's lack of anchoring voice-over narration or obvious narrative structure, the repeated phrase begs the question of subjectivity, evoking both the ventriloquist video hacker of the British and American versions of the 1980s TV's *Max Headroom* and the authoritarian 'control voice' of the opening credits of the 1960s US science fiction TV series *The Outer Limits*. The repeated utterance, built from a pastiche of voices from critically disdained TV genres (confessional talk shows, game shows, talking-head financial news programmes, South Asian movie musicals, *Baywatch* clones, and sentimental children's melodramas), is shown interrupting and frustrating traditional viewing routines. Later in the 60-second commercial, the phrase becomes highly directive, apparently commanding an in-gathering of passers-by to a shop window containing scores of TV sets displaying the same phrase, à la newsman Howard Beale's messianic broadcast voice in the 1975 film *Network*. While the commercial offers an arch and humorous catalogue of vaguely pathetic TV viewers, its own opacity has the effect of leaving viewers in the same confusion about who is speaking and what is on offer as the hapless audience members represented in the ad itself.

Each of the succeeding 30-second commercials in the WebTV campaign, which highlighted a single feature of the relaunched interactive service (customized stock reports, intelligent programme guides, programme-embedded Web links, programme schedule reminders, and interactive quiz shows), is built around a vignette depicting the inadequacies of the traditional TV viewing experience and its technologically obsolete viewer. In each vignette, a TV actor on-screen breaks out of the inscribed diegesis to confront directly the startled on-screen viewer, and this aggressive and fanciful literalization of 'interactive television' evokes the fearful associations of broadcast technology within the home that have been the stuff of innumerable speculative fictions since domestic television was imagined in the 1920s. The interactivity promised in the WebTV commercials invokes both the familiar advertising trope of a thrilling spectator immersion in the television image and the long tradition of dystopian visions of electronic simulation, from the supposed pathological para-social interaction of radio soap opera fans of the 1930s to the Orwellian telescreen, the television monitor that performs perfect surveillance of the viewer. The WebTV commercials' refusal or inability to offer an affirmative vision of the new technological capabilities of television, along with the contradictory and highly affective cultural myths the commercials evoke, suggest the continuing cultural ambivalence about the place of electronic media in the home.

Despite Microsoft's efforts to reposition the WebTV service via its extensive marketing campaign, by October 2000, trade journals were reporting that 'the WebTV brand itself has a limited future, its mission confined to the slow business of dial-up Internet access through the TV set', and in March 2001 Microsoft announced that WebTV, previously a semi-autonomous corporate subsidiary based in Silicon Valley, would be brought into the MSN group and moved to Microsoft's corporate headquarters in Redmond.[12] One columnist remarked that 'Microsoft Corp. took the remnants and detritus of Web-TV, screaming and kicking, to Redmond for a decent burial', and many observers saw the move as Microsoft's admission of the failure of WebTV to move beyond a niche market and of the limited appeal of Internet access on television.[13] At the same time, Microsoft folded the existing WebTV technology (and sales staff) into a new product, immodestly called Ultimate TV, which was launched, after several delays, in early 2001.[14] Ultimate TV combined WebTV capabilities with a two-tuner digital video recorder integrated into a DirecTV satellite TV set-top box, allowing viewers to pause live TV, digitally record thirty-five hours of programming, and record two programmes simultaneously. Microsoft spent eighteen months and $20 million developing the proprietary Ultimate TV microchip, part of the estimated total of $100 million that its WebTV subsidiary spent developing its interactive television products.[15] As one industry reporter noted, Microsoft's launching of Ultimate TV 'sounds a quiet death knell for WebTV'.[16]

Microsoft's shifting digital television strategies were part of the company's larger rethinking of its traditional business model; faced with slower growth in the PC business (one analyst in March 2001 estimated growth in PC sales of only 60 per cent over the next five years[17]) and greater resistance among PC users to upgrade to new software releases, Microsoft had little choice but to look beyond the traditional PC platform for its accustomed rate of growth.[18] In January 2001, Bill Gates used a consumer electronics trade show in Las

12 Mike Yamamoto and Stephanie Miles, 'Picture Imperfect: WebTV: How Microsoft Lost its Vision with WebTV', CNET News.com, 12 Oct. 2000. http://news.cnet.com/news/0-1006-201-2950148-1.html.

13 'A Hitch and a Glitch Leaves Bluetooth no Sales Pitch', *Bangkok Post* (5 Apr. 2001), n.p.

14 Bill Gates promised an industry group in January 1998 that 'you will see a WebTV box that has DSL in the coming year', something that was still not on offer three and a half years after his speech; see Michael Kanellos, 'Gates: WebTV, PCs to get DSL', CNET News.com, 28 Jan. 1998. http://news.cnet.com/news/0-1003-200-326014.html; Dominic Gates, 'Microsoft's Ultimate Delay', *Industry Standard* (13 Nov. 2000), n.p.

15 'Microsoft Designs New WebTV Chip', ZDNet News, 24 Aug. 2000, n.p. www.zdnet.com/zdnn/stories/news/0,4586,2619528,00.html.

16 Shim, 'Microsoft's Ultimate Challenge in Interactive TV', CNET News.com, 27 Mar. 2001. http://news.com.com/2100-1040-254788.html.

17 Alex Pham, 'Gates Hopes Xbox is Key to the Living Room', *Los Angeles Times* (8 Jan. 2001), C1.

18 Microsoft CEO Steve Ballmer told journalists that he expected that most of the firm's revenues would come from Web-based subscriptions and services within four to ten years; see Wylie Wong and Stephen Shankland, 'Ballmer Learns from Past Microsoft Missteps', CNET News.com, 28 Sept. 2000. http://news.cnet.com/news/0-1003-201-2887282-0.html.

Vegas to introduce Ultimate TV, as well as the company's new video game system, the Xbox. The company's move into the consumer electronics industry reflected a strategic shift from the PC platform alone to six potential software platforms: telephones, hand-held computers, television, video games, and the Internet (as well as new partnerships with Starbucks, LazBoy, and Lego); the shift also represents Microsoft's risky move into the highly competitive business of consumer electronics manufacturing, against formidable established firms including Sony.[19] At the same time, Microsoft's launch of Ultimate TV marked an expensive new wager on the general economic prospects for interactive television; one technology analyst noted that 'a lot of eyes are watching how well Ultimate TV does. This will be the first indicator of whether this market is real or that there's nothing here and we need to move on. It's a major litmus test for this market genre.'[20]

In September 2000, Microsoft CEO Steve Ballmer explained the company's shift in interactive television strategy in terms of the wider repositioning of Web access and television viewing: 'I actually think that the current WebTV service is interesting but not overwhelming. What we do today is let you get Internet on TV, as opposed to enhancing the TV experience. . . . Ultimate TV . . . is much more about enhancing the TV experience. . . . You get the Internet on TV, but it's more about enhancing the way you watch TV, recording shows, pausing. I'm bullish on that,' Ballmer said.[21] *Variety* connected Microsoft's repositioning of its interactive television products to wider changes in the cultural and strategic position of the television set: 'While its Web TV service was always aimed at computer users, MS execs say Ultimate TV is aimed squarely at TV watchers. As broadband Internet programming continues to disappoint, the TV that was uncool 18 months ago is once again hip with media execs.'[22] In its substantial advertising campaign for the new Ultimate TV service, Microsoft positioned the product more as a digital video recorder than an Internet-access device, thus aligning it in direct competition with the two-year-old TiVo device.

Like digital video recorder pioneers TiVo and ReplayTV, which had been advertising eighteen months before the launch of Ultimate TV, Microsoft faced special challenges, as well as possible rewards, as pioneers in an entirely new product category. *Advertising Age* quoted Forrester Research's chief analyst, Josh Bernoff, in the autumn of 2000: 'You will see an insane amount of brand advertising, especially for TiVo, and probably for Microsoft Ultimate TV, because what's going to happen in the next twelve months is the concept of video recording will be associated in the minds of consumers with a brand name.'[23] In July 2001 the *Financial Times* estimated that Microsoft was pouring $50 million into marketing Ultimate TV, and one analyst warned in

19 Kelly Zito, 'Microsoft Branches out: Software Maker Opens Windows to Video Games, Cellular Phones and More', *San Francisco Chronicle* (15 Jan. 2001), B1; Pham, 'Gates Hopes Xbox is Key to the Living Room', C1; Dori Jones Yang, 'Why Gates is Smiling', *U.S. News & World Report* (5 Mar. 2001), 38.

20 Rob Enderle of the Giga Information Group, quoted in Pham, 'Gates Hopes Xbox is Key to the Living Room', C1.

21 Wong and Shankland, 'Ballmer Learns from Past Microsoft Missteps', n.p.

22 Christopher Grove, 'Interactive Tube's Future Looks Hazy', *Daily Variety* (21 July 2000), A2.

23 Tobi Elkin and Hillary Chura, 'PVRs Revolutionizing TV Ad Buys', *Advertising Age* (18 Sept. 2000), 16.

March 2001 that 'Ultimate TV will have to do a really good job in marketing this type of enhanced TV product because they are out ahead of everyone else a bit . . . so they'll not only have to define their product but really this entire category. . . . TiVo and ReplayTV had some troubles with this.'[24]

The five national television commercials that launched Ultimate TV in March 2001, produced by the Rodgers Townsend advertising agency in St Louis (one of three different ad agencies Microsoft hired and fired to market interactive television in the first five months of 2001 alone), each foreground a single function of the device's digital video recorder capabilities; at the same time, none of the commercials even mentions Ultimate TV's email or Internet-access features.[25] Microsoft's vice-president of consumer products addressed the decision to omit Ultimate TV's interactive television features in its advertising, by explaining that 'the combination of parts is greater than the individual services, but [DVR] will be the selling point'.[26] According to the Ultimate TV account supervisor at Rodgers Townsend, Ultimate TV's interactive features were seen by both Microsoft and its advertising agency to be too difficult to explain in a brief commercial spot, and of too little appeal beyond a niche market of potential users.[27] Especially compared to Microsoft's flamboyant WebTV campaign the previous year, the subsequent print (to date only seen in DirectTV's programme guides) and television advertising campaign for Ultimate TV is exceedingly modest and self-effacing in tone, depicting a variety of TV households seamlessly integrating the digital video recorder into their daily routines. These scenes include a couple programming the recording of two different programmes while preparing to go out for the evening; a man pausing a live TV broadcast to check on a baby in a crib; a family using the 'my shows' feature to distract their dog at dinner time; a man in bed with a cast on his leg appreciating the 35-hour recording capacity; and a housewife watching a soap opera using the instant replay feature to rehear lines of dialogue drowned out by her husband's lawnmower outside her window. Despite its ambitious name, the marketing of Ultimate TV suggests Microsoft's lowered expectations for the immediate prospects of PC-like interactivity of the traditional television set.

While Microsoft's overall involvement with interactive television is certain to continue in some form, the first half of 2001 saw intense speculation in the financial press about the company's apparent desire to shed Ultimate TV altogether as part of a proposed deal by News Corporation's Rupert Murdoch to acquire satellite broadcaster DirecTV from General Motors' Hughes Electronics subsidiary. Under the complex plan, which emerged after more than a year of negotiations, Microsoft would supply News Corp.

---

24 Paul Abraham, 'Television's Revolution Postponed: Digital Video Recorders were Supposed to Replace Analogue Machines. But they Remain a Cult', *Financial Times* (7 July 2001), 11; Gartner analyst Mark Snowden, quoted in Shim, 'Microsoft's Ultimate Challenge in Interactive TV', n.p.

25 For Microsoft's controversial moves among ad agencies working on the Ultimate TV account, see 'For the Record', *Advertising Age* (12 Mar. 2001), 37; Stuart Elliott, 'Stuart Elliott in America', *Campaign* (16 Mar. 2001), 27; Stuart Elliott, 'Microsoft Shakes up Beleaguered San Francisco Agencies by Shifting its Account for Ultimate TV', *New York Times* (11 May 2001), C5.

26 Shim, 'Microsoft's Ultimate Challenge in Interactive TV', n.p.

27 Telephone interview with Gary Shipping, Ultimate TV account supervisor, Rodgers and Townsend Advertising, St Louis, Mo., 12 Apr. 2001.

with $3 billion for the DirecTV acquisition and transfer Ultimate TV to Murdoch's new satellite service; Microsoft would in turn become the 'preferred supplier' of software for future interactive services on the platform.[28] The *Los Angeles Times* noted that 'the deal also would allow Microsoft to exit gracefully from the interactive television business after spinning its wheels for a decade without much success', despite spending an estimated $1.5 billion since its 1997 acquisition of WebTV.[29] For Murdoch, the acquisition of DirecTV would double the reach of his Sky Global Networks to 200 million households across the globe, which currently reaches every major population area except China and the USA.[30] While the *Los Angeles Times* reporter noted that 'few analysts expect interactive television to be much of a business for years', she also suggested that 'some on Wall Street are expecting Murdoch to jump-start the interactive television business if he gains control of DirecTV by giving away boxes as he has in Britain', where Murdoch's BSkyB reported interactive revenues for the nine months ending 31 March 2001 of £60 million, of which £55 million related to sports betting via television.[31] Even though the Microsoft–Murdoch DirecTV deal was never consummated, the plan indicated how far the immediate business prospects for interactive television had diminished in the eyes of the giant software firm by early 2001.

Digital technologies and changing TV programme forms	If the experience in interactive television of a company as large and market shaping as Microsoft suggests the dangers of overestimating the public appetite for enhanced TV services, it is nevertheless clear that at least some of TV's new digital technologies are already having an effect on programme forms and advertising practices. In fact, while the number of purchasers of the new television systems remained relatively small (for example, TiVo reported only 229,000 subscribers by August 2001), industry executives and media pundits alike were busy predicting winners and losers in the new media environment.[32] In particular, the digital video recorder, launched by TiVo and ReplayTV in 1999, was quickly heralded by several media analysts as a powerfully destabilizing new tool enabling viewers to evade traditional television advertising. The *New York Times Magazine* August 2000

28 The News Corp.-DirecTV merger was complicated by the August 2001 rival bid for DirecTV from competing satellite service Echo Star Communications; see Kris Hudson, 'Echo Star Drama Gets Complicated. Ergen has Several Cards up his Sleeve, Analysts Say', *Denver Post* (19 Aug. 2001), K1.

29 Sallie Hofmeister, 'News Corp. to Make New Bid for DirecTV', *Los Angeles Times* (20 Apr. 2001), C1; also see Jim Rutenberg and Geraldine Fabrikant, 'Dream Prize Draws Closer for Murdoch', *New York Times* (7 May 2001), C1.

30 Hofmeister, 'News Corp. to Make New Bid for DirecTV', C1.

31 Ibid.; for a profile on the European interactive television market, see William Echikson, 'Europe's I-TV Advantage', *Business Week* (19 Feb. 2001), 16. The BSkyB results are reported in a 9 May 2001 press release at **www.corporate-ir.net/ireye/ir_site.zhtml?ticker=bsy.uk&script=410&layout= 0&item_id=174017**; the fall in News Corp. advertising revenues and share price following the 11 Sept. 2001 World Trade Center terrorist attack cast new doubt on the viability of Murdoch's bid for DirecTV; see Andrew Clark and John Cassy, 'On the Brink of War: Media: Murdoch may Lose DirecTV Bid', *Guardian* (3 Oct. 2001), 26.

32 TiVo, Inc., *Quarterly Report* (SEC form 10-Q), 14 Sept. 2001. **http://biz.yahoo.com/e/010914/tivo.html**.

cover article by Michael Lewis about TiVo was subtitled 'The End of the Mass Market', accompanied by the spectacular cover image of an exploding cereal box.[33] The following summer a *Brandweek* reporter noted: 'If there's an antichrist for advertisers, thy name is TiVo', citing the device's potential to 'allow viewers to exorcise Madison Avenue's finely focus-grouped and carefully crafted work'.[34]

Indeed, the mere threat of the digital video recorder has encouraged a range of new technological and advertising countermeasures to the digital recorder's ability to evade traditional TV commercials. In the first half of 2001, the contracting advertising market for network television brought about by a general economic slowdown (total US advertising expenditures in the first half of 2001 were down 5.9 per cent from the previous year), and the 11 September 2001 terrorist attack on New York's World Trade Center caused national advertising revenues to plunge even more steeply (within weeks after the attack, one analyst predicted that total US advertising industry revenues would fall 9 per cent for 2001).[35] In this inhospitable economic climate, the advertising and television trade presses were filled with calls for sponsors and broadcasters to develop advertising vehicles that would rebuff the expected assault from digital recorders via what TiVo itself calls inescapable 'embedded commerce', including on-screen banner ads, intensive use of conventional product placement, and the move to single-sponsor infomercials and entertainment programming.[36] May 2001 saw the announcement of the first planned use of so-called virtual product placement in dramatic programming, marked by an agreement between Princeton Video Images and the TBS cable network to offer sponsors the opportunity to insert digitally on-screen virtual products within reruns of *Law and Order*.[37] A Princeton Video Images executive predicted that within two years, the majority of its business would involve inserting virtual products into syndicated programming; 'We don't call it product placement, we call it product presence, because it's such a seamless way of including the brand', he said.[38] To the same end of frustrating the ad-evading powers of the digital video recorder, others in the industry predicted the development of digital

33 Michael Lewis, 'Boom Box', *New York Times Magazine* (20 Aug. 2000), 36–41.

34 Becky Ebenkamp, 'Peyton Placement', *Brandweek* (4 June 2001), S10.

35 Claudia Deutsch, 'Study Details Decline in Spending on Ads', *New York Times* (5 Sept. 2001), C2; Stuart Elliott, 'An Agency Giant is Expected to Warn of Lower Profits, and Analysts Darken their Outlook', *New York Times* (2 Oct. 2001), C2; see also Harry Berkowitz, 'Media Firms Report Big Losses; Companies Pulled Ads in Tragedy's Wake', *New York Newsday* (3 Oct. 2001), A53.

36 TiVo press release; for an account of increased interest among advertising-supported cable networks in advertiser-supplied programming, see Jim Forkan, 'On Some Cable Shows, the Sponsors Take Charge; Advertiser-Supplied Programming Trend Focuses on Outdoorsy and Family Genres', *Multichannel News* (4 June 2001), 53; on the growth of product placement, see Wayne Friedman, 'Eagle-Eye Marketers Find Right Spot, Right Time; Product Placements Increase as Part of Syndication Deals', *Advertising Age* (22 Jan. 2001), S2.

37 David Goetzi, 'TBS Tries Virtual Advertising', *Advertising Age*, 21 May 2001; weeks later, there was still confusion about the final status of the *Law and Order* deal, including permission from the show's joint production companies; see Stuart Elliott, 'Reruns may Become a Testing Ground for Digital Insertion of Sponsor's Products and Images', *New York Times* (23 May 2001), C6. In an indication of the unsettled and over-hyped industry environment of digital television in this period, the widely announced PVI-TBS deal for *Law and Order* never materialized.

38 'Digital Television Advertising', *Financial Times* (5 June 2001), 12.

encryption schemes that would limit the digital video recorder's ability to play back specific programmes or disable the device's fast-forward function during TV commercials.[39]

The deteriorating advertising market and the technological threat of the ad-thwarting digital video recorder in 2001 combined to create a climate of increased network accommodation to advertiser wishes in prime-time programming. As we have seen, TiVo itself already offered advertisers several areas of branded content that would negate the commercial-avoiding capabilities of its own device in the form of TiVo Direct, Network Showcases, TiVolution Magazine, and *TiVo Takes*. TiVo's merging of advertising and programme content was seen as emblematic of a larger trend; *Broadcasting and Cable* quoted one analyst who saw TiVo's blending of entertainment and advertising content as a sign of the future of advertising: 'We've already seen a blurring of the lines between providing information and advertising. . . . Advertisers and programmers are going to have to blur those lines even further in the future.'[40] These so-called 'embedded commerce' features have increasingly become the model for network programming as well, especially as the networks faced a weakening upfront advertising market in the spring of 2001; with costs per thousand expected to fall 12–15 per cent and the possibility of talent strikes looming, the major television networks undertook new efforts to accommodate the marketing needs and creative ideas of advertisers directly into the autumn 2001 prime-time season programmes.[41] At ABC's presentation to advertisers and ad agencies in Los Angeles in March 2001, the network announced that it would send every one of its comedy and drama pilot scripts directly to advertisers, something that the co-chairman of the ABC Entertainment Group characterized as a 'little unprecedented'.[42] A few months earlier, the producer of ABC's daytime serial *The View* shrugged off objections to the product placement of Campbell Soup in the programme, telling the press, 'We're willing to plug shamelessly, but we have limits. The integrity of the show has to be maintained.'[43] In January 2001, the USA's sixth largest network, UPN, made a deal with Heineken beer to be the sole sponsor of the evening's prime-time line-up, as well as to provide product placement within the evening's half-hour sitcoms.[44]

39 Jon Healey, 'Digital Living Room: Copyright Concerns are Creating Static for Digital TV', *Los Angeles Times* (22 Mar. 2001), T7; a TiVo executive told a group of advertisers that disabling the capacity to fast-forward through commercials might not be technologically possible and warned his audience that they might not want to be the network or sponsor that disabled the viewer's remote control; Ken Ripley, national director, advertising sales, TiVo, at personal video recorder panel, 2001 Association of National Advertisers Television Advertising Forum, 29 Mar. 2001, Plaza Hotel, New York City. In a chapter entitled 'Friction-Free Capitalism' in his 1995 best-seller *The Road Ahead*, Microsoft CEO Bill Gates wrote approvingly about 'software that lets the customer fast-forward past everything except for the advertising, which will play at normal speed' when Internet-delivered full-motion video becomes available; Bill Gates, *The Road Ahead* (New York: Penguin, 1995), 171.

40 Lee Hall, 'Coming Soon to a PVR near you; TiVo to Provide Uploadable Advertisements, while Giving Customers the Means to Skip them', *Broadcasting and Cable* (26 Feb. 2001), 40.

41 Michael Freeman, 'Networks Ready for Strikes', *Electronic Media* (26 Mar. 2001), 2.

42 Louis Chunovic, 'Advertisers go Deep in New TV Shows', *Electronic Media* (26 Mar. 2001), 3.

43 Ibid.

44 Gloria Goodale, 'Ads you can't Subtract', *Christian Science Monitor* (19 Jan. 2001), 13.

At least some in the creative community seemed unperturbed about the growing practice of product placement; the executive producer of *The Drew Carey Show* told the *Christian Science Monitor* in January 2001: 'If someone wants to step up and pay for my show, it doesn't bother me to find a way to put their product in my show.' The same producer told the paper that he was considering having the show's star make live product pitches in the next TV season's special live broadcast.[45] Another sign of growing network accommodation to the wishes of television advertisers was CBS's August 2001 decision to withdraw several repeat episodes of its prime-time dramatic series *Family Law* after one of the programme's major sponsors, Procter and Gamble, threatened to withdraw its advertisements from episodes dealing with what the *New York Times* called 'politically or socially charged issues', including handgun regulation, the death penalty, abortion, and interfaith marriage.[46]

The spectacular popularity of quiz programmes and reality-TV shows in US network prime time in the late 1990s also encouraged more intrusive product placement, greater creative roles for sponsors, and increased experimentation with commercial applications of interactive television. A March 2001 report on interactive television by Jupiter Media Metrix advised clients to continue investing in the 'interactive-friendly' genres of sports, game shows and news, while warning that drama and comedy genres would be more challenging.[47] The case of CBS's reality-TV hit *Survivor*, where a number of sponsors paid $12 million each to place products in the programme, was reported to be a very happy one for network and advertisers alike, with one network executive especially proud of arranging for the emaciated contestants to compete for a special prize of Mountain Dew soft drink and Doritos snack food: 'It's probably the most creative use of product placement in TV', the CBS spokesman boasted.[48]

Concerns over the threat of the digital video recorder, the financial potential of product placement and viewer interactivity, and new levels of network–sponsor accommodation converged in the 2001 trade discussion concerning an upcoming ABC reality-TV series, *The Runner*, which the *New York Times* called 'almost surely the most ambitious reality series so far conceived'.[49] After being pitched in 2000 by actor-writer-producers Matt Damon and Ben Affleck, in mid-2001 ABC announced that the programme would be launched in January 2002. *The Runner* was to feature an incognito individual contestant who moves across the country fulfilling a series of network-assigned tasks over twenty-eight days, motivated by a reward of up to a million dollars if he or she can accomplish the assignments and elude

45 Gloria Goodale, 'Ads you can't Subtract', *Christian Science Monitor* (19 Jan. 2001), 13.

46 Bill Carter, 'CBS Pulls Show over Concern from P. & G.', *New York Times* (17 Aug. 2001), C1.

47 Jay Lyman, 'Study: Interactive TV to Boom Despite Barriers', *NewsFactor Network*, 27 Mar. 2001. www.NewsFactor.com/perl/story/8465.html.

48 CBS spokesperson Chris Ender, quoted in Gail Collins, 'Public Interests; Elmo Gets Wired', *New York Times* (24 Apr. 2001), A19; also see Bill Carter, 'New Reality Show Planning to Put Ads between the Ads', *New York Times* (30 Apr. 2001), A1.

49 Bill Carter, 'The New Season: Television and Radio: The Annotated List: France Liberated, Laughs Generated and Reality Revisited', *New York Times* (9 Sept. 2001), B23.

capture by viewers seeking the same prize money. (Viewers would sign up as 'licensed agents' and track clues and location updates on the programme's Internet site.) By July 2001, the show's website was already reporting 30,000 visitors a week, including those seeking to download application forms to become either a runner or one of the agents seeking his or her capture.[50]

Broadcasting and Cable called the show 'the most expensive and ambitious reality series to hit network television yet', and warned that 'it also might be the most dangerous if not executed properly,' conjuring *Fahrenheit 451*-inspired scenarios of telescreen-linked vigilantes pursuing the breathless hero through panopticon streets.[51] The TV critic of New York's *Daily News* noted that 'the potential for mob scenes, assaults, mistaken-identity confrontations and other assorted mayhem seemed limitless', and *Daily Variety* reported that 'exactly how the runner will be caught—and not harmed in the process—is still being hammered out. But ABC execs are confident they'll be able to work out that detail, as well as find a way to use hidden cameras to track the runner's progress without alerting the public to the runner's whereabouts.'[52] After noting that viewers would be invited to participate by either helping or hindering the runner, the *Toronto Star*'s TV critic argued that 'given that there are cash rewards for the latter, but not the former, I can't see this guy getting more than a mile or so before he gets turned in. Or shot.'[53] In response to a press question about what was to stop viewers who think they've spotted the fugitive from attempting a potentially injurious capture, one of the programme's executive producers stated, 'If you impede the runner, you not only will be prosecuted to the full extent of the law, but you can't win any money.'[54] ABC hired Michael Davies, the producer of *Who Wants to Be a Millionaire*, to help run the show, and stage managing what was to be a 28-day televised national manhunt was turned over to Roger Goodman, a veteran of ABC's sports, news, and special event programming (including the network's coverage of the 1991 Gulf War and its *ABC 2000* global millennium event). As one ABC vice-president explained to *Daily Variety*, the network was essentially 'creating a gigantic sporting event', to which the network would enjoy exclusive rights. 'It's rife with logistic and liability issues', the executive told the paper.[55]

Beyond the daunting privacy, logistical, and personal safety issues involved in producing *The Runner*, the proposed programme also attracted considerable press attention by the unusual lengths to which the network and the show's producers announced they were willing to go to integrate advertising material into the programme itself. These efforts were repeatedly justified as responses to the increased ability of TV viewers to escape

50 David Bloom, 'The Digital Dozen', *Variety* (23–9 July 2001), 29.

51 Joe Schlosser, 'Safety First for Runner: ABC being Cautious with Series that Sends Viewers on Manhunt', *Broadcasting and Cable* (9 Apr. 2001), 24; Ray Bradbury, *Fahrenheit 451* (New York: Ballantine Books, 1976), 138–9.

52 Eric Mink, 'Rundown on "Runner" ', *Daily News* (24 July 2001), 67; Josef Adalian, 'ABC's "Runner" Making Stride', *Daily Variety* (21 Mar. 2001), 1.

53 Rob Salem, 'Everyone's Offering a Dose of Reality', *Toronto Star* (25 Aug. 2001), J3.

54 Noel Holston, 'On ABC Family, a Different Type of Diversity', *Newsday* (25 July 2001), B35.

55 Adalian, 'ABC's "Runner" Making Stride', 1.

traditional television commercials through devices like the digital video recorder. ABC's president of programme sales told the *New York Times* that such concerns 'sent us down the road into evaluation of what kind of programming we might have that could integrate their products into the content. . . . This show does it organically. That's the beauty of it.'[56] The co-chairman of ABC Entertainment described the show as 'one of the best ideas for a television show I have ever heard', in part because of its potential for product placement, which, he told the *Times*, 'occurred to us about a nanosecond after we heard Matt and Ben describe the show'.[57] The same executive told a group of network advertisers: 'Is the runner going to wear Nikes? Is the runner going to wear Reeboks? Is the runner going to wear Adidas? You guys get to decide.'[58]

By May 2001, ABC had closed an $8-million-dollar deal with Pepsi as *The Runner*'s exclusive soft drink. *Newsweek* reported that 'Pepsi was intrigued by ABC's "open invitation" to actively help create the scenarios for product placements', and according to a Pepsi vice-president 'we are going to work very closely with them to make this different and unusual'.[59] The show's producers suggested putting clues to the runner's location in Pepsi's TV commercials and were reportedly also pursuing product placement deals with advertisers in eight other product categories, including 'a clothes store, a car firm, a fast food chain, a financial services company and a wireless communications brand'.[60] In September 2001 *Broadcasting and Cable* reported that ABC had also made a deal with Chrysler for product placement on *The Runner*.[61] An executive for the show's production company told the press, 'We don't look at it as product placement, we look at it as product integration.'[62] *Newsweek* concluded: 'with *The Runner*, ABC is offering advertisers much more [than traditional product placement]—a chance to help decide how the plot of the series will unfold, in some cases on an episode-by-episode or even scene-by-scene basis'.[63] The network invited advertisers to suggest plot ideas and incidents tailored to their products; 'We would absolutely love to hear the advertisers' ideas', ABC's president of sales told the *New York Times*.[64] A Pepsi spokesperson told Britain's *Guardian* newspaper in July 2001: 'What really is the most intriguing aspect of the show is how we'll fit in and that Pepsi products can be used as a part of the plot. For example,

56 Carter, 'New Reality Show Planning to Put Ads between the Ads', A1.

57 Ibid.

58 Chunovic, 'Advertisers go Deep in New TV Shows', 3.

59 Margaret McKegney, 'U.S.: Is Reality TV a Survivor?', *Ad Age Global* (1 June 2001), 6; Johnnie L. Roberts, 'This Space Available', *Newsweek* (7 May 2001), 42.

60 Wayne Friedman, 'ABC Puts Ads on Run; Reality Show "Runner" Pitches Product Placement', *Advertising Age* (30 Apr. 2001), 3; Gillian Drummond, 'Meet TV's Newest Stars', *Guardian* (23 July 2001), 6.

61 Joe Schlosser, 'Have we Got a Deal for you: Adjusting to Bear Market, Networks Offer Sponsorships, Product Placements, Other Value-Added Lures this Fall', *Broadcasting and Cable* (3 Sept. 2001), 5.

62 Joanne Weintraub, 'Show and Sell: Products a Bigger Part of the Plot', *Milwaukee Journal Sentinel* (5 June 2001), 1E.

63 Roberts, 'This Space Available', 42.

64 Carter, 'New Reality Show Planning to Put Ads between the Ads', A1.

[the runner] may have to go to a store and purchase a Pepsi.'[65] ABC also announced plans to promote *The Runner* across its programme schedule, with on-screen bugs and lower-third crawls updating clues and the current bounty amount throughout the network's programming and allowing advertisers to sponsor branded programme updates.[66] Dismissing critics of the planned show's intensive use of product placement, co-producer Ben Affleck told the *Financial Times* in August 2001: 'As if you had some inalienable right to have commercial-free television! What do you think pays for this show?'[67]

Conclusion

Some in the TV industry viewed the unprecedented willingness of *The Runner*'s producers and network to integrate programme and advertising as merely a taste of things to come, as advertisers respond to the increasing ability of viewers to evade traditional 30-second commercials, and networks make new business and creative accommodations to advertisers in a weak TV ad market. In addition, several industry executives pointed to the value of product placement at a time when more and more viewers are seen to be increasingly sceptical of conventional advertising forms; one ad executive told *Brandweek*: 'It's far more effective in bypassing the usual alarms that go off; the critical part of the brain shuts down. . . . When you're aware someone's trying to get to you, you're more guarded. When you're not, stuff just seeps in.'[68] In support of the practice the same executive pointed to the recent federally funded efforts by US anti-drug tsar General Barry McCaffrey to place surreptitious anti-drug messages in prime-time programmes as an alternative to traditional public service commercials.[69]

Surveying the new technological and economic climate for television advertising, an NBC executive told *Broadcasting and Cable* in September 2001: 'I think everybody realizes that they have to do business differently and they have to be more open than they were before. . . . Whether it's buying advertiser-supplied programming, whether it's integrating further into a show than you have before, or getting promotional consideration in another media . . . I just think the whole state of the business is changing.'[70] As an example of the industry's new programming models, the magazine pointed to WB network's mid-season 2002 reality series *No Boundaries*, sponsored by the automobile manufacturer Ford, featuring contestants driving and winning Ford Explorer SUVs; the programme's title itself echoes the

65 Gillian Drummond, 'Meet TV's Newest Stars', *Guardian* (23 July 2001), 6; Drummond quotes a LivePlanet executive claiming that 'the sponsors are not determining the content of the show, but they are integral to the content. That's a fine point . . . the runner is not going to go into a store to buy a Pepsi. That would be a gross way of doing this.'

66 Roberts, 'This Space Available', 42.

67 Katja Hofmann, 'LivePlanet', *Financial Times* (7 Aug. 2001), 4. Plans to air *The Runner* were shelved by ABC after the terror attacks of 11 Sept. 2001.

68 Ebenkamp, 'Peyton Placement', S10.

69 Ibid.; for a discussion of McCaffrey's efforts, see Daniel Forbes, 'Prime-Time Propaganda: How the White House Secretly Hooked Network TV on its Anti-Drug Message', 13 Jan. 2000. www.salon.com/news/feature/2000/01/13/drugs/index.html.

70 Schlosser, 'Have we Got a Deal for you', 5.

advertising slogan in Ford's ongoing multi-million-dollar marketing campaigns.[71] In August 2001, the *New York Times* reported that UPN, owned by Viacom, was considering offering sponsors the ability to superimpose logos and brand names as on-screen bugs during the network's prime-time programming 'as a bonus [to advertisers] for buying large blocks of time to run traditional commercials during regular breaks'.[72] While one advertising executive denounced UPN's proposed ad bugs as 'shockingly crude and inappropriate . . . A sign of desperation', another industry executive argued that 'history has shown that when consumers are exposed to advertising in places where advertising has not been in the past, they initially react negatively—then accept it'.[73] Addressing a more general trend, a product placement broker told a British reporter that advertisers' direct involvement in TV programming was likely to increase, with the development of 'single advertising shows', where sponsors produce their own TV programmes and integrate their products into the dramatic content, 'right around the corner'.[74]

The prospect of heightened commercial creative censorship, intrusive ad bugs, sponsor-supplied programming, and enhanced product placement, all fuelled by the fearful prospect of the ad-evading digital video recorder and growing advertiser power in a recessionary TV ad market, has provoked some misgivings within the television industry, including fear of provoking increased consumer resistance to all advertising. Such contemporary trade anxieties resonate with an older and wider public debate about the limits to commercialization in twentieth-century culture. An executive at one product placement firm admitted that its growing use in television programmes is 'only going to work if there isn't a backlash among consumers', and an editorial in *Brandweek* called the trend toward more product placement 'dangerous, for brands, for TV and yes—you and me'.[75] Several industry commentators referred to a 2001 Roper-Starch Worldwide survey of TV viewers which pointed to growing public aversion to advertising; according to the survey, the percentage of television viewers who switch channels at commercial breaks had roughly tripled to 36 per cent since 1985, and the percentage of viewers who mute commercials had tripled to 23 per cent during the same period.[76] The Roper survey reported that 64 per cent of respondents characterized advertising as a 'nuisance' that 'clutters up' TV, up 5 points since 1998, and 76 per cent felt advertising is 'shown in far too many places now, you can't get away from it', up 10 points from 1998.[77] More broadly, according to a September 2000 *Business Week*-Harris poll, 82 per cent of consumers see 'entertainment and popular culture . . . dominated by corporate money, which seeks mass appeal over quality'.[78]

71 Schlosser, 'Have we Got a Deal for you', 5.

72 Stuart Elliott, 'UPN Weighs Ad Logos in Prime Time', *New York Times* (23 Aug. 2001), C1.

73 Ibid.

74 Drummond, 'Meet TV's Newest Stars', 6.

75 Ibid.; Karen Benezra, 'In Reality, Television is Overrated', *Brandweek* (4 June 2001), n.p.

76 Matthew Grimm, 'Reality Bites', *American Demographics* (July 2001), 56.

77 Ibid.

78 Aaron Bernstein, 'Too Much Corporate Power?', *Business Week* (11 Sept. 2000), 144; cited in Grimm, 'Reality Bites', 56.

As Raymond Williams noted in 1960, public complaints that advertisers 'have gone about as far as they can go' date back at least to the mid-eighteenth century, and there is a poignant *déjà vu* quality to some of the debates around contemporary television's emerging advertising forms.[79] The two previous periods of sustained business expansion in the twentieth century—the 1920s and the 1950s—coincided not only with advertisers' eager exploitation of the new media of radio and television, respectively, but with the widespread expression of popular unease about the role of advertising in everyday life and cultural media.[80] Several contemporary observers have noted the ironic echo of earlier broadcast advertising practices in the new world of digital television, including the return of single sponsorship, the integration of commercial and programme, and the reprise of the celebrity pitch man.

The sometimes fevered trade and public discussions of the observed and anticipated changes in broadcast television's commercial and programme forms in 2000–1 were linked by many commentators to a wider cultural anxiety about the place of advertising in modern life, ranging from literary critics' outraged and parodic responses to Fay Weldon's 2001 novel *The Bulgari Connection*, which pioneered modern literary product placement, to the widely reported attempt by a New York couple to auction the naming rights of their unborn child to corporate marketers the same year.[81] Such wider cultural anxieties suggest that the ultimate fortunes of the various new technological capabilities of digital television will depend on more than questions of technology and market power. In the fog of marketing hype and economic uncertainty around technological innovation in the first years of the twenty-first century, it is important to note that the reaction of TV viewers to the increasingly desperate attempts of advertisers and broadcasters to integrate commercial message and programme form remains largely untested, and crucial to any eventual outcome.

79 Raymond Williams, 'Advertising: The Magic System', in *Problems in Materialism and Culture* (London: Verso, 1980), 172.

80 See, for example, Ralph Borsodi, *This Ugly Civilization* (New York: Simon and Schuster, 1929); Fred Manchee, *The Huckster's Revenge: The Truth about Life on Madison Avenue* (New York: Nelson, 1959).

81 A small sample of the Weldon debate includes John Balzar, 'Sold! A Literary Soul, Now Mud', *Los Angeles Times* (5 Sept. 2001), B13; *Boston Herald*, 'Editorial; Author Should Play by the Book' (9 Sept. 2001), 24; Jenny Lyn Bader, 'Brand-Name Lit: Call Me Tiffany', *New York Times* (9 Sept. 2001), D2; Don Campbell, 'For Author, the (GE) Light Dawns', *USA Today* (10 Sept. 2001), 17A; for the attempted corporate-naming auction of the unborn child, see Matthew Purdy, *New York Times*, 'Our Towns; A Boy Named Soup?' (1 Aug. 2001), B1; Arthur Asa Berger, 'Sponsor Me: Selling out or Subverting?', *New York Newsday* (17 Aug. 2001), A49; 'Editorial: Ad Mad: The Parents who Offered Naming Rights for their Baby are not the Problem', *Pittsburgh Post-Gazette* (15 Aug. 2001), A13.

11

'Too Easy, Too Cheap and Too Fast to Control': Intellectual Property Battles in Digital Television

Introduction

MANY OF THE PREVAILING assumptions about the future of moving-image culture in the United States which emerged out of the consumer prosperity and booming capital markets of the 1990s were suddenly subjected to new scrutiny in the wake of economic recession and military mobilization at the end of 2001. This chapter examines some of the implications for media scholars and educators of the media landscape transformed by the precipitous declines in share prices, advertising expenditures, and consumer confidence. The first years of the new millennium were marked by additional disruptions in an already unsettled environment for technological innovation within moving-image industries in the United States. The psychological and economic effects of the terrorist attacks of 11 September 2001, the unfolding global consequences of the over-bidding and over-building which marked the high-tech stock bubble of the late 1990s (including the bankruptcies in 2002 of ITV Digital in the UK and the Kirsch media empire in Germany), and the still-unanswered questions regarding consumer appetites for a range of present and prospective digital devices and services, have combined to create an unusual level of uncertainty across the industries of programme production, information technology, and consumer electronics. The year 2001 in the United States witnessed a nearly unprecedented drop in network television advertising revenues as well as the first-ever declines in personal computer sales, the number of cable subscribers served by the top six firms, and the number of Americans subscribing to Internet service providers.

The uncertain economic conditions have sharpened rivalries within and across these industries, sparking new commercial conflicts, legal actions, and legislative battles. While the ensuing trade and policy debates evoke enduring, if disputed (and always self-serving), figurations of the television apparatus, viewer, and nation, the consequences of the current disputes may be of unprecedented significance for citizens and media scholars alike. This chapter considers the way in which emerging digital delivery and storage devices in the home have brought into stark relief the divergent interests of the distinct sectors of the moving-image economy and outlines some of the legal, policy, and professional stakes of the battles they have provoked. The ongoing legal and legislative battles between Hollywood and the information technology and consumer electronics industries have inevitably enlisted long-established competing cultural constructions of the computer user and television viewer and the private and public sites of media consumption. For media historians, such disputes may do more than offer insights into the implications of such long-running discursive practices; indeed, their concrete legislative outcomes may have a direct effect on how film and television teachers and researchers might accomplish their work.

Threatening technologies

Two technologies—one notorious, if still tangential to motion pictures, and the other a presence in less than 1 per cent of American homes—currently haunt what is variously called the 'creative content industry', the 'content industry', or the 'copyright industry', in the blunt term of Jack Valenti, long-time president of the Motion Picture Producers' Association of America (MPPA). The first is Napster, the infamous Internet file-sharing service, more broadly defined as P2P or peer-to-peer (or 'pirate-to-pirate', in the content industry's view, or indeed 'prisoner-to-prisoner' as some wags have suggested, if the industry achieves its legislative goals). An unnamed technology expert at Rupert Murdoch's News Corp. predicted in January 2002 that 'within five years, music will be a cottage industry',[1] and an MPPA executive vice-president, quoted in an April 2002 *Christian Science Monitor* article entitled 'Web Pirates Pillage Hollywood', proclaimed that 'with Napster, we learned that we have seen our future, and it's terrifying'.[2] Disney CEO Michael Eisner called Internet piracy 'the most devastating thing that's happened to the entertainment business in . . . the last 75 years'.[3] AOL-Time Warner CEO Richard Parsons told the Senate Judiciary Committee in the spring of 2002 that 'unfortunately, right now, with the advent of services like Napster and more recent peer-to-peer file swapping sites, a generation of young people is growing up thinking it's all right to steal. At an average cost of $80 million per movie, that is simply not O.K.'[4] In June 2002 a Disney vice-president warned: 'We need to get a reasonably secure environment before 50 million Americans get used to downloading their movies for free.'[5] As early as July 2000, News Corp. president Peter Chernin was warning, in speeches to the Republican and Democratic party platform committees, that 'infringement has become too easy, too cheap and too fast to control'.[6] The

1 Mike Godwin, 'A Cop in Every Computer: The Content and Technology Industries Differ over an Initiative that would Build Infringement-Sniffing Powers into New Computers', *IP Worldwide* (16 Jan. 2002), n.p.

2 Gloria Goodale, 'Web Pirates Pillage Hollywood', *Christian Science Monitor* (12 Apr. 2002), 13.

3 Quoted in Richard Raysman and Peter Brown, 'Computer Law: Are Federal Digital Security Standards the Answer to Illegal Copying?', *New York Law Journal* (9 Apr. 2002), 3.

4 Testimony of Richard Parsons, Senate Committee on the Judiciary, 'Competition, Innovation, and Public Policy in the Digital Age: Is the Marketplace Working to Protect Digital Creative Works?', 14 Mar. 2002. http://judiciary.senate.gov/testimony.cfm?id=197&wit_id=259.

5 Disney executive vice-president Preston Padden, quoted in Mike Musgrove, 'Copyfight Renewal; Owners of Digital Devices Sue to Assert the Right to Record', *Washington Post* (7 June 2002), E1.

6 Jill Goldsmith, 'Chernin Addresses the Digital Threat', *Daily Variety* (14 July 2000), 5.

MPPA, citing an unnamed consultant's study, in April 2002 estimated that 350,000 unauthorized digital movie files were being downloaded daily, with the number expected to reach 1 million by the end of 2002 as broadband Internet access expanded.[7] As MPPA president Valenti inimitably summed up in March 2002 in the *Wall Street Journal*: 'With what velocity will this avalanche of thievery roar when broadband is more widely used?'[8] As we shall see, such apocalyptic visions among studio executives of peer-to-peer video file sharing represent at least the ostensible motivation behind Hollywood's recent productive trips to Washington.

The second technological spectre haunting Valenti's 'copyright industry' is the digital video recorder and its possible progeny, various labelled the 'home media centre', the 'personal home network', or the 'home network asset management system'. This multi-purpose device would combine the time-shifting and commercial-avoiding capabilities of the digital video recorder with Internet and intranet broadband links to download and distribute on-line, broadcast, and cable- and satellite-delivered audio-video content. The new multimedia appliance would also incorporate or link satellite and cable set-top boxes, DVD players, MP-3/CD jukeboxes, video game consoles, personal computers, digital camcorders and still cameras, IP-based telephones, and personal data assistants. While it might seem premature to ponder the technological and commercial successor to the barely three-year-old digital video recorder, which has sold less than 2 million units in the USA by the middle of 2002, the prospect of the new media hub device seemed to condense and multiply Hollywood's fears concerning the entire product category of digital storage and display devices.

The digital video recorder, despite its initial modest commercial success, by 2002 had already generated remarkable attention from industry leaders and pundits, who predicted that the device would bring about the end of the traditional television commercial (and spur new efforts to devise inescapable advertising in the forms of conventional and virtual product placement, advertiser-supplied programmes, and Internet-style bugs and banner ads, as we have seen). As discussed in earlier chapters, some observers pondered the digital video recorder's effect upon the entire economy of mass marketing and the extinction of 'live' television reception as instrument of national identity.[9] Disputing such claims for the decisive impact of the new device, Britain's *New Statesman* in 2002 noted the slow uptake of the digital video recorder and found in the phenomenal worldwide success of the more conventional DVD player salutary consumer resistance to the widely trumpeted communications revolution in favour of 'our archaic habit of squirreling away physical copies of conventionally constructed artifacts'.[10] However, most industry observers remained sanguine about the ultimate commercial future of the digital video recorder. US media executive Barry Diller in early

7 Goodale, 'Web Pirates Pillage Hollywood', 13.

8 Jacob Heilbrunn, 'Copyright Law: Hollywood Embraces Big-Brother Tactics', *Los Angeles Times* (31 Mar. 2002), M3.

9 'To Infinity and Beyond', *The Economist* (13 Apr. 2002), n.p.

10 David Cox, 'The Future has been Canceled: Experts Said we would Surf the Net on TVs and Watch Films on Mobiles. But we Still Prefer the Cinema', *New Statesman* (21 Jan. 2002), n.p.

2002 called the impact of the digital video recorder 'the most profound change taking place in TV'.[11] A front-page *New York Times* article in May 2002, 'Skip-the-Ads TV Has Madison Ave. Upset', quoted the chief executive of Turner Broadcasting who sternly warned viewers that 'the free television that we've all enjoyed for so many years is based on us watching these commercials. There's no Santa Claus. If you don't watch the commercials, someone's going to have to pay for television and it's going to be you.'[12]

In the context of such alarmist industry rhetoric, it is important to separate the general prospects for the digital video recorder from the fortunes of any particular hardware platform, business model, and corporate actor. As discussed in the previous chapter, Microsoft's expensive entry, and quick exit, from the sector, in the form of its inauspiciously named Ultimate TV, suggests the need for such caution. TiVo, the digital video recorder market leader, relies upon the distinct revenue paths of subscriptions and advertising sales, and has signalled its desire to accommodate advertisers in several ways: by omitting a 'skip' button on the device's remote control, by creating branded-content areas across its programme guide and speciality channels, and, according to some reports, by experimenting with telescoping ad windows which would zoom to full-screen display of advertising text and logos during fast-forwarding. Another US firm announced plans to offer discounts on digital cable service in exchange for the mandatory viewing of a certain number of commercials for each thirty minutes of digitally recorded material.[13]

Indeed, the fundamental revenue models and technological platforms for the digital video recorder remain unsettled. TiVo models introduced in 2002 incorporate the Real Media player and subscription service, and the company announced plans to offer AOL Instant Messaging, interactive gaming, and video-on-demand. Meanwhile, there is an ongoing debate about the viability of the digital video recorder as a stand-alone device, versus its integration into a satellite or cable set-top box, a DVD player, a game console, or even the television set itself. Such multimedia devices, merely the latest artefact in the endlessly hyped convergence of computer technology and electronic entertainment in the home, provoked a great deal of both fear and anticipation in the consumer electronics, computer, and creative content industries in the early years of the twenty-first century.[14] As one enthusiastic industry consultant put it, 'if the '90s were all about managing information on your PC, then this decade is going to be all about managing your entertainment content on your entertainment computer. We see the television as an entertainment computer.'[15] Pointing to what he called the 'consumerization of technology' over the next five-to-ten years, one stock analyst told *Business Week* in 2002 that 'the future isn't about

11 'Big Brother is you, Watching', *The Economist* (13 Apr. 2002), n.p.

12 Amy Harmon, 'Skip-the-Ads TV Has Madison Ave. Upset', *New York Times* (23 May 2002), A1.

13 Jeff Howe, 'Total Control', *American Demographics* (July 2001), 28.

14 Edward C. Baig, 'Gadgets Go Way beyond VCRs, CDs', *USA Today* (25 June 2002), 6E.

15 Ian MacLean, vice-president of iTV Lab, a division of Montreal-based Media Experts, quoted in Peter Vamos, 'Will PVRs be a Boon to Spot Production?', *Playback* (8 Jan. 2002), 1.

IBM selling more mainframes . . . it's about MP3 players, digital video, and the like'.[16]

In the context of general industry interest in such multimedia consumer appliances, Microsoft announced plans to launch a new PC-based home entertainment network system built upon its proprietary software; an unnamed industry insider was quoted in *Electronic Engineering Times* in January 2002 that '[Microsoft CEO Bill] Gates is passionate about this. He was passionate about the Xbox last year, and this is his thing for 2002.'[17] The best-of-show product of the January 2002 consumer electronics trade show was the Moxi Media Center (an integrated digital video recorder, DVD player, digital jukebox, cable or satellite receiver, and broadband modem), the much-anticipated first product from WebTV co-founder Steve Perlman's new firm. Moxi, having burned through most of its reported $67 million in start-up capital before the product's launch, was subsequently acquired by Paul Allen's Digeo interactive TV company; Allen is majority owner of Charter Cable, the nation's fourth largest cable operator. The Moxi Media Center has been described as a Trojan horse for the shift to a pay-per-view media economy, and cable operators, who describe the media hub as a 'home network asset management system', are eager to enter the nascent market. As *Newsweek* magazine noted in January 2002, such a device 'may even help in realizing the dream of record labels and movie studios (like AOL): a "pay per view" world where every listen of a Lucinda Williams tune or viewing of a "Get Smart" rerun racks up another nickel on the cable bill'.[18]

On one level, the prospect of an entirely new domestic product category, as the digital video recorder morphs into the home media server, has provoked a rush of competing suppliers inspired by yet another vision of the networked home. In May 2002 the *New York Times* announced that a new 'battle for control of your living room is about to be waged by consumer electronics makers, developers of personal-computer hardware and software, and set-top-box designers that sell directly to cable and satellite providers', and a trade magazine declared around the same time that 'at stake is not only a massive market but also control over how entertainment content will flow to and be consumed within the home'.[19] On the other hand, the new integrated digital storage devices have sparked visions of Napster-like ruin among studio executives and network programmers; the fear that such machines could 'leak copyrighted material all over the world . . . has them terrified', according to a counsel for a software industry lobbying organization.[20] In addition, as Disney head Michael Eisner explained to the Senate Commerce Committee in March 2002, the motion-picture studios fear the creation of new electronic gatekeepers in the form of proprietary encryption systems controlled by satellite, cable, or PC-based home network

---

16 Merrill Lynch & Co. analyst Steven Milunovich, quoted in David Rocks, 'The Tech Outlook: Home Entertainment', *Business Week* (11 Apr. 2002), 203.

17 Rick Merritt, 'M'soft Drives Home with Info Appliance', *Electronic Engineering Times* (7 Jan. 2002), 1.

18 Steven Levy, 'A Couch Potato's Digital Dream', *Newsweek* (14 Jan. 2002), 55.

19 Wilson Rothman, 'Mission Control for the Living Room', *New York Times* (9 May 2002), G1; Steven Fyffe, 'Home Ownership: Who Controls the Household Entertainment Hub?', *CommVerge* (1 May 2002), 20.

20 Godwin, 'A Cop in Every Computer', n.p.

systems.[21] Other have warned that even the 'open standards' which Eisner advocated for such security schemes have a history of evolving into closed, proprietary systems under anti-competitive market pressures, as seen in Microsoft's appropriation of Java and HTML.[22] Notwithstanding the fears of the content industry over the new entertainment servers, *Business Week* warned in early 2002: 'Networked home-entertainment products are coming, whether the industry likes them or not, and they are going to get cheaper and easier to use. We can only hope the entertainment industry fails in its efforts to kill these new products before they have a chance to thrive.'[23]

Legislative battlegrounds

These simmering conflicts over digital storage devices between the creative content industry on one side and the information technology and consumer electronics industries on the other came to a head in March 2002 when Senator Ernest 'Fritz' Hollings and four co-sponsors introduced the Consumer Broadband and Digital Television Promotion Act. The bill, strongly supported by Disney, the News Corp., and the MPPA (and reportedly written by Disney lobbyists),[24] revised earlier draft legislation entitled the Security System Standards and Certification Act, which was proposed, though not introduced, in late 2001; autumn hearings on that measure were postponed as a result of the US Capitol's anthrax scare. The 2002 bill would impel the information technology, consumer electronics, and creative content industries to devise and agree upon within eighteen months a series of 'open standard' security measures to protect copyrighted audio-visual material from unauthorized duplication and distribution and would mandate the inclusion of such hardware and software measures on all digital devices subsequently sold in the United States capable of converting, storing, or transferring such digital material. The legislation would also impose notorious 'anti-circumvention' provisions, prohibiting the dissemination of information or software which would frustrate such prohibitions, with penalties of five years in prison and $500,000 in fines for each offence. Despite the bill's title, the devices covered in the legislation would in no way be limited to broadband or digital television; indeed, as the *New York Law Journal* noted, the bill's 'language appears capable of encompassing every kind of hardware device that can copy, manipulate, transfer or store digital information, including storage media such as CD-ROMS, floppy disks and DVDs, all kinds of computers ranging from mainframes and PCs to PDAs and digital devices such as digital television, cell phones and e-book readers, as well as any software associated with such hardware devices'.[25]

---

21 Testimony of Michael D. Eisner, Chairman & CEO, The Walt Disney Company, Before the Committee on Commerce, Science & Transportation, United States Senate, 28 Feb. 2002. http://commerce.senate.gov/hearings/hearings0202.htm.

22 Testimony of Joe Kraus before the Senate Judiciary Committee, 'Competition, Innovation, and Public Policy in the Digital Age: Is the Marketplace Working to Protect Digital Creative Works?', 14 Mar. 2002. http://judiciary.senate.gov/testimony.cfm?id=197&wit_id=340.

23 Stephen H. Wildstrom, 'This Video Recorder Has Some Enemies', *Business Week* (14 Jan. 2002), 18.

24 'The Anti-Mammal Dinosaur Protection Act', *DVD Report* (1 Apr. 2002), n.p.

25 Raysman and Brown, 'Are Federal Digital Security Standards the Answer to Illegal Copying?', 3.

As *Business Week* pointed out, the proposed legislation 'has made allies of the rivals in the living room/home office battle—consumer-electronics manufacturers and PC makers—who say that anti-piracy measures would limit consumer choice and hurt their ability to sell gear'.[26] The proposed legislation also served to divide California from north to south, as outraged executives from the consumer electronics and information technology industries complained that they would shoulder the entire financial burden and legal exposure in a futile legislative attempt to protect the financial assets of another industry. Benny Evangelista, the *San Francisco Chronicle*'s technology reporter, argued that 'the bill, if enacted, would be a major departure in the way copyright law has evolved because instead of trying to control how people use the technology, the proposal focuses on controlling the technology itself'.[27] Evangelista complained that 'the real power behind the Hollings bill is the six companies that now control most of the media we consume every day, including music, movies and television. They are worried that their profits will be diminished, and, like King Canute by the seaside, they have stamped their little feet and demanded that information become a private commodity.'[28] The *Washington Post* technology columnist criticized 'the absurd logic of the Hollings bill. It says the only way to prevent people from using stolen content is to require all software and hardware to verify that nothing's been stolen. In other words, you are presumed guilty until proven innocent.'[29] As one trade journalist noted, 'the outrage being expressed . . . is less concerned with the draconian bill becoming law than with Hollywood's sheer audacity in proposing it', and one website quickly labelled the bill the Anti-Mammal Dinosaur Protection Act.[30]

Even if intended merely as Hollywood's warning shot across the bow of the computer and consumer electronics industries, the bill's introduction demonstrated the political power of the copyright industry in Washington, where South Carolina's Senator Hollings was the third largest recipient of the industry's campaign contributions during his most recent electoral race in 1998.[31] The ensuing congressional debate, including extensive testimony before Hollings's Senate Commerce Committee and the Senate Judiciary Committee chaired by Vermont Democrat Patrick Leahy, indicates the degree of mistrust and antipathy between the three sectors of the new digital media industry, involving disputes over national economic policy, figurations of the domestic consumer, and competing normative constructs of the location and uses of electronic media devices in the home. Disney's Eisner complained to the Hollings committee that 'at least one high tech executive has described illegal pirate content as a "killer application" that will drive

---

26 David Rocks, 'The Tech Outlook: The Digital Revolution is Shaking up the Pecking Order', *Business Week* (11 Apr. 2002), 203.

27 Benny Evangelista, 'Proposed Copyright Law Raises Controversy', *San Francisco Chronicle* (8 Apr. 2002), E1.

28 Jon Carroll, 'Jolly New Threat to our Freedoms', *San Francisco Chronicle* (11 Apr. 2002), D14.

29 Rob Pegoraro, 'As Copyright Gets a Starring Role, We're Cast as the Villains', *Washington Post* (31 Mar. 2002), H06.

30 'The Anti-Mammal Dinosaur Protection Act', n.p.

31 John Davidson, 'File-Swapping Dyke Has a Hole', *Australian Financial Review* (2 Apr. 2002), 34.

consumer demand for Broadband', and that computer makers like Gateway and Apple (with its 'Rip, Mix, Burn' advertising campaign) encouraged their customers to use their PCs to violate copyright.[32] Gateway, in response to the Hollings bill, launched an April 2002 ad campaign promoting the downloading and burning of on-line music files and conducted consumer clinics on digital downloading in its 277 stores nationwide.[33] Meanwhile, many in the software and computer manufacturing industries were sceptical of any quick technological solution to the problem of digital piracy; the chief technology officer of one Internet security firm told the press in June 2002: 'You're trying to make water not wet. . . . The natural law of cyberspace is that bits are copyable.'[34]

Strategic constructions of television's apparatus and user

Some in the information technology side of the debate were eager to point to wider cultural differences between their industry and Valenti's 'copyright industry', evoking the conventional gendered oppositions between computer user and television viewer, itself built upon older figurative oppositions going back to the days of early wireless. Leslie Vadasz, executive vice-president of chip maker Intel Corporation, told the Senate Committee that 'the IT industry is all about innovation; we embrace and champion technological progress. The content community, by contrast, has historically feared technology—from the advent of sound recording, to the development of the VCR, the DVD, the PC and other digital devices.'[35] Roger Parloff, a contributing editor at *American Lawyer*, argued that 'there are cultural distinctions between a consumer's passive relationship with the single-function consumer electronics devices of the past (a TV, VCR or CD player) and the consumer's interactive relationship with today's computers and software. . . . It is more important to lock the government outside of our computers than it ever was to lock it outside of our appliances.'[36] Intel's Vadasz warned committee members: 'do not buy into a view of content protection that will deprive consumers of the ability to get the full benefit of the capabilities of the PC by neutering it—when it comes to content management—to be nothing more than a more expensive version of a "dumb" DVD player.'[37] These rhetorical antipodes of the passive and neutered domestic appliance versus the heroic and adventurous electronic tool have their roots, as we have seen, in the earliest conflicts between radio amateurs and early commercial broadcasters.

32 Eisner, Senate Commerce Committee testimony.

33 Michelle Megna, 'Copy Catfight: A New Plan to Restrict Digital Duping Raises Concerns about Consumers' Rights', *Daily News* (21 Apr. 2002), 6.

34 Bruce Schneier, founder and chief technology officer of Counterpane Internet Security Inc., quoted in Musgrove, 'Copyfight Renewal', E1.

35 Testimony of Leslie L. Vadasz, Executive Vice President, Intel Corporation, President, Intel Capital, Hearing on 'Protecting Content in the Digital Age: Promoting Broadband and the Digital Television Transition', Senate Commerce Committee, 28 Feb. 2002 http://commerce.senate.gov/hearings/hearings0202.htm.

36 Roger Parloff, 'The Hollings Bill Doesn't Compute', *Recorder* (15 May 2002), 4.

37 Vadasz, Senate Commerce Committee testimony.

Reinforcing the notion of a cultural gulf across the sectors of high-tech, many in the information technology and consumer electronics industries were eager to point out the MPPA's history of technological scare-mongering, especially its earlier opposition to the videotape recorder. Intel's Vadasz told the Senate Commerce Committee: 'In 1981, Mr Valenti bemoaned the prospect that the industry would be overwhelmed by "millions of little tape-worms" eating at the very heart and essence of copyright(s). . . . Substitute "digital" for "tape" in Mr Valenti's comments in 1981 and the arguments are the same,' Vadasz argued.[38] Other observers delighted in citing Valenti's famous 1981 formulation that 'the VCR is to the motion-picture industry what the Boston strangler is to the woman alone', while inevitably noting that after losing the Betamax case the Hollywood studio plaintiffs eventually realized far greater revenues from videotape and DVD sales than they would from the domestic theatrical box office.[39]

If members of the information technology community responded to the Hollings bill by reviving gendered oppositions between their industry and its customers and the traditional contexts of television reception, executives from the consumer electronics industry often framed their critiques by insisting upon the traditional split between the private domestic site of media reception and the 'public' space of the Internet and public performance. In this regard as well, contemporary intellectual property debates in digital media evoke long-standing cultural oppositions constructed by the experience of earlier electronic media. Robert Perry, vice-president of marketing for Mitsubishi Digital Electronics America, and a board member of the Home Recording Rights Coalition, an organization founded in the early 1980s to oppose the studios in the Betamax litigation, told the Senate Commerce Committee that 'the movie industry agendas from which consumers need protection go well beyond dealing with external connections to the Internet. Rather, they extend *internally*, inside the home, into the heart of the consumer home network.'[40] James Meyer, former chief operating officer and current special adviser to Thomson Multimedia, laid out for the Senate Commerce Committee Thomson's plans for its Personal Home Network, which would link an array of digital devices controlled by a new 'smart card' access system called 'SmartRight': 'the SmartRight system would permit a consumer to view, record, and store digital content for his own use within what is called a personal private network.'[41] Justin Hughes, a UCLA law professor, told the Senate Judiciary Committee in March 2002 that any remedy to the problem of copyright piracy 'should be one that focuses on stopping unauthorized distribution over the Internet and leaves alone what some people have called the "home net"—the integrated system of personal

38 Vadasz, Senate Commerce Committee testimony.

39 Danny O'Brien, 'Hollywood Attacks the TV Pirates', *Sunday Times*, 14 Apr. 2002.

40 Statement of Robert A. Perry, Vice President, Marketing, Mitsubishi Digital Electronics America, Inc., on Behalf of the Home Recording Rights Coalition, 'Protecting Content in the Digital Age—Promoting Broadband and the Digital Television Transition', Senate Commerce Committee, 28 Feb. 2002. http://commerce.senate.gov/hearings/hearings0202.htm.

41 Written Statement of James E. Meyer, on Behalf of Thomson Multimedia, Before the US Senate Committee on Commerce, Science, and Transportation, 28 Feb. 2002. http://commerce.senate.gov/hearings/hearings0202.htm.

computers, display devices, and audio equipment that private homes will increasingly have'.[42] Underscoring the crucial legal implications of the shifting borders between public and private in the new networked home, a senior intellectual property attorney for the Electronic Frontier Foundation argued that the Hollings bill would give content firms control far beyond that of traditional copyright law, which addresses only public performance and display: 'The [legislation] would permit content purveyors to use digital rights management technology to reach into a citizen's home and control what she can do with her books, movies or CDs.'[43] In May 2002 the Electronic Frontier Foundation filed a federal suit against the TV networks and Hollywood studios defending the right of consumers to evade viewing TV commercials through the digital video recorder; according to Electronic Frontier Foundation lawyer Fred von Lohmann, 'the point we want to make here to Hollywood is, when it comes to television, we're not in their movie theatres, they're in our living rooms'.[44]

Many in the information technology and consumer electronics industries view the proposed Hollings legislation as less an attempt to maintain control over their intellectual property in the face of new digital threats than an attempt to impose new restrictions upon long-established consumer practices. Joe Kraus, the founder of Internet website Excite and president of a lobbying group, DigitalConsumer.org, organized in response to the proposed Hollings legislation, told the Senate Commerce Committee that 'under the guise of "preventing illegal copying" I believe Hollywood is using the legislative process to create new lines of business at consumers' expense. Their goal is to create a legal system that denies consumers their personal use rights and then charge those consumers additional fees to recoup them.'[45] James Meyer of the consumer electronics manufacturer Thomson argued before the Senate Commerce Committee that 'just because we move to digital delivery doesn't mean that we should run roughshod over law abiding consumers'.[46] Jonathan Taplin, CEO of Internet movie distributor Intertainer (and producer of films by Martin Scorsese, Gus Van Sant, Wim Wenders, and the Coen Brothers), told the Senate Judiciary Committee in March 2002 that 'content providers [are] looking to stonewall digital distribution until they find a way to become the digital gatekeepers'.[47] Indeed, Jack Valenti explicitly outlined the content industry's aims: 'simply put, in order to transport movies on a rent, buy, or pay-per-view basis, computers

42 Testimony of Prof. Justin Hughes, Visiting Professor of Law, University of California, Los Angeles, Before the Senate Judiciary Committee, 'Competition, Innovation, and Public Policy in the Digital Age: Is the Marketplace Working to Protect Digital Creative Works?', 14 Mar. 2002. http://judiciary.senate.gov/testimony.cfm?id=197&wit_id=341.

43 Fred von Lohmann, quoted in Megna, 'Copy Catfight', 6.

44 Quoted in Nick Wingfield, 'Fight for Right to Turn off Ads', *Australian Financial Review* (8 June 2002), 16; also see Jon Healey, 'Liberties Group Sues Studios over Consumers' Use of Digital Devices', *Los Angeles Times* (7 June 2002), C2.

45 Testimony of Jonathan Taplin, CEO, Intertainer, Inc., before the Senate Judiciary Committee, 'Competition, Innovation, and Public Policy in the Digital Age: Is the Marketplace Working to Protect Digital Creative Works?', 14 Mar. 2002. http://judiciary.senate.gov/testimony.cfm?id=197&wit_id=343.

46 Perry, Senate Commerce Committee testimony.

47 Taplin, Senate Judiciary Committee testimony.

and video devices must be prepared to react to instructions embedded in the film'.[48] Critics in the information technology and consumer electronics industry warned that the repercussions of the Hollings bill would include disabling control over video material in the home that viewers have enjoyed for decades. The content industry's technological proposals included 'forensic tracking' of networked programming, with substantial privacy implications, 'selectable output' control (which would allow content owners to disable or degrade digital and analogue output feeds on a programme-by-programme basis, to limit generational recording, create time restrictions on the life of any recording, or to prevent recording altogether), and software to prevent the fast-forwarding of advertising messages on digital video recorders. Precedent for the latter feature is found in the hardware mandates of the 1996 Digital Millennium Copyright Act, allowing studios to disable the consumer's DVD player's fast-forward function during the studio's commercial trailers.

While the copyright industry was again demonstrating its political power in Washington, it was also enjoying some preliminary success in its legal battles against digital video recorder manufacturer Sonicblue. Sonicblue (manufacturer of Rio MP3 players and Go Video double-VCR decks), acquired ReplayTV in August 2001, and it introduced digital video recorders equipped with both the licensed proprietary Commercial Advance system to automate the fast-forwarding through commercials and a broadband port to enable the sharing of recorded shows with other Replay devices via the Internet. Even before the new Replay models were available to consumers, a suit was filed against Sonicblue by Viacom, Disney, AOL-Time Warner, and NBC, objecting to its use of Commercial Advance and its file-sharing abilities.[49] In April 2002 a federal magistrate in Los Angeles gave Sonicblue sixty days to begin collecting information from each user 'about what works are copied, stored, viewed with commercials omitted or distributed to third parties [and] when each of those events took place', with the information to be handed over to the plaintiffs.[50] The *Baltimore Sun* reported that 'privacy advocates reacted to this news like a pack of wolverines—not without reason'.[51] Jeff Joseph, vice-president of the Consumer Electronics Association, told the press: 'This whole thing just smacks of Big Brotherism. It's just insane', and DigitalConsumer.org's Joe Kraus protested that the media companies are 'trying to make the argument that consumers have signed a contract to watch the television commercials. . . . If we ban that [ReplayTV commercials skipping] feature, then we should be asking ourselves what the next step is: to ban the fast-forward button on the VCR?'[52] An explicit answer to Kraus's hypothetical question is found in the MPPA executive

48 Danny O'Brien, 'Hollywood Attacks the TV Pirates', *Sunday Times* (14 Apr. 2002), n.p.

49 Christopher Stern, 'It May Finally be Showtime for DVRs', *Washington Post* (18 Jan. 2002), E1.

50 Benny Evangelista, 'Sonicblue Chafes at Ruling: Maker of ReplayTV Told to Gather Data', *San Francisco Chronicle* (4 May 2002), B1. A federal judge later reversed the decision; see Michelle Kessler, 'Hollywood, High-Tech Cross Swords over Digital Content', *USA Today* (25 June 2002), 1E, and Jon Healey, 'Order to Monitor Viewing Habits Overturned', *Los Angeles Times* (4 June 2002), C 2.

51 Mike Himowitz, 'ReplayTV's Features have Entertainment Industry Ticked', *Baltimore Sun* (9 May 2002), 1C.

52 Evangelista, 'Sonicblue Chafes at Ruling', B1.

vice-president Fritz Attaway's April 2002 statement that 'this is the first I've ever heard that there's an inalienable right to fast-forward a film'.[53]

While leaders of the content industry protest that the goal of introducing the Hollings bill is merely to prod the efforts to reach a consensus among the three industries on measures to ensure copyright protection (Valenti described the Hollings bill to the *Hollywood Reporter* as 'only the beginning of the beginning'),[54] some industry observers warned that the bill had a real possibility of passage. While similar legislation was introduced in the House, the outlook in the Senate was complicated by the issue of committee jurisdiction. The Senate Judiciary Committee, which traditionally has jurisdiction over copyright issues, was chaired by Patrick Leahy, who vowed to prevent the passage of Hollings's bill in 2002; however, the *Hollywood Reporter* noted that the Judiciary Committee's ranking Republican, Orrin Hatch, was considering backing the Hollings bill, effectively transferring jurisdiction from the Judiciary to the Commerce Committee.[55] According to *Communications Daily*, UC-Berkeley law professor Pamela Samuelson believed that although Hollings's bill 'was unlikely to pass this year, Hollywood would be back year after year, with a good chance of winning similar protections technology by technology, until eventually it had prevailed across the board'.[56]

The end of fair use?

The ongoing legal and legislative battles around intellectual property in emerging digital media systems in the home underscore the legal and political fragility underlying many long-established practices among domestic viewers and media scholars and educators. As Mike Snider concluded in a March 2001 article in *USA Today*:

> Ironically, Napster and similar online file-sharing programs, once heralded as the ultimate liberating technology, might instead become the final nail in the coffin of the vague, constantly shifting set of rights known as 'fair use'. What the entertainment industry once tolerated as penny-ante pickpocketing is now envisioned as theft on a massive global scale.[57]

DigitalConsumer.org's Joe Kraus told the Senate Judiciary Committee in March 2002 that 'many in the copyright community will not admit that there is such a thing as fair use',[58] and even the UCLA law professor testifying in opposition to the Hollings bill admitted that the concept of fair use, legally codified only in 1976, 'is about as far from a bright line test as statutory law

---

53 Goodale, 'Web Pirates Pillage Hollywood', 13.

54 Brooks Boliek, 'Hollings Delivers Net-Piracy Bill: Calls for H'wood, Silicon Valley to Agree on Digital Standard', *Hollywood Reporter* (22 Mar. 2002), n.p.

55 Brooks Boliek, 'Hatch Mulls Backing Piracy Bill: Senator Studying Hollings Measure that has H'wood Support', *Hollywood Reporter* (27 Mar. 2002), n.p.

56 'Berkeley Policy Maven fights Hollings on Many Fronts', *Communications Daily* (10 May 2002), n.p.

57 Mike Snider, 'No Copying, no Trading? No Kidding: Copyright Fight Might Narrow our Options', *USA Today* (6 Mar. 2001), 1D.

58 Kraus, Senate Judiciary Committee testimony; also see Kraus's testimony to the House Energy and Commerce Committee on 25 Apr. 2002, available at http://DigitalConsumer.org/testimony-20020425.html.

should wander'.[59] Yet it is precisely this thin legal reed which protects not only the widespread consumer practices of time- and space-shifting music and images, but also many of the quotidian and fundamental practices undertaken by media scholars and educators. More than mere spectators to the current costly and elaborate legal and legislative efforts of the copyright industry, media researchers and teachers may become their most conspicuous victims. In this regard, the most unsettling aspect of the contemporary US debates around fair use in the new digital environment is the relative absence of the voices or interests of the media studies community, or indeed of consumers generally. Mike Godwin concluded in a January 2002 intellectual property law journal article:

> What gets lost in the debate is the voice of consumers—whatever they are called. Maybe they are willing to trade away open, robust, relatively simple digital tools for a more constrained digital world in which they have more content choices. But maybe they aren't. The Hollings bill is unlikely to attract them to the debate, pitched as a 'security standard' rather than as a new copyright law. . . . And if and when peace talks begin between the two sides, there's no guarantee that the rest of us will have a seat at the table.[60]

The stakes for media scholars of the outcomes of the sometimes arcane technical and legal debates associated with a new generation of digital delivery, storage, and display devices are clear; what remains to be seen is whether this community will stir itself into action.

---

59 Hughes, Senate Judiciary Committee testimony.

60 Godwin, 'A Cop in Every Computer', n.p.

Conclusion

WHILE ENCOMPASSING A CENTURY of technological innovation, the lessons of the distinct historical case studies in this book speak to the specific context of early twenty-first-century media culture. The historian's task of tracing the complex determinants of technological innovation in electronic media seems especially urgent during the present era of rapid technological change and institutional realignment, when the popular experience of a media text may take the successive or simultaneous forms of a theatrical film, television programme, comic book, interactive website, video game, and theme-park ride, challenging conventional notions of textual form and intellectual property. As new multinational corporate strategies traverse the traditional boundaries of media artefact and nation state, it is important not only to address the formal and historical discontinuities presented by contemporary digital media but also to analyse their institutional and discursive links to the past. To this end, this book has excavated the historical antecedents of the recent controversies over digital media, moving away from traditional history's allegiance to the autonomy of specific media forms—cinema, radio, television, digital communication—in favour of an examination of how all these media have addressed and constructed the gendered communities of audience, fan, hobbyist, and citizen. As we have seen, this excavation involves addressing the 'dream life' of twentieth-century electronic media, the ways in which popular fantasies anticipated and incorporated both positive and fearful capabilities of communications media, and considering how these fantasies illuminate the wider ideological and psychic contexts for media reception. These fantasies —prosaic, euphoric, and dystopian—are embodied in diverse historical sites, including the institutional self-representations of media industry advertising, popular fiction and film, the trade and popular press, and the legal and legislative records. Rather than offering a seamless narrative of technological progress and commercial triumph, this book has instead analysed a handful of distinct moments of industrial and ideological tension and crisis within the media industries. The questions raised in each case study, from the earliest experiences of wireless at the end of the nineteenth century, through the hesitant mid-twentieth-century launch of commercial television, to the decidedly mixed commercial success of contemporary digital media, involve the perennial historiographic challenge of relating technological change to industry structure and aesthetic form. In part, the attention in these chapters to the striking discursive continuities across the early experiences with the historically disparate media of radio, television, and digital communication is a rebuttal of the ubiquitous claims of historical novelty which have accompanied the promotion of a variety of digital media over the past two decades.

Notwithstanding claims for the unprecedented nature of technological change confronting contemporary media industries and audiences, the record of previous moments of media innovation over the past 100 years suggests that popular responses continue to be shaped by a remarkably consistent set of anxieties and aspirations. The tendency toward the hyperbolic and apocalyptic and the investment in new media technologies of extravagant hopes for the transformation of personal and public life has characterized a century of media innovation. This sense of historical *déjà vu* has been noted by many media historians, including Tom Gunning, who, in his analysis of early cinematic expressions of popular anxieties arising from the new forms of transportation and communication at the end of the nineteenth century, saw a parallel with our contemporary media landscape:

> Now at the close of another century, with new technological topologies confronting us, I believe we look back at the first experiences with technology with an uncanny sense of *deja vu*. Not only do we confront the same ambivalence of optimism and anxiety, but the scenarios constructed around these primal ambiguities seem even more clearly legible.[1]

The point of this historiographic *déjà vu*, however, as Lynn Spigel argues, 'is not to argue that history repeats itself, but rather that the discursive conventions for thinking about communication strategies are very much the same'. As Spigel concludes, 'our culture still speaks about new communication technologies in remarkably familiar ways'.[2]

Despite a century of popular anticipation and experience with electronic communication in the home, electronic media in their various forms still have the power to fascinate and disturb. As we have seen, the shift of the personal computer over the past decade from a computational tool to a communications device brought it into a new, and, for many, uncomfortable relationship with the domestic television receiver. At the same time, the shift also brought to the personal computer new fearful associations of invasion and contamination, from Internet porn to commercial spam, echoing responses to the entry of earlier electronic media into the home. The networked computer, like television and wireless before it, seemed to threaten boundary definitions of domestic and public, self and community, nation and other, and the domestic artefacts of electronic communication continue to be psychically charged objects, invested with the work of constructing personal and social identities. Whatever specific hardware devices, business models, and aesthetic forms eventually triumph in the emerging digital moving-image economy, the implications of such fundamental tensions are unlikely to recede.

The industrial and textual forms emerging out of the current transition from analogue to digital moving-image media in the USA and elsewhere remain difficult to discern, in spite of the cacophonous commercial promotion of new digital products and services, much overheated media punditry, and extensive journalistic reports from an extremely unsettled media market place. As Bertolt Brecht argued in his 1932 article 'Radio as a Means of

---

1 Tom Gunning, 'Heard over the Phone: *The Lonely Villa* and the de Lorde Tradition of the Terrors of Technology', *Screen*, 32/2 (Summer 1991), 185.

2 Lynn Spigel, *Make Room for TV: Television and the Family Ideal in Postwar America* (Chicago: University of Chicago Press, 1992), 186, 182.

Communication', in a capitalist economy 'one can invent and perfect discoveries that still have to conquer their market and justify their existence', and media history is littered with still-born product launches spurned by recalcitrant consumers.[3] In any event, the recent instability and contention within the US TV industry has at least had the salutary effect of making clear that 'television' as we have so long understood it and taken it for granted has in fact always been historically and ideologically contingent. As the present intra-industry disputes demonstrate, technological change affects distinct sectors within the media industries in very different ways, provoking revealing clashes among the competing actors and public constructions of the medium. However, television as an informal nexus of textual practices, commercial and regulatory institutions, popular attitudes, and audience practices may prove to be more robust and long lived than the current ubiquitous prophets of the medium's imminent demise imagine. The prevailing social meanings of television and other media are complex and deep seated, and may not be exclusively, or even especially, driven by changes in technology.

3 Bertolt Brecht, 'Radio as a Means of Communication', in John Hanhardt (ed.), *Video Culture* (Rochester: Visual Studies Workshop Press, 1990), 53.

Index